I0489304

An Easy Introduction to Economics:
Microeconomics

quantum scientific publishing

An Easy Introduction to Economics:
Microeconomics

SUSAN M. CARLSON

quantum scientific publishing

An Easy Introduction to Economics: Microeconomics

ISBN-13: 978-1481874021
ISBN-10: 1481874020

Published by quantum scientific publishing

Pittsburgh, PA | Copyright © 2012

All rights reserved. Permission in writing must be obtained from the publisher before any part of this work may be reproduced or transmitted in any form, including photocopying and recording.

Cover design by Scott Sheariss

QUANTUM
SCIENTIFIC
PUBLISHING

Table of Contents

Unit One

Unit Two

Unit Three

Unit Four

Unit Five

Unit Six

Appendix

An Easy Introduction to Economics: Microeconomics Answer Key   234

Unit One

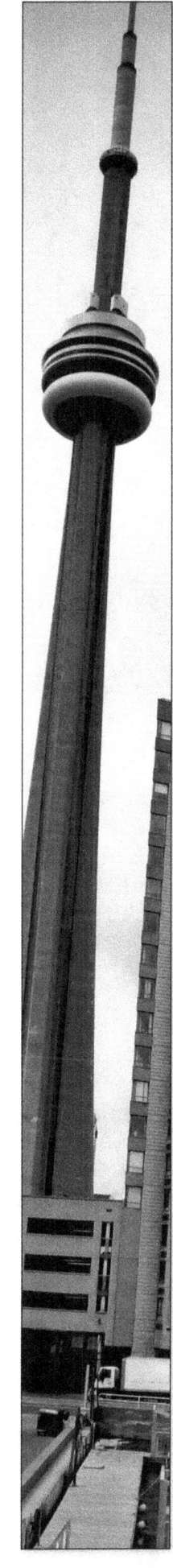

Section 1.1 – Introduction to Economics

Section Objective:

- Define economics

Economics affects every person in the world every day of our lives. It is important to have a full understanding of how economics impacts each of us on an individual level as we make decisions about how to use our resources.

Economics is a social science. Economists develop theories about economies and economic systems. More specifically, economics is the study and management of the production, distribution, and consumption of goods and services within economies and economic systems.

Everything you produce, buy, sell, and consume is part of your economy.

The term economics is derived from the Greek words *oikos*, which means house, and *nomos*, meaning custom or law. When combined, they mean "rules of the house."

Modern economics was defined by Lionel Robbins in 1932. According to Robbins, economics is the study of human behavior and how we decide how to use scarce resources to meet our goals. Every time you buy something, you're making a decision about how to use the scarce resource of money.

What does all that mean? **Economics** is a social science, meaning it is a study of human behavior and human systems. It is studied at the micro (small) and macro (large) scales. Ultimately, economics is the study of how individual human behavior and choices affect individual, local, corporate, national and international economies. The human activities that affect the economy are production, distribution, exchange and consumption of goods and services. This covers a LOT of human activity.

Why is it necessary to study economies? The basic premise of economics is one of scarcity, meaning that the demand for goods and services is higher than the available supply. If everyone has access to everything they want or need, there is no need to study scarcity and there was no need for the field of economics to develop. Since this is not the case and there is scarcity, economic theories are used to understand past economic events and predict future economic behavior.

The study of economics on a large scale is called **macroeconomics.**

Macroeconomics is concerned with national and regional economies. Topics of study include income, productivity, diversity of economic sectors, imports, exports, relationships with other countries, and any activities that affect the national economy of a country. Macroeconomists study aggregated (combined) indicators such as gross domestic product, unemployment and employment rates, price indices, national income, output, consumption, inflation, savings, investment, and international trade and finance.

What about the topic of this book – **microeconomics**? The prefix "micro" indicates that microeconomics is economics on a small scale. In other words, microeconomics is the study of different pieces of the national economy, like individual companies, individual people, and individual households. Your family finances, for example are of interest in microeconomics.

Now what does this mean? It means that microeconomists study how individuals, families, households and companies make decisions to allocate limited resources. Each of you is interesting to the microeconomist because of your individual patterns of decision-making. How do you allocate scarce resources? How do you decide which goods and services will serve you the best? Decisions made by individuals accumulate to contribute to the patterns of supply and demand for goods and services that micro-economists study. Micro-economists analyze how prices are established in an environment of limited resources and how resources are allocated in these conditions. Other areas of interest to micro-economists are market failure and how it occurs, theoretical conditions for perfect competition, elasticity of products within the market system, and how the market regulates itself. We will be exploring microeconomics throughout the rest of this course.

Concept Reinforcement:

1. Define economics.

2. Define microeconomics and macroeconomics and describe how they differ.

Section 1.2 – Early Economic Systems

Section Objective:

- Trace the general history of early economic systems

Early Economic Systems

An economic system is simply the way a society manages the production, distribution and consumption of goods and services for its members. The system consists of both individual people and organizations (governments, companies, etc.) and their relationship to the resources that can be used to produce the goods and services needed by the members of the society. Economics is the way in which scarcity of resources and demand of consumers is managed.

Qin Shi Huang was the emperor of China who unified the nation in 221 B.C. Part of his reforms for China included the establishment of a single uniform currency. To further aid the economy, he standardized weights and measurements and improved roads and canals connecting the provinces.

One of the oldest forms of economic systems is the barter system, in which two individuals agree to an exchange of goods and/or services that meet each of their needs. The important thing to understand in a barter system is that each exchange will assign a perceived value to the good or service that is based solely on the perspective of the person making the decision. This eventually led to some standard of value being established for certain resources. For example a cow may have become an accepted standard of exchange for an acre of land.

In addition to the practical aspects of economics – i.e. people getting what they want and need – theories and systems of economics developed beginning back in ancient Mesopotamian, Greek, Roman, Indian, Chinese, Persian and Arab civilizations. Philosophers, such as Aristotle, Thomas Aquinas, Chanakya, Qin Shi Huang and Ibn Khaldun were influential through the 14th century, when the late scholastics developed economic theories of money, interest and value in the context of natural law, which is law that is considered to apply everywhere because it is set by nature.

Qin Shi Huang

The late scholastics were followed by two groups – mercantilists (16th-18th century) and physiocrats (18th century).

Mercantilists followed the economic model that a nation's wealth is directly dependent upon its accumulation of gold and silver, which could either be mined (if the resource was available to the nation) or traded for using other goods or services the nation was able to produce. This led to the gold standard, which was used to ensure the value of currency until the mid 20th century. This philosophy also encouraged import of cheap raw materials for manufacture of goods and tariffs (an import tax) on imported manufactured goods. This philosophy resulted in complex and burdensome governmental regulation and oversight of trade.

Physiocrats were a group of people who believed that there was a natural order that properly governed society and that land should be the basis of all wealth. They developed the idea of the economy as flowing in a circle in the 18th century. The circle is a relationship between income and output. This group believed that only agricultural production generated a true profit (surplus over cost), therefore that agriculture was the basis of all wealth. Physiocrats disagreed with the mercantilist concept of promoting manufacturing and trade at the expense of agriculture, as well as that tariffs should not be imposed on imported goods. Physiocrats also proposed the idea of a land tax, which is a single tax on land owners, to replace the complex tax system generated by the mercantilist theories, and introduced the concept of *laissez faire,* which discouraged governmental interference and regulation of trade.

Modern economic systems were first described in a 1776 publication by Adam Smith called "The Wealth of Nations." Adam Smith was a philosopher who was interested in how resources were allocated to meet the needs and wants of the consumers. His work provided the rationale for free trade and capitalism as effective economic models and he is acknowledged as the father of economics. He defined land, labor and capital as the three primary factors of production and the major contributors to the wealth of a nation. Smith promoted a self-regulating free-market system that would automatically meet the needs of the people and businesses. This idea is based on the concept that individuals, while pursuing their own self-interests, will produce the greatest benefit to society as a whole. This idea is also described as the "invisible hand" of the market encouraging individuals to fulfill their own self-interests, resulting in the greatest societal gain. This is a paradox: an individual pursuing selfish interests also advances broader societal interests.

Adam Smith

Concept Reinforcement:

1. Describe an economic system.

2. Describe the general changes in economic systems from the ancient Greek and Roman systems to the beginning of modern economic thought.

Section 1.3 – Three Basic Economic Questions

Section Objective:

- Describe the three basic economic questions

Three Basic Economic Questions

There are three basic questions that must be answered in any economy:

- What will be produced?

- How much will be produced?

- For whom will it be produced?

These are all questions of resource allocation. Let's look at them one at a time.

What will be produced? This question will be answered by asking more questions. What does the society already produce? What resources are available to the society? Are those resources appropriate for production of goods and services that will be used by the society or traded to another one? The decision about which goods and services to produce is driven by the availability of resources and the potential benefit to the society of producing specific goods or services.

As an example, a traditional society has domesticated a crop from which they are able to make very durable clothing. The neighboring society does not have access to that crop, but has a need for the durable clothing. Is it in the best interests of the traditional society to produce clothing or the neighboring group? It depends upon whether the neighboring group has something that they are willing to trade to the traditional society AND they have something that is of value to the traditional society.

Tribal groups in South America established trade routes between the mountains and the seashore thousands of years ago. The tribes living near the ocean had access to a ready supply of shells that would wash in from the ocean. These were used for decoration and eventually became a form of money when trading with the mountain tribes. The mountain tribes had products that the tribes living near the ocean wanted, but did not have ready access to the seashells. As a result, the shells became valuable to the mountain tribes and were used by the ocean tribes to trade for the products produced by the mountain tribes (clothing, meat, food crops, etc.).

American colonists used wampum as currency when they engaged in trade with Native American tribes.

How much will be produced? This is a question that requires an assessment of the supply of resources available, the costs incurred to produce a good and the demand for that good. What is the benefit to the group that is producing the good? Is it worth the energy and resource expended to produce the good? Is the demand high enough to produce the good? Is there a benefit to the society of restricting production of a good that is in high demand? In low demand? Is it worth using scarce (valuable) resources to produce this good or service? Is there a reason to be conservative with the use of the resource?

Oil production occurs because the cause of drilling and processing the oil is less than the price the consumer will pay for the resulting gasoline and other petroleum products.

The last question–**for whom** will the good be produced? Questions to ask before answering this include: Is this an essential good? Is this a luxury good? Are there concerns about justice of distribution, meaning will the good get to the people who will benefit from it? Is the good made from scarce resources or are the resources sufficient to meet demand? Will this benefit the society, the individual or both?

These are questions that often come up in discussions about new medical treatments. New medical treatments are expensive, however, they often have the potential to alleviate the suffering of many people living in poverty or without access to the newest clinical therapies. The question here is: is justice served if a new medical treatment is not made available to patients who might benefit if they cannot afford the treatment? This is a question that is vigorously debated. There is no right answer – each situation is different and must be assessed individually.

Concept Reinforcement:

1. What are the three basic economics questions?

2. Discuss how these questions raise more questions before they can be answered appropriately.

Section 1.4 – The Role Of Entrepreneurs

Section Objective:

- Discuss the role of entrepreneurs

What is an Entrepreneur?

Entrepreneurs are people who organize, operate and assume the risk for a business venture. An entrepreneur can be the chief executive officer (or CEO) of a big company or a high school student who mows lawns for a fee.

Entrepreneurs

The most important characteristics of entrepreneurs are that they are:

- profit-seeking, meaning that they want to earn money by increasing the value of the resources they use,

- decision makers, meaning that the entrepreneur decides what projects will be pursued and how they will be conducted, and

- ultimately responsible for the success or failure of the business they are engaged in.

In the case of the CEO of a large company, there are a lot of other people working to carry out the goals and projects set by the CEO. The CEO's job is to look to the future to decide what activities will best serve the success of the business.

Some questions CEOs consider when making decisions about the future of the company are:

- What is the market for the goods or services produced by the company?

- Will the demand for the product stay steady, increase or decrease? Is there a seasonal demand?

- Is technology affecting how the goods and services of the company are able to compete in the marketplace?

- Does the company need to upgrade its products to maintain its competitiveness?

- Does the company need to consider developing new goods and services?

- Does the company need to discontinue existing goods and services?

These questions all boil down to one idea: finding the opportunities the company can use to increase the values of the resources used and generate profits.

How does this idea apply to the teenager with the lawn mowing service? The teenager will have to consider the same questions as the CEO of a large company when deciding what services to provide his/her customers. Let's take each of the questions above and look at them from the perspective of the teenager's lawn mowing service:

- What is the market for the goods or services produced by the company?

It depends upon where the business is located. Are there lawns that need cutting?

If the teenager lives in a desert area where everyone does xeriscaping (using native plants only), there is not likely a demand for lawn mowing because desert plants do not include the type of grasses that make up the average American lawn. There may be other opportunities for a lawn service, such as maintaining the native plants (weeding, planting, etc), but mowing the lawn is unlikely to be a needed service.

On the other hand, if the teenager lives in the Midwest, lawns, whether they consist of grass or weeds, grow quickly and need to be maintained. There is likely to be high demand for a lawn mowing service, especially if it is priced competitively.

- Will the demand for the product stay steady, increase or decrease? Is there a seasonal demand?

This is an assessment of the market where the entrepreneur looks at the number of possible business opportunities. If our teenage lawn service owner lives in an established neighborhood, demand is likely to be relatively steady. No new houses are being built. The size of the lawns in the neighborhood is probably not changing, etc. There might be a little variation in demand as individuals decide whether they want to engage a lawn service or not, but there will not be a lot. If the entrepreneur's family just moved into a newly-developed subdivision where houses are still being constructed, the demand for lawn service is likely to increase as more homes are built and people move into them. A decrease in demand could occur if a neighborhood is on the decline as a result of an economic downturn where people are conserving resources. Depending upon where the entrepreneur lives, the demand for lawn services may also be seasonal. The climate in Wisconsin is much different from that in Florida, for example. Wisconsin lawns only require care when they are actually growing, which is from about April to October. Florida lawns, on the other hand, grow all year round because they do not go dormant in the winter. This will affect the demand for lawn mowing service. Wisconsin winters, however, provide a different business opportunity for our teenage entrepreneur in the form of snow removal. People who have lawns typically have sidewalks and driveways, too. When it snows, the snow needs to be removed to allow people to walk and drive their cars without getting stuck.

Is technology affecting how the goods and services of the company are able to compete in the marketplace?

- Does the company need to upgrade its products to maintain its competitiveness?

- Does the company need to consider development of new goods and services?

- Does the company need to discontinue existing goods and services?

The questions above are all questions about the changing trends in the marketplace. The technology used for lawn mowing is typically a gas-powered mower. These can be push mowers or riding mowers. The increasing prices of gasoline are causing a shift from gas mowers to rotary mowers or electric motors that do not use gasoline. The entrepreneur will need to be sensitive to the trends in how people use lawn mowers and also how they perceive the use of gasoline, rotary or electric mowers in a moral sense. Many people are trying to reduce their "carbon footprint" on the planet and are engaging services that actively reduce hydrocarbon use and emissions. Again, this will depend upon the market the entrepreneur is serving. Does the trend away from gas-powered machines offer an opportunity to the lawn service?

Concept Reinforcement:

1. Define the term entrepreneur.

2. What is the most important role of the entrepreneur in a business?

Section 1.5 – Scarcity and Choice

Section Objective:

- Discuss why scarcity and choice are basic problems of economics

Scarcity and Choice

It is important to first understand exactly what the terms scarcity and choice mean in the economic setting. From the perspective of an economist, **scarcity** is the problem of the unlimited human wants and needs in an environment of finite resources. Society is unable to fulfill all of the wants and needs because it does not have enough resources to produce the goods and services in demand. If society had enough resources to meet all of the wants and needs of every person, scarcity would not exist.

Scarcity can also refer to the concept that society is unable to pursue all of its goals at the same time. This applies at all levels, from the individual to the national government. In this situation, scarcity of resources results in decisions being made about how to best use existing resources. These decisions are also known as trade-offs.

Scarcity can also lead to rationing. If you remember reading about World War II or the energy crisis of the early 1970s, you may recall that certain scarce resources were strictly rationed to those who needed them. Gasoline was sometimes rationed so that each person could only get a certain amount, but so that each person who needed some gasoline could obtain it. During World War II, food resources were rationed. Civilians were limited to certain amounts of specific basic foods to ensure that the armed forces had enough of those resources to feed the soldiers who were fighting the war.

Gasoline vouchers

Choice comes into play when an individual who has limited resources must decide how to use those resources to maximize their benefit to the individual. As an example, a person earns $2,500 per month working at a job. The $2,500 is the resource the person has to purchase the goods and services he needs for the next month. How will the person allocate the $2,500 to meet his wants and needs? Typically, the first choices will ensure his basic needs of food and shelter are met. This reduces the cash resource available for fulfilling other wants and needs. If food and shelter use 40% of his income for the month, he has fewer resources ($2,500 – ($2,500*.4) = $1,500) remaining to fulfill his other wants and needs. Other needs that are not as critical as food and shelter, but may still be needs, are clothing and transportation. Transportation costs for a month are $400 and clothing is $350. This reduces his available resource from $1,500 to $750 ($1,500 – ($400 + $350)=$750). As you can see, his money resource is becoming scarcer. Our individual will make his remaining choices based on the level of satisfaction of wants or needs he receives from using his financial resources to obtain specific goods or services. His decisions will be influenced by the price of goods and services, and availability of alternatives that will meet his needs or wants. This is the basis of the economic concept of supply and demand.

Concept Reinforcement:

1. Define scarcity in terms of economics.

2. Define choice in terms of economics.

3. How do choice and scarcity affect purchasing decisions?

Section 1.6 – Factors of Production

Section Objective:

- Describe land, labor and capital as three factors of production

Three Factors of Production

How are decisions made regarding what to produce and how much to produce? The decision to produce goods and services is based upon demand for the good or service and the availability of the resources required to produce them.

Three of the basic factors of production are land, labor and capital. Why are these three items critical?

Land is essential for the physical infrastructure required to produce the product. Production requires buildings for the workers and machines required to make the goods, as well as for storage. In order to have buildings, the business must have the land on which to build the buildings and related infrastructure of parking lots, green space, offices, and any other things necessary for the business to produce goods. The amount of land required for producing different products varies. A lumberyard, for example, requires a large amount of land for storing the logs required for making the boards used in construction projects. A restaurant, on the other hand, requires enough space for the building (kitchen, bar, seating area) and parking for employees and patrons.

Labor is essential for the production of goods and services. The infrastructure will not be productive without the people required to operate the machines and do the other tasks required to produce the goods. You may need skilled or unskilled labor for your particular production process. When considering where to locate a production facility, it is important to define the skill level required for your production process and whether an appropriate labor pool is available where you want to locate your business. Another consideration when looking at the labor pool available to you is the cost of the labor. If the cost of labor is too high, you will not be able to produce your goods at a cost that will result in a price that the consumers will pay for the product you produce. You will also need to consider the costs of labor for employees who are in support roles, such as administrative and sales people.

Unskilled labor

Skilled Labor

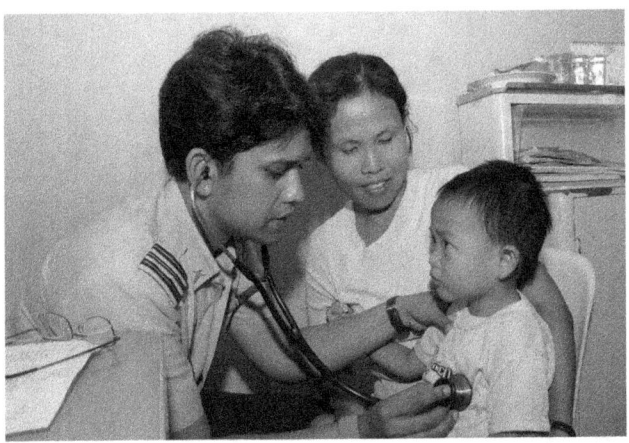
Professional Labor

Capital is the money available to pay for the production of your goods. Capital is required to acquire land, build buildings, pay workers, and transport the goods to their final destination. Capital is available from a few sources: self-financing, bank loans, venture capitalists, and others. The type of capital you use will depend upon your unique situation and the business you are establishing.

Self-financing occurs when you rely on financial assets you have built up yourself to finance your business venture. The benefits of this approach are that you do not have to repay loans or give part of your company (and profits) away to other investors (venture capitalists).

Venture capitalists are people who are interested in investing their resources in new ventures that need financing. These new ventures are often high risk, early stage technology businesses that have large startup costs. These might include expensive lab equipment, highly-trained staff, or complex software.

These three factors of production must all be in place at the appropriate levels for a good or service to be produced. If one is missing or not available at a sufficient level, the production process will not work efficiently if it works at all.

Concept Reinforcement:

1. List the three factors of production.

2. Discuss why each factor is essential to production of a good.

Section 1.7 – Types of Capital

Section Objective:

- Describe the two types of capital

Two Types of Capital

Financial capital is financing provided by lenders and investors to businesses. Financial capital may be borrowed from a bank or a credit union in the form of a loan. Sometimes it is even possible to get financial capital in the form of grants from state or federal governments to start a small business. Grants are beneficial because they are gifts – not loans that require repayment. It is also possible to self-finance a business if you have been able to save enough money or build sufficient assets to support your business venture. Financial capital is considered a liability to a company if it is from a loan that requires repayment. It may also be considered shareholders' equity if venture capital is involved. Venture capital is an investment made by a person called a venture investor, who is someone who invests in young businesses with the hope of making a profit when the business becomes established. Equity is ownership. A person who provides 25% of the funding required to start a business is likely to have 25% ownership equity in the business. Remember that both liabilities and shareholders' equity represent funds that will eventually leave the company, either in the form of loan payments or dividend payments.

Real capital takes the form of the tools required to perform the task. Real capital includes the buildings, tools, equipment and other physical things required to produce goods. Real capital is considered an asset. Real capital is wealth that can be represented in financial terms. A savings or investment account has a financial value associated with it. Real estate and financial securities (stocks, bonds, CDs, and other financial instruments) may be considered real capital. Real assets are owned by the company and have value, meaning that they can be used as collateral for loans or sold for cash, if necessary. It is important to use caution when considering a sale of real capital because you need to maintain the infrastructure required to produce your good or service.

Liabilities in financial terms are obligations for previous transactions to be settled at a later time. These can be debts or settlements for wrongful acts.

Equipment needed to run a business can be considered real capital.

The following table is a very simple example of how assets and liabilities are shown on a financial report.

Item	Liability	Asset
Real Capital		100,000
Loan	25,000	
Investor funds	75,000	

Concept Reinforcement:

1. Define the two types of capital.

2. Discuss the primary differences between the two types of capital.

3. Define equity.

Section 1.8 – Decisions and Trade-offs

Section Objective:

- Identify why every decision involves trade-offs

Decision-making

Think about the things you consider when making the decision to purchase a book or a piece of sporting equipment. What are the questions you ask yourself?

- Do I need or want this item enough to use my scarce resources (money or time) to acquire it?

- Is the price I will pay for the item appropriate for the value I place on it?

- Will I gain more from having the item than I pay for it, in terms of survival, work productivity or pleasure?

- Is acquisition of this item high enough priority for me to forego other purchases?

- If I purchase the item, will I be unable to purchase something else that I need to survive?

Each person and business approaches the decision making process based upon their own sets of values, needs and wants. A mechanic will place a much higher value on a piece of equipment or parts he needs to complete a repair job than will someone who does not know how to use the tool or what the part does to help the vehicle move.

The concept of a trade-off is a result of scarcity of resources. In many cases, people and businesses have limited resources available to acquire what they need or want. Since human beings have unlimited wants, they must learn to make trade-offs to obtain what they need and want within the resources available to them.

Let's look at an example. A student wants to purchase a new bicycle to ride to school and her part-time job. The student really likes a high-end, expensive racing model that she saw at the local bike shop, even though she does not race bicycles. The bicycle she really likes is very lightweight, has high quality rims, tires, gears, derailers, and brakes, and costs $2,000. The student has $2,000 but does not want to spend all of her money purchasing the bicycle because she is saving money to go to college. There are other bicycles out there that will serve her purposes just as well. She sees another bicycle that looks nice, is a little heavier, and probably more practical for carrying books and other things to school because it has a rack on the back. This bicycle costs $350. She decides to purchase the less expensive bicycle after she assesses the two options she has identified.

What are the trade-offs? She gave up the high-end racing features of the bicycle she first wanted (light weight, high quality rims, gears, etc.) for a less expensive, heavier, and probably slightly lower quality bicycle because she placed more value on saving money to go to college than having the high-end bicycle. The end result is that she has a bicycle that allows her to get from home to school and work and she still has $1,650 in the bank to help her pay for college.

The same idea can be applied to all aspects of economic decision-making. The people making the decisions consider the resources available, the options available, and make a decision about how to use the resources to provide the most benefit/profit to the business and, hopefully, the end user.

Trade-offs are not always strictly financial. Many companies are now considering the impact they have on the environment and are changing their business practices because they value the environment enough that they are willing to pay more to reduce their long-term environmental impact. This has been driven in large part by demand on the part of the consumers who are worried about environmental degradation and are making purchases from companies that are actively working to reduce their environmental impact.

Other areas where consumers have had an impact on corporate decision-making are personnel practices, where they obtain their raw materials, how they market their goods, and compensation of workers and executives.

Concept Reinforcement:

1. Describe the concept of a trade-off in decision-making.

2. Describe how consumers impact the way companies make decisions.

Section 1.9 – Types of Profit

Section Objective:

- Distinguish between the different types of profit in economics

Types of Profit

An **equity** is any ownership interest in an economic venture such as common or preferred stocks and bonds.

There are four fundamental types of profit in the study of economics. These are normal profit, economic profit, accounting profit, and social profit.

Normal profit occurs when total revenues equal total costs. In other words, the company is breaking even. A company that is making normal profits is bringing in enough revenue to ensure that the investors in the company are not losing money. The rate of return (profit) is at the minimum level required by the investors to maintain their level of investment. Normal profit is considered one of the two components that compose the cost of capital. There is no economic profit to the business owner in the condition of normal profits.

Economic profit occurs when revenues of a company exceed the total opportunity costs of the inputs required to produce the company's goods or services. In this case,the costs include the cost of the equity (loans, venture capital) that are included in normal profit, as well as the costs of raw materials, labor, overhead, and the other costs related to production. Economic profit occurs when the average cost of production is less than the price of the product or service to the consumer.

Accounting profit is a calculation of the company's total earnings, including costs such as depreciation, interest and taxes. Accounting profits tend to be higher because they do not include the opportunity cost of engaging in the business venture.

Opportunity costs are the income you did not earn as a result of your decision to pursue the goals of the business. For example, if you invest $75,000 in a business, and earned $100,000 in profit, your accounting profit would be $25,000. If you had been employed during that time and earned $40,000, the opportunity cost would be calculated as profit-investment-lost earnings. In this case, it would be $100,000–$75,000–$40,000 = -$15,000. The opportunity cost is $15,000.

Social profit is defined as the normal profit plus or minus any effects of the production activity on society. If a company engages in production processes that result in damage to the environment, use unfair employment practices, or do other things that result in a negative social effect, the social profit will be negative. If, on the other hand, the company works to maximize both profits and social good by minimizing environmental impact, engaging in fair employment practices, and doing other things to improve society, the social profit will be maximized.

Reducing the amount of pollution a factory creates can have a positive social effect on a company's business.

Concept Reinforcement:

1. List the four primary types of profit in economics and describe how they differ.

Section 1.10 – Careers Based In Economics

Section Objective:

- Discover a career based in economics, such as store manager

Careers Based in Economics

All careers are based in economics in some way, either as a result of demand for specific types of labor or as generator of products and services that result in profit.

There are some careers that are more affected by economic conditions than others. Careers that are less affected by economic conditions are those that provide fundamental services to the community. For example, safety services (fire, police, emergency medical services), government positions (administrative, educational, regulatory) and other positions that keep society working at a minimal required level are not as subject to economic downturns as those that rely on consumer spending. Why do you think these careers are called recession-proof? Regardless of the economy, people will always need fire, police and emergency medical services. These career fields may be affected somewhat by the economy, but are likely to be less impacted than others.

US Air Force Fire Fighters

Careers that are more susceptible to changes in economic behavior are those that rely on consumer spending. Economic downturns tend to decrease consumer spending and up-swings tend to increase consumer spending.

Think about careers that might be susceptible to economic changes. If consumer spending is a measure that can affect a career, there are some obvious careers that would be affected. What do you think they might be? Where do you think consumers cut back when they are concerned about conserving resources? Many of these careers are in the service industry. Some of these careers are in lawn care, house cleaning, retail, restaurants, and other service industries, as well as management of those industries.

Waitress

Why do you think these careers are susceptible? What are the first things consumers cut back on when they are conserving resources? Unnecessary expenditures are typically the first expenses to be cut. Housekeeping, lawn care, and entertainment are usually considered unnecessary expenses when people have to choose between necessary expenses, such as food, shelter and transportation, and luxury items, such as lawn and home services and eating out. Because they are unnecessary, or things people can do themselves if they need to, services in this area are more likely to be cut when financial conditions become more restrictive.

Those who manage service industries, such as store managers, need to be aware of the economic conditions of their community and how those conditions will affect sales at the store. Let's look at an example of a clothing store that is located in a neighborhood that is undergoing a cultural shift. In this situation, the families the store has relied on in the past are becoming fewer because of deaths or people moving to other places. This reduction in the original population often leads to an influx of new people. In some cases, the influx of people is people of a specific cultural group that has different wants and needs from the original people who lived there. In order for the store to survive and thrive, the store manager must be aware of the changing customer base and adapt the store's merchandise and sales approach to suit the culture style of the new clients. She needs to consider income level, cultural style, age groups of the clients, and any other variables she can use to successfully transition from the old client base to the new one. If she is not able to manage the store through these changes, fewer customers will visit the store, fewer purchases will be made, and the store is likely to go out of business.

Concept Reinforcement:

1. Explain why some careers are more susceptible to economic downturns than others.

2. Describe how a business can weather an economic downturn by understanding the needs and wants of the client base.

3. Why are publicly funded careers less impacted by an economic downturn than others?

Section 1.11 – Real World Applications of Economics

Section Objective:

- Explore real world applications of economics

Real World Applications of Economics

Business cycles are a fact of life for everyone. Business goes through periods of expansion and recession. What causes these cycles? Business cycles can be predictable – for example, the seasonal nature of certain jobs in climates that have a harsh winter. They can also be the result of other factors, such as changes in the political landscape, addition or departure of large employers from a geographic area, and a shortage or surplus of a key raw material, labor or capital. There are many other factors that can influence the business cycle, but we do not have room to discuss all of them in this section.

Seasonality is a key component of many economic situations. Think about agriculture. All agricultural businesses rely on the rhythms of nature to ensure a successful crop. If all goes well, the crops are planted, grow and are harvested in a predictable cycle. One of the major challenges of agriculture is the unpredictability of Mother Nature. Crops are dependent upon good conditions to grow to a harvestable state. What do you think happens when there is drought, flooding, unusually cold or warm weather, disease outbreaks, or pest infestations? The crop does not follow a predictable pattern, which may result in a smaller crop than expected or no crop at all. Seasonality of jobs, such as those in tourist areas or in agricultural situations, can be predicted and managed. The problems crop up when unexpected situations such as extreme conditions or economic recession occur.

Drought can cause economic changes when farmers
are unable to produce their goods.

Political change can result in economic disruption. Think about what happens in a time of war or when a key economic resource is limited. In a time of conflict, essential resources are segregated to support the war effort. Examples of this include manufacturing capacity for war materials (weapons, vehicles, clothing, and other commodities required by the military), food, fuel, and other basic necessities of life. This can result in rationing that affects the entire economy of the nation at war. Another example of economic disruption occurred in the 1970s with the energy crisis. The supply of gasoline to fuel vehicles was extremely limited, resulting in high prices and fuel shortages.

How do these things affect the economics of the individual person? Let's look at the effect of the Iraq war on gas prices in the 2000s. In the year 2000, gas prices were about $1.50 per gallon. At that time, this was an extremely high price to pay for a gallon of gasoline. In 2008, gas prices nearly reached $4.00 per gallon. How do you think this affects the economic situation of the average consumer?

Let's look at the inflation rate relative to gasoline prices since 2000. Average inflation rate is the average of the monthly inflation rates for a year. For example, for the year 2000, the sum of the inflation rates for all twelve months of the year was divided by 12 (the number of months) to calculate the average inflation rate for the year.

The average inflation rates for each year are:

2000: 3.38%

2001: 2.83%

2002: 1.59%

2003: 2.27%

2004: 2.68%

2005: 3.39%

2006: 3.24%

2007: 2.85%

What would you predict 2008 gas prices to be based on the above inflationary rates?

2000: $1.50

2001: $1.54 (1.50 × 1.0283)

2002: $1.56 (1.54 × 1.0159)

2003: $1.60 (1.56 × 1.0227)

2004: $1.64 (1.60 × 1.0268)

2005: $1.70 (1.64 × 1.0339)

2006: $1.76 (1.70 × 1.0324)

2007: $1.81 (1.76 × 1.0285)

2008: $1.87 (1.81 × 1.0339)

We have seen significant economic changes as a result of political activities since 2001, when the terrorist attacks on New York City and Washington DC occurred. This event, commonly known as 9/11, has been the rationale behind many decisions that have had an impact on the U.S. and worldwide economies. Think about the effects of the War on Terror on both the domestic and international economies. How has the War on Terror affected the ability of the U.S. to engage in international commerce? How has the effect of the international economic and political scene filtered down to the individual?

Concept Reinforcement:

1. Describe an economic cycle.

2. Explain how political decisions affect individual and business economics.

3. Describe how natural events can affect the economics of the agricultural industry.

Section 1.12 – Pricing and the Free Market

Section Objective:

- Evaluate the role of prices in the free market

Pricing and the Free Market

A free market is a market where prices are established based purely on the supply and demand for a good or service. The price is established where the supply and demand curves meet. The chart below shows supply and demand for a fictional product.

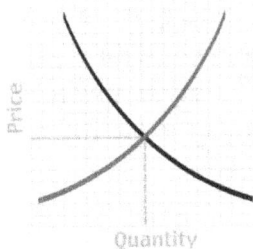

The key point you need to understand from this chart is that the intersection of the supply and demand lines represents equilibrium of both supply and demand, which is the price the market will bear for that product.

What do you think will occur if the price is set at an amount higher than the market will bear? Demand for the product is likely to decrease because fewer people will feel that the price of the product is worth the benefit gained by purchasing the product.

What do you think will happen if the price is set lower than equilibrium? Demand may outstrip the available supply, causing a shortage of the product.

Businesses sometimes intentionally set prices too high or too low. Businesses who want their product to be perceived as a **luxury product** are likely to set their price higher than equilibrium to increase the **perceived value** of the product. Examples of this are expensive purses and designer clothing. Are these clothes truly worth more than those that are priced at equilibrium? They may or may not be, but the **brand name** gains value if the product is perceived as a luxury.

Why would a business set a price that is lower than equilibrium? This happens when a brand new product is being introduced to the market and the producer wants to make sure that the product is priced at a level that will encourage as many people as possible to purchase it, who then rely on the product. After consumers accept the product, they may be willing to pay a higher price for the product and the producer may increase the price to equilibrium.

Grocery and retail stores use the concept of a loss-leader to attract consumers to the store. A **loss-leader** is a product that consumers want and that is priced significantly below market value. The store loses money on the loss-leader, but anticipates that the consumer will make other purchases while in the store that will make up for the initial loss.

Other basic factors that affect prices are supply of raw materials, the ease or difficulty of production, the availability of production facilities, and market demand for the good or service. A sudden change in the availability of raw materials, typically a shortage, usually results in a rapid increase in the price of the product to the consumer. Likewise, a surplus of a raw material may drive the price down.

Concept Reinforcement:

1. Describe the factors that affect price.

2. Discuss how a free market defines price based on market variables.

Section 1.13 – Microeconomics and Macroeconomics

Section Objective:

- Distinguish between macroeconomic concerns and microeconomic concerns

The field of economics is divided into two primary areas of study: microeconomics and macroeconomics. Microeconomics is the study of the effect of individual decisions on the economy. Macroeconomics is the study of economies on the macro, or large, scale of economic systems.

Microeconomics

The field of microeconomics is concerned with the behavior of the individual economic entity, including individual people, households, and businesses. Microeconomics also includes the study of individual economic factors, such as employment, unemployment, prices, and labor economics. Each person reading this book is interesting to a microeconomist. Each of you makes decisions about how you use your resources (money and time, primarily) to acquire goods and services differently. One person may value a microeconomics text more than another person, which influences how much each person is willing to pay for the book. The person who values the book might be willing to pay two or three times as much for it as a person who does not value it. A microeconomics text may not be the best example here because most people only read them because they are required to for class. Think about other goods or services that you find valuable or not valuable. Does your perception of value for each item match that of your best friend?

Small independent businesses lining a street

Macroeconomics, on the other hand, is the study of economic systems. Topics of interest to a macroeconomist include national economies, large portions of a national economy, production and distribution systems, indicators of the health of the large system (overall income and productivity of an economy), and the relationships that exist between different parts of the economy.

Economic news is often based in macroeconomic theory. Discussions of markets, recession, inflation, gross domestic product, and national debt are all based in macroeconomics.

Microeconomics and macroeconomics both affect the individual consumer, just in different ways. Microeconomics is the economy of the individual household or small business. Each person creates his own unique economy based on income and the choices he makes as far as how he uses this financial resource. It is possible to create a very strong personal economy if he uses his financial resources to acquire the necessities of life (food, shelter, transportation, clothing, etc.), save for the future, and generally lives within his income. It is also possible to create a very weak personal economy if he makes unwise choices about how to use his money. Some people place more importance on having the "right" things than taking care of basic necessities. This leads to debt and other financial problems.

The combined behavior of all the individuals in a country drives the larger economic trends that macroeconomists are interested in. For example, if the majority of individual consumers are not confident about having continued employment, they will scale back their spending, conserving their resources in case they need them later. This, in turn, impacts the businesses that no longer generate sales because people have reduced their spending. The ripple effect of these behaviors eventually leads to changes in the indicators that macroeconomists use to understand the behavior of the national economy.

Concept Reinforcement:

1. Define microeconomics and discuss the primary concerns of the microeconomist.

2. Define macroeconomics and discuss the primary concerns of the macroeconomist.

3. Discuss how microeconomics and macroeconomics both affect the individual.

Section 1.14 – Positive and Normative Economics

Section Objective:

- Distinguish between positive economics and normative economics

Positive economics are also referred to as scientific economics. This field of study attempts to determine what is actually happening in the economy. The scientific method is used to gather and assess data to answer a specific question, or hypothesis, the researcher developed. The hypothesis is developed based on extensive research and a thorough understanding of the topic under study.

For example, a person who is studying positive economics may hypothesize that the price of energy will decrease when the weather is warm. The scientist is then able to develop a series of data points that will help validate or invalidate the hypothesis once the data are analyzed. There are some key variables that need to be included in the data analysis:

- Historical data about seasonal energy costs (price) per unit of energy.

- Historical data about seasonal energy usage (demand) per unit of energy.

- Recent trends in energy costs per unit of energy.

- Recent trends in energy usage per unit of energy.

There are likely to be many other factors that are important, as well. The researcher must take the time to fully understand the topic and select all of the relevant variables for measurement and analysis.

Notice that the data types listed above are all measured in the same units – unit of energy. This makes it easier for the scientist to directly compare the data and determine if the hypothesis is valid or invalid. The essence of positive economics is that we can analyze objective data to determine whether a hypothesis is correct.

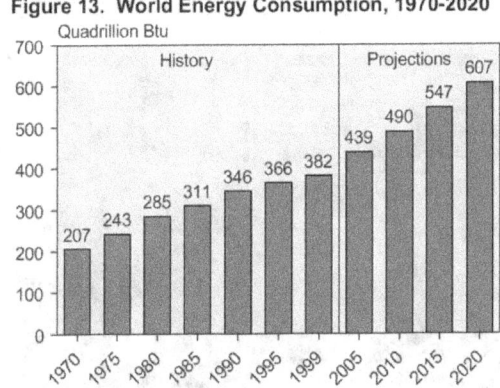

Figure 13. World Energy Consumption, 1970-2020

Sources: **History:** Energy Information Administration (EIA), Office of Energy Markets and End Use, International Statistics Database and *International Energy Annual 1999*, DOE/EIA-0219(99) (Washington, DC, January 2001). **Projections:** EIA, World Energy Projection System (2001).

Normative economics add ethical, or value, judgment to the methods used in positive economics. Normative economics are often used to advocate for policy changes based on a specific point of view. The statements used in normative economics are about "what could be" if certain conditions are met. For example, a person might say that if all U.S. citizens are provided comprehensive health care at no charge, the total cost of health care will be reduced. Do you think it is possible to prove or disprove this statement? A key aspect of normative economics is that the statements made in support of a particular point of view cannot be proved or disproved using data. This happens because personal values are introduced to the conclusions made. Personal values cannot be proved right or wrong because they are based on opinion and not data.

For example, a person might state that hybrid cars are more valuable than traditional cars. How are the "values" of the hybrid and traditional cars determined? There are certain data points that can be gathered relatively easily. These include purchase price, fuel efficiency, maintenance costs and hauling capacity. Values are introduced when a person places higher ethical value on using a hybrid vehicle as opposed to a car powered by a traditional combustion engine. How is the "ethical value" of a hybrid quantified (made into a number)? There is no way to do so. As a result, when positive economics add considerations of ethical value to the analysis, it is only possible to develop an opinion based on the values and data. Companies actually take advantage of the perceived benefit of something like a hybrid vehicle when marketing products. Is a hybrid SUV that gets 20 miles per gallon and costs $35,000 to buy a more "valuable" vehicle than a compact car with a combustion engine that gets 40 miles to the gallon and costs $15,000 to purchase? It depends on how much you value the concept of driving a hybrid.

It is important to assess claims you hear in the media so you understand if they are based on positive economics (fully fact-based) or normative economics (positive economics plus unquantifiable values).

Concept Reinforcement:

1. Define and describe positive economics.

2. Define and describe normative economics.

Section 1.15 – Economic Profit vs. Accounting Profit

Section Objective:

- Distinguish between economic profit and accounting profit

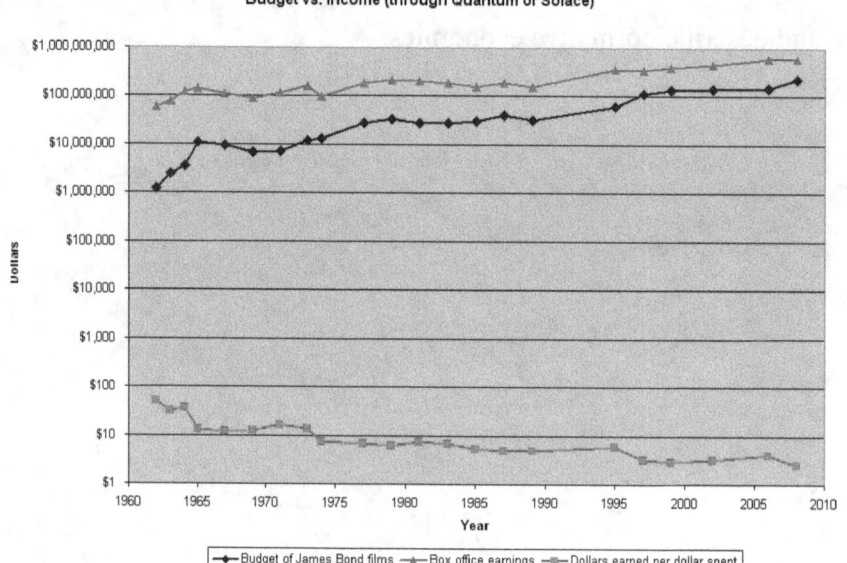

Budget vs. Income (through Quantum of Solace)

Accounting profit is the result of calculating revenue minus costs for the company for a specific time frame, which is typically a year. Accounting profit includes the payments made to investors to ensure a specific rate of return on their investment in the company. This means that what you might logically consider profit is actually listed as a cost because it must be paid out to the investors before the business actually makes a profit. The formal term for this cost is the **cost of capital.** If the firm's income is greater than the costs, it is making an accounting profit.

Economic profit adds the concept of opportunity cost to the calculation. Economic profit includes accounting profit (revenue – costs for a time frame) and the opportunity cost of doing business. Economic profit occurs when the revenue generated by a business exceeds the total of expenses plus opportunity cost.

Opportunity cost is the cost of pursuing one option instead of another option, which may be equally interesting or appealing. What do you think is the opportunity cost of purchasing a new vehicle? If you pay cash for the vehicle, it might be the interest you would have earned if you had left the money in the bank. Alternatively, what do you think the opportunity cost of purchasing a used vehicle might be? Let's say you pay half the amount for a used car that you would for a new car. What happens if the used car requires a significant number of repairs that end up costing you more than the new car would have? The opportunity cost is the difference between the amount you actually paid for the used car plus the repair costs minus the amount you would have paid for a new car.

Revenue is the actual amount of money a business receives during a given period of time. This is also known as gross income.

It is possible for a company to make an accounting profit, but not an economic profit. It is not possible for a company to make an economic profit if it does not make an accounting profit. This is the case because economic profit includes accounting profit plus the opportunity cost of engaging in the business.

Concept Reinforcement:

1. Define and describe economic profit.

2. Define and describe accounting profit.

3. Describe opportunity cost.

Unit Two

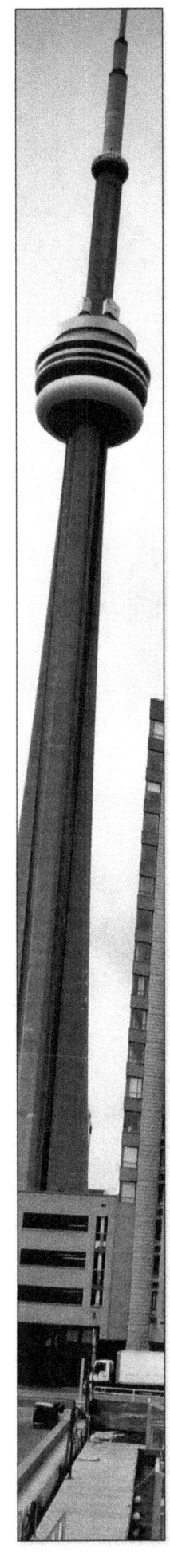

Section 2.1 – Production Possibilities Curve

Section Objectives:

- Demonstrate how production possibilities curves show efficiency, growth and cost

- Interpret a production possibilities curve

Production Possibilities Curve

The production possibilities curve shows all the possible combinations of total output. Opportunity cost is a key component of the production possibilities curve. Each point on the curve represents a trade-off between the use of one resource and another to produce a good.

The production possibilities curve assumes three things:

- Utilization of a fixed amount of productive resources.

- Resources are used fully and efficiently.

- A specific state of technical expertise.

The chart below shows several different possibilities based on the resources available to produce guns and butter. The points on the curve (B, C, and D) represent full utilization of the available resources to produce varying amounts of guns and butter. Production at point B will result in a much higher output of guns than butter. Point D represents equal production of guns and butter.

Remember that the curve represent maximum efficiency in the use of resources to produce the products. What to you think points A and X represent? Point A is under the curve, meaning that the available resources are not being fully utilized or are being wasted. Point X is outside the curve meaning that there are not enough resources available to produce the goods at that level.

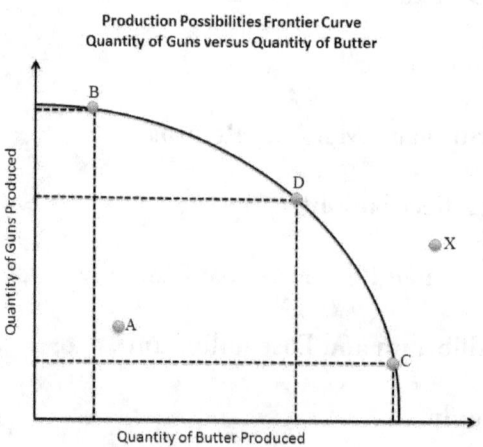

The production possibilities curve will give an indication of where pricing will increase or decrease. Remember that the larger the supply of a good or service relative to demand for that good or service, the lower the price will be. Conversely, the smaller the supply of a good or service, the higher the price will be.

The last concept we will address is how the production possibilities curve reflects economic growth. What do you think will happen if an economy grows, increasing the resources or efficiency available to produce the guns and butter? The curve will push out to reflect the increased production capacity as you see in the chart below. Draw a line from the x axis and y axis so the lines start from the axis lines and cross the curves. What do you see in the relationship between the original production possibilities curve and the new one that is the result of the additional resources available in the economy? You should note that anywhere you draw lines, the new production possibilities curve allows for a higher level of production of both guns and butter. Production possibility curves do not always increase in this way. It is possible for the resources to produce the guns to increase without the resources for producing butter increasing. This could result in the original and new production curves actually intersecting.

Concept Reinforcement:

1. Define production possibility curve and describe what it represents in relationship to efficiency, growth, and cost.

Section 2.2 – Production and Societal Values

Section Objectives:

- Study that a country's production possibilities depend on its available resources and technology

- Evaluate the societal values that determine how a country answers the three economic questions

Production Possibilities

Hopefully it makes sense to you that the production possibilities curve for a specific country will depend upon the natural, technical, and human resources available.

Natural resources are the resources available from the natural environment. Different areas have different combinations of natural resources available for use in production of goods and services. Think about the different resources that might be available in a tropical area and a desert area. A tropical area will have an abundance of plant and animal life and a sufficient supply of water. A desert area will not have the same abundance of life forms and water, but has other natural resources that could be equally valuable for production of a good or service. Think about generation of power using wind or solar power collectors. Is there a mineral deposit under that sand that is valuable? What about all of the sand? Each geographic area has a unique grouping of natural resources that can be utilized for producing goods and services to stimulate the economy.

Technical resources include the infrastructure and expertise required to produce a good or service. Economies that use basic technologies of production are usually not able to take advantage of the increased efficiencies resulting from improvements in production technologies. Think about the differences between developing and developed countries. Is the production capacity different? If so, how? Developed countries have more technically advanced production and money management systems than developing countries, which typically lead to more efficient systems.

Human resources, which are also known as human capital, are the people available to do work. The number and skill level of the people available to do work has a strong influence on the production capacity of a country. A highly-educated workforce is able to produce more complex products that have a high value to the consumer. A workforce that does not have a strong education or specialized technical skills will be able to do a lot of work, but not take advantage of the benefits provided by technological advances and higher education.

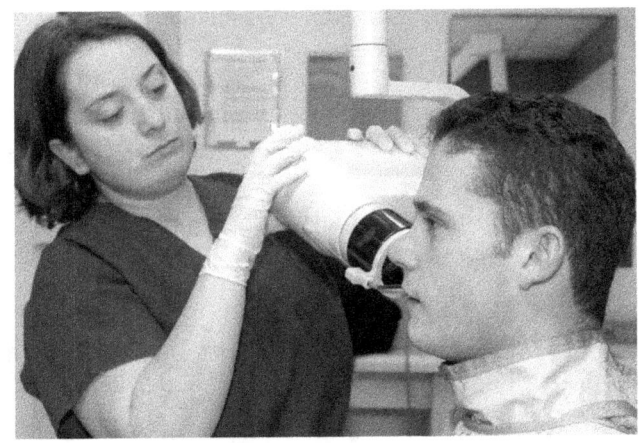

Infrastructure includes the basic physical and organizational structures necessary for the operation of an entity, either governmental or private. Offices, roads, sewers, and information systems are examples of infrastructure.

Societal Values contribute to the decisions made about production of goods and services. For example, in times of war, a society may choose to sacrifice availability of certain consumer goods to support production of the resources needed to support the war effort.

Three basic economic questions drive the decision about what goods and services a society will produce. These three questions are:

- What goods and services should be produced?

- How should the goods and services be produced?

- For whom should the goods and services be produced?

Societal values will impact how these decisions are made. A society that values ensuring that all people in that society have their basic needs met will make decisions to support that goal. A society where the decision makers care only about personal gain will produce the goods and services that benefit the few (decision makers) and not the majority of the people, who are the ones actually producing the goods and services.

Of course, all of these production decisions are made based on the natural and technical resources available. A country that is rich in energy will make production decisions based on those natural resources. A country that is rich in highly-skilled labor and technical resources will make its production decisions based on those resources and the availability of the raw materials required to produce their products.

In theory, a society should be able to manage its resources so that all of its members have what they need to survive and be healthy. If the people making the decisions about production are not interested in the well-being of the society as a whole, the decision will probably serve the selfish interests of the decision makers.

Supply and demand is a basic theory of economics that is used to explain how the value of a good or service is determined. The essential concept of supply and demand is that the price of a good or service will be set at the point where demand for the good equals supply for the good. If supply is greater than demand, price drops. If demand is greater than supply, price increases.

Concept Reinforcement:

1. Describe how the resources available in a country influence its ability to produce goods and services.

2. What societal pressures influence society's decisions to produce specific goods or services.

Section 2.3 – Free Enterprise

Section Objectives:

- Describe the basic principles of the United States free enterprise system

- Describe the role of the consumer in the United States free enterprise system

Free Enterprise

Free enterprise is also known as capitalism. A basic precept of free enterprise is that each individual in a society has the right to produce goods and services and engage in trade without interference from the government. A pure free enterprise system is not viable given societal needs and pressures to ensure that the basic needs of its members are met. In a pure free enterprise system, those who are able to produce what people want at the highest possible price will benefit and those who are unable to do so will fail. This does not work in a society where the individual is valued regardless of his or her capacity to be productive.

A free enterprise system is based on competition without regulation by the government. The only restrictions on a free economy are supply and demand. In a free enterprise system that is operating without regulation, a company will work to provide a good at the highest possible price the market will bear.

A key characteristic of a free economy is that people choose to do what they feel is best for them, which results in a benefit to the overall economy. The individual person/company will choose to produce the goods or services that benefit society the most because this is likely to provide the greatest economic benefit to the producer.

Free enterprise systems typically consist of four components: households, businesses, market, and governments.

Households in a free market control the majority of resources and decide how to use them. People may think that the government actually controls most of the resources, but this is not the case. Households control money (income that they spend) and labor, which they sell to companies in exchange for wages or to develop their own businesses. **Consumer sovereignty** means that consumers vote with their dollars about the way resources are used to produce goods and services.

Businesses organize economic resources to produce goods and services. The entrepreneurs organize and innovate, always trying to find new products, services and markets for their products. Successful businesses grow. Those that are not successful fail because there is either not a market for the product or because the entrepreneur is unable to generate demand for his product.

Markets facilitate free trade by providing a place for buyers and sellers of goods and services to interact with one another. The free market has three types of markets: resource, produce and financial markets. Resource markets involve sale of labor from households to businesses. Product markets are used by businesses to sell goods and services to households. Financial markets are used by households and businesses to manage money, both in the form of investment and loans.

Governments are not a factor in a true free enterprise economy because the economy is supposed to be free of governmental interference. In reality, government plays the role of protector. When one person's freedom conflicts with another person's freedom, society must have some way to manage that conflict. A Supreme Court Justice, William O. Douglas, once described this as, "My freedom to move my fist must be limited by the proximity of your chin." In other words, society must develop and enforce standards of behavior to enforce the rules of society. The other important role of government is to provide the capability to enforce the rules of society (military, police) so that everyone is free to pursue a profit.

The American consumer

The U.S. consumer votes with her dollar. Consumers make choices every day about how to use their resources. Free markets are an extension of personal freedom, which is the result of people making decisions that benefit themselves. A market that is providing what the consumer needs at a reasonable price will thrive. A market that is unable to provide what the consumer needs will not thrive.

Another way to look at this problem is from the perspective of the individual business. A business may choose to engage in ethical behavior or unethical behavior, which is based on societal norms. A business that chooses to engage in ethical behavior may have a competitive advantage in attracting clients, which will contribute to the behavior of the market.

The consumer also drives the market based on fundamental needs for survival. A consumer will allocate resources to provide for basic needs before providing for unnecessary purchases.

Concept Reinforcement:

1. Define the free enterprise system in the U.S.

2. Describe how the consumer affects the freeenterprise system.

Section 2.4 – The Law of Demand

Section Objectives:

- Discuss the law of demand

- Interpret a demand graph using demand schedules

The Law of Demand

The law of demand states that as the price for a good or service increases, demand will decrease. It also states that as the price for a good or service decreases, demand will increase. An alternative way to state this law is that, given a consistent supply, increased demand will increase price and vice versa. In other words, the price of a good or service drives consumer demand for that commodity.

Demand Graphs and Demand Schedules

A demand schedule is a table that lists the quantity of a good or service that potential buyers would purchase at different price points. The information in a demand table reflects the purchasing behaviors of a specific individual, business, or group for that particular product. In terms of microeconomics, the data included in demand graphs is often a composite of data collected from a large number of individuals or businesses.

Let's look at a demand schedule for a fictional product, the Catercizer. The Catercizer was developed to help out of shape housecats get exercise. The Catercizer has been tested on a number of housecats, who responded favorably to it, indicating that there will be demand for the product. Based on the market research, the demand schedule for this product was developed.

Catercizer demand schedule:

Price	Monthly Demand
$100	5
$75	8
$50	20
$25	50

Demand schedules can be graphed to show the trend demand based on price.

Catercizer Demand Curve:

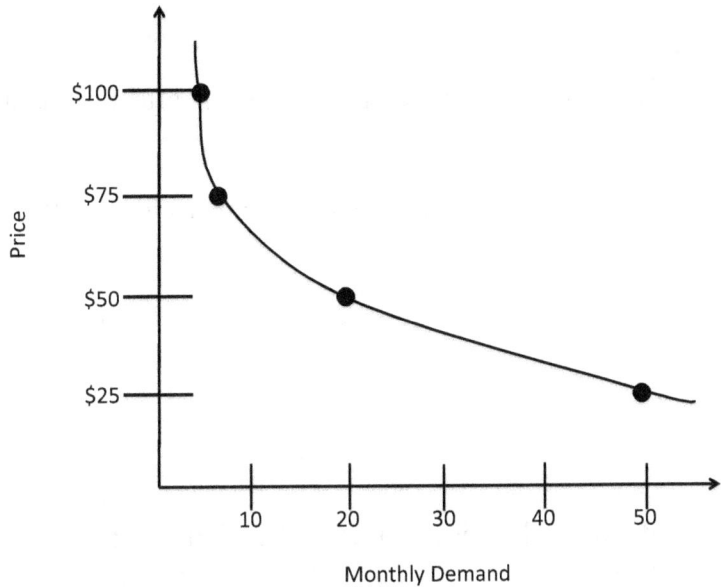

Catercizer Demand Curve

The above chart shows demand (quantity) on the *x*-axis and price (dollars) on the *y*-axis. This demand curve shows low demand at a high price and increasing demand as the price drops.

Concept Reinforcement:

1. State the law of demand and discuss how increases and decreases in price are related to demand.

2. Use the following demand schedule for the product "Flower Power" to draw a demand curve for the product.

Price	Demand
$50	0
$40	1
$30	5
$20	20
$10	100
$0	175

Section 2.5 – Demand Curves

Section Objectives:

- Discuss how the change in the price of one good can affect demand of a related good

- Describe the determinants that create changes in demand and that can cause a shift in the demand curve

- Changes in the price of a good or service can affect the demand for related goods or services

What Causes a Shift in the Demand Curve?

The demand curve shifts when there is a change in the relationship between price of a good and quantity. This change in the relationship can be caused by a number of factors, such as preferences, population, prices of other goods services, incomes, and perceptions of future prices.

Let's take these one at a time.

Preferences: Societal preferences tend to change over time, which affects demand for products. In the 1970s, for example, people covered their hardwood floors with shag carpeting. Wood floors were considered to have a lower status than carpet, so people added carpet to their homes when they remodeled. In the 21st century, wood floors are very popular and a sign of quality. As you might imagine, the demand curve for shag increased in the 1970s and decreased as wood floors came back into fashion.

Population: Populations change over time. These changes can be a result of normal growth. They may also be the result of an influx of people from another place as a result of a natural disaster or economic downturn. Finally, the composition of population changes over time. The U.S. is currently experiencing a rapid growth in the population of people over age 65 as the baby boomers are retiring. Each of these population changes has the potential to shift the demand for products.

Prices of Other Goods and Services: Related goods or services are those that substitute easily for on another. Consider what will happen, for example, if pork drops sharply in price compared to related products, such as beef, chicken and fish. In this situation, the demand for the higher priced beef, chicken and fish will fall while the demand for the cheap pork is likely to increase. This occurs because pork is a substitute for other meats.

A similar effect may occur when a complementary product, which is one that is typically used in conjunction with another product (hot dogs and buns, for example), has a sudden increase in price. If the price of hot dogs increases dramatically, we will expect to see a drop in demand for both the hot dogs and the buns.

> **Income** for an individual is any money earned either through employment, interest, or dividends. For a business, it is revenue minus all costs.

When introducing a new product, the price of the new product must be at a level where the consumer finds it beneficial to substitute the new product for an old product. This has occurred frequently in the home entertainment electronics area. VCR players gave way to DVD players, and then to the new Blu-Ray technology, in the period of about 20 years.

Income: Increases or decreases in income will affect demand for goods and services. As people have more income (resources), they demand higher quality goods and services and want to enjoy an improved lifestyle. As income decreases, people conserve resources by reducing their demand for goods and services. Normal goods are those for which demand increases as income increases. Inferior goods are those for which demand decreases as income increases. An example of this is a store brand versus a name brand food or household item.

Perception of Future Prices: If people think that the price of a good is going to increase dramatically in the future, demand for that good is likely to increase if it is something people are able to store for future use. For example, if the price of rice is expected to double because of a natural disaster that destroyed a major portion of the world's rice crop, one would expect the demand for rice to increase as people stock up on it. This factor affects goods more than services because it is not likely that a service can be hoarded.

The graph below shows shifts in the demand curve, both positive and negative.

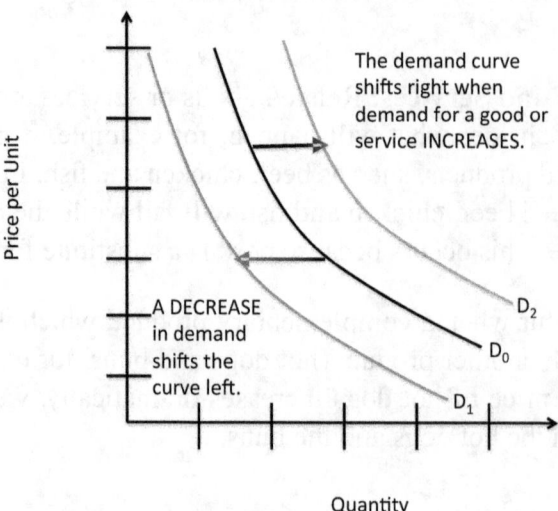

Shifts in the Demand Curve

Demand and price are related concepts. There are some fundamental factors that affect demand curves, causing them to shift in a positive or negative direction.

Concept Reinforcement:

1. Describe how the change in price of a product can change the demand for complementary products.

2. Discuss the impact of drastic price changes on related products.

3. List and describe the primary factors that cause a shift in the demand curve.

Section 2.6 – Quantity and the Demand Curve

Section Objectives:

- Study the difference between quantity demanded and a shift in the demand curve

- Recognize outside effects on demand

Quantity demanded represents any point on a demand curve and is a relationship between price and quantity. As price increases on a demand curve, the quantity demanded falls. Likewise, as price decreases on a demand curve, the demand increases

A shift in the demand curve is a result of a fundamental change in the relationship between price and demand. The demand curve may shift down or up. A negative shift in the demand curve means that there is less demand for a good or service. The demand at a specific price point decreases. For example, if demand for car tires decreases because people are driving less, the demand for tires at specific price will decrease. A positive shift in the demand curve means that there is an increased demand for a good or service at that same price point.

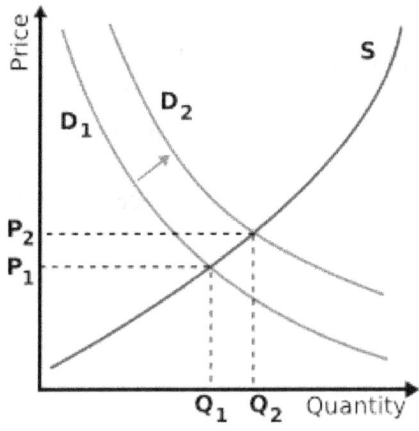

Outside Effects on Demand

Many factors can affect demand for a good or service. Politics, raw materials or component availability, labor issues, natural disasters, and a number of other factors can affect demand.

Consider the demand for transportation, health care, food and housing after Hurricane Katrina hit New Orleans. The hurricane wiped out all of these services in the city, resulting in a huge demand for them from other parts of the country. Those who evacuated New Orleans had to travel a very long distance to find a hotel room. The demand for transportation and housing in other areas soared as these people were displaced. The hurricane had a very strong outside effect on demand.

Labor disputes in manufacturing industries often have a huge impact on demand for the components of the product. The auto industry has experienced this on several occasions. Labor strikes at assembly plants reduced the demand for the components used by the assembly plant until the strike was over. Likewise, strikes at factories that make key components affect the demand for workers at assembly plants, often resulting in layoffs of workers.

The availability of raw materials for a product, especially a shortage of a material, has the potential to shift the demand curve. If the raw materials required to manufacture a product are expensive, that cost will be passed on to the customer. Additionally, if the raw materials required to produce a product are in short supply, fewer of the product are likely to be produced, which can sometimes lead to a shift in the demand curve as consumers assess whether the product is worth the increased price.

Demand is affected by a number of variables, including availability of products and the price charged for them. A shift in the demand curve is a result of a fundamental change in the relationship between price and quantity demanded.

Concept Reinforcement:

1. Compare and contrast quantity demanded and a shift in a demand curve.

2. Describe a situation in which a demand curve might have negative movement.

3. Describe what effects you think political processes might have on a demand curve.

Section 2.7 – Elasticity of Demand

Section Objectives:

- Discuss how to calculate elasticity of demand

- Discuss the law of supply

Elasticity of Demand

Elasticity of demand is the change in demand for a good or service based on changes in price. Elasticity of demand is the degree to which an increase or decrease in price will change the quantity demanded.

There are three degrees of elasticity: unitary elasticity, elasticity, and inelasticity.

Unitary elasticity occurs when the percentage increase in price results in an offsetting decrease in demand. Conversely, a decrease in price will result in an offsetting increase in demand.

Let's look at an example. A farmer sells a gallon of milk for $2.00 and sells 500 gallons per week at this price. If he doubles his price to $4.00 per gallon because his milk is organic and he thinks he can charge more because of that, the demand will decrease to 250 gallons per week. He may also choose to halve the price of his milk to $1.00 per gallon. In a situation of unitary elasticity, the demand will increase to 1,000 gallons per week. What do you think happens to the revenue? The table below shows the results.

Number of Gallons	Price per Gallon	Revenue
250	$4.00	$1,000
500	$2.00	$1,000
1,000	$1.00	$1,000

> **Elasticity** is the amount of change in demand or supply as a reaction to changes in price. If a change in price does not have an effect on the demand or supply, an item is said to be **inelastic**.

If you are in a situation of perfectly elastic demand, there is not any motivation to produce a higher volume of product because the revenues always stay the same. This is extremely rare in the real world.

Elasticity is a situation in which a reduction in price increases demand sufficiently to increase revenue. Using our example above, if a $.50 decrease in price doubles the demand, what do you think happens? You have a $500 increase in revenue.

500 gallons x $2.00/gal = $1,000   1,000 gallons x $1.50/gal = $1,500

Inelastic demand occurs when a price increase does not increase revenue. As an example, let's say our gasoline prices are reduced to $1.50/gallon, but the demand only increases 10%. This will lead to a reduction in revenue. Let's look at the numbers.

500 gallons x $2.00/gal = $1,000

If we reduce the price to $1.50 and the demand increases 10%, the numbers change a bit.

(500 x 1.10) x $1.50/gal = ??

550 x $1.50/gal = $825

The actual revenue fell by $175.

The Law of Supply

The law of supply states that there is a direct relationship between the price of a good or service and the amount of it offered for sale. In other words, all other factors being equal, as the price of a good or service increases, the quantity of goods or services offered by suppliers will increase. Conversely, as the price of a good or service decreases, suppliers are less motivated to provide the good or service for sale. If the price drops too low, the company will no longer provide the good or service because there is no opportunity for profit. Higher prices induce producers to offer more of a good or service for sale. The minimum price for a good or service must at least be equal to the opportunity cost of using the resources required for production of the good or service. In other words, the producer is going maximize profit by utilizing the resources available in the most efficient manner. If the producer cannot make a profit, the good or service will not be produced. As the price for the good or service increases, the producer has incentive to increase the supply, which can lead to a surplus if the supply outstrips the demand.

Supply Curve

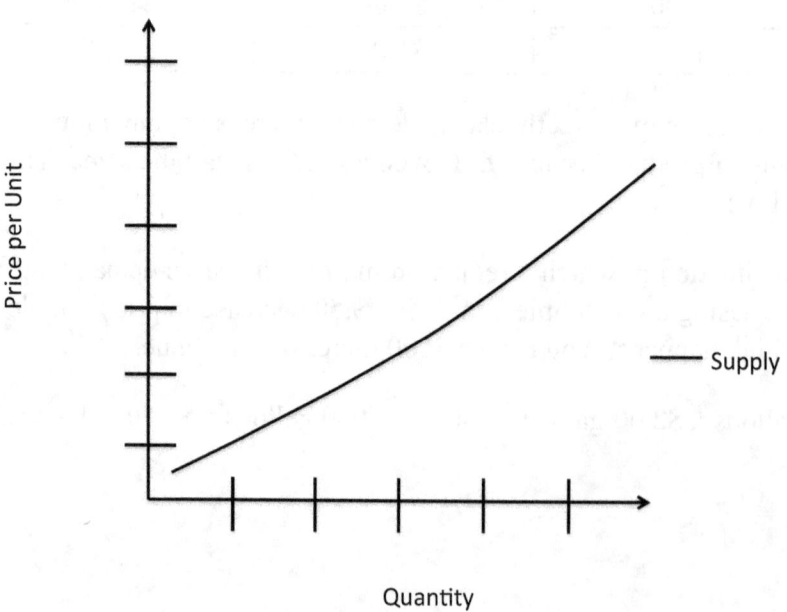

Supply and demand are related concepts in microeconomics. The consumer demand for a good or service and the willingness of a producer to supply a good or service is directly related to the price of the end product. If the price is high, there is motivation for the producer to increase supply. However, if the price is too high, the consumer will not purchase the goods or services, reducing demand. Likewise, if the price is low, consumer demand may increase, but the supply may decrease.

Concept Reinforcement:

1. Define elasticity of demand and describe the three types of elasticity studied in microeconomics.

2. Discuss the law of supply and how price affects the supply of goods and services to the market.

3. Solve the following problems and state which type of demand elasticity it represents.

   $Demand_1=10; Price_1=\$50$

   $Demand_2=30; Price_2=\$150$

   $Demand_3=20; Price_3=\$100$

4. Calculate the revenue for each of the price and demand combinations and specify which type of elasticity of demand is shown for this set of problems.

   $Demand_1=50; Price_1=\$35$

   $Demand_2=75; Price_2=\$30$

5. Calculate the revenue for each of the price and demand combinations and determine which type of elasticity of demand is shown here.

   $Demand_1=100; Price_1=\$150$

   $Demand_2=110; Price_2=\$100$

Section 2.8 – Elasticity of Supply

Section Objectives:

- Discuss the relationship between elasticity of supply and time

- Interpret a supply graph using a supply schedule

Supply elasticity is related to the speed with which suppliers are able to respond to changes in price and demand. Production facilities typically have fixed capacity to produce goods and it takes effort, money, and time to increase capacity. This may require bringing in additional equipment, hiring new workers, increasing supply orders or building new buildings to accommodate the increased production capacity.

If a supplier is able to plan for an increase in production, the company is better able to respond when the price changes. However, if the change in price is sudden, the supplier will require time to adjust the production capacity of the factory.

In general, it is less expensive to expand production capacity slowly because careful planning and cost estimation will allow the expansion to be done at the lowest possible cost. If the production capacity expands quickly, it often costs more because of the speed with which the work is done. Once production capacity is established, it is efficient for the company to produce products at different levels, usually lower than the maximum capacity of the plant, while still retaining the ability to ramp up production if necessary to increase supply.

Let's look at oil supply as an example. OPEC (the Organization of Petroleum Exporting Countries) has the infrastructure required to provide oil to the world at a certain level of production. It is very efficient for OPEC nations to provide oil at levels equal to or less than the infrastructure will support. However, if demand increases to a level above that which can be supported by the existing infrastructure, the price per unit will increase because the infrastructure cannot supply more without significant, rapid (high cost) investments to increase production capacity.

Suppliers are able to adjust production levels over time. The more time that passes, the better they adjust to the change in production.

Supply Graphs and Supply Schedules

A supply schedule is simply a display of the amount of goods or services a producer is willing to supply at a given price. It is the same concept as a demand schedule, but from the perspective of the producer rather than the consumer. A supply schedule assumes that all things are held constant except for the price and quantity of the product. In the example below, we show a series of prices for widgets (a fictional product) and the number of widgets the producer is willing to manufacture at each price point.

Price per widget	Number of widgets produced.
$5.00	1,000,000
$4.00	750,000
$3.00	500,000
$2.00	250,000
$1.00	0

The supply graph is generated by placing the values for price on the *y*-axis (vertical) and the value for quantity on the *x*-axis.

Every point on the supply curve shows the amount of product the producer is willing to manufacture for each price point. As price goes up, the willingness of the company to produce goods increases. As price drops, the company becomes less willing to produce goods. Keep in mind that the supply curve represents the relationship between supply and price without taking other factors that may affect price and supply into consideration, such as production capacity and technology, cost structure, prices of substitutes and complements, and perception of future prices.

Concept Reinforcement:

1. Define elasticity of supply.

2. Discuss how producers of goods and services respond to increases or decreases in price, both in the long and short term.

3. Create a supply curve from the following supply schedule.

Price per unit	Number of units manufactured
$25.00	3,000
$20.00	2,800
$15.00	2,300
$10.00	1,500
$5.00	750
$1.00	0

Section 2.9 – Entrepreneurship and Marginal Returns

Section Objectives:

- Recognize the entrepreneur's effect on supply

- Relate downsizing to diminishing marginal returns

Before we get into the entrepreneur's effect on supply, we need to define the term "entrepreneur." An entrepreneur is a person who starts a new business venture and assumes all of the risk of the venture's success or failure. Small business owners are considered entrepreneurs, as is anyone who is self-employed.

How does this relate to supply? Entrepreneurs combine the factors of production (capital, labor, and land) to produce specific goods and services. These goods and services become part of the supply chain for the companies that use them. For example, let's say that your school needs to purchase new instruments for band. They will probably look for a music store in your area as a source for the instruments. The entrepreneur who owns and runs the music store is critical to the process of the school acquiring the instruments. If the entrepreneur did not provide the service of instrument sales, the school might have difficulty finding a good resource from which to purchase the trumpets, saxophones, flutes, and other instruments it needs for the music program.

Downsizing and the Law of Diminishing Returns

Production includes two types of inputs: fixed and variable. Fixed inputs are the costs of the building, equipment, and other fixed assets that are required to produce the good. Variable inputs are those that change based on the volume of goods being produced. The primary variable inputs are labor and raw materials.

The **law of diminishing returns** is related to production. It states that a production system with fixed and variable inputs will receive proportionally less benefit from additional variable inputs after a certain point. For example, consider what happens if you plant a garden. If you space the plants according to the growing instructions, you will maximize the amount of vegetables you are able to harvest. If you space the plants twice as close as the growing instructions state, you will have twice the plants, but will not end up with twice the output of vegetables because the plants will not be able to grow to their full size and produce as much fruit as they are capable of. You are still likely to have more vegetables, but not twice as many. You may achieve a harvest of 25%, 50%, or 75% more food rather than 100% more food. The same concept applies to labor. Labor efficiency is maximized at the point where each person is producing as much product as possible while maintaining standards of quality. If demand for a product increases or decreases, the demand for labor to produce that product does the same.

Reduction in demand for a good or service often leads to downsizing of production capacity, including labor and raw materials. When this occurs, companies will downsize their operations to maximize efficiency and profits. A reduction in demand reduces the efficiency of the production process. This happens because the available resources are not being used at their full capacity for manufacturing the product. In other words, there is idle time for the equipment and labor used in the production process. Fixed assets are not easily reduced, so they are typically allowed to be idle for some period of time before the sale of the assets is considered. Labor, on the other hand, is a resource that can be increased or decreased to meet the needs of the production. This ability is, of course, dependent upon the available labor pool. Assuming that everything but demand stays constant, the company will be able to downsize (lay off employees) when demand decreases and scale up (hire employees) when demand increases.

Downsizing is a response to the law of diminishing returns. A company is motivated by profit and seeks to maximize profit by minimizing production costs through efficient use of resources. Downsizing will also have a negative effect on the entrepreneurs who are supplying the raw materials used in production of a good. If demand for the product decreases, the demand for raw materials decreases, which means that suppliers of the raw materials have reduced demand for their products.

Concept Reinforcement:

1. Define entrepreneur and describe the role entrepreneurs play in the economy.

2. Describe how fixed and variable inputs are affected by increases or decreases in demand for a good.

3. Discuss how the law of diminishing returns and downsizing are related, including how they contribute to production efficiency and profit maximization.

Section 2.10 – Factors that Affect Supply

Section Objectives:

- Evaluate the effects of other factors that affect supply

- Describe how determinants, such as input costs, create changes in supply

What Affects Supply?

There are a number of factors that affect supply. The primary factors are capacity and technology, cost structure, prices of substitutes and complements, and perceptions of future prices. Other factors include politics, and cost and availability of raw materials. We'll go through these one by one in this section.

Capacity and Technology:

Capacity is the ability of an industry to produce goods and services. When a product is new to the market, the capacity for production is limited. Production capacity will increase as the product gains acceptance by the market and the price is in line with what consumers are willing to pay for the product. Production capacity also increases as additional producers are able to add to the available supply of product. Sometimes, as with the telecommunications industry in the 1990s, the industry developed too much capacity (overcapacity). This made it possible for the companies to increase the supply of goods and services produced for a specific, lower price point because they had the infrastructure in place to make their production processes highly efficient. Technology is closely related to capacity. In order for a company to remain competitive, it is critical to improve the technology used to produce the good or service provided. Companies that invest in technological improvements improve their efficiency and capacity. Overcapacity can occur within one company or across and entire industry.

The reverse also holds true. If a company or industry has too little capacity, too few producers, or is behind in technological innovation, the supply will decrease.

Cost Structure:

The factors of production (labor, raw materials, and equipment) all have a cost to the producer. These are also known as input costs. If any one of these decreases or increases, it affects the amount of goods the producer is willing to supply to the market. An increase in the cost of one or more factors of production will decrease the amount of product supplied to the market. Likewise, a decrease in the cost of one or more factors of production will increase the amount of goods supplied to the market.

Price of Substitutes and Complements:

This concept is applied differently by producers than consumers, but is based on the same concept of efficiently using resources. Whereas consumers will purchase substitute or complementary products to maximize their purchasing power, a producer will supply substitute or complementary products to maximize the efficiency of their production process and maximize profits. For example, if a farmer grows both wheat and corn, he will maximize his profits by planting the crops in ratios that reflect the value of the crops to the market. A recent example of this is the increase in corn production to support the production of corn-based ethanol for fuel. Farmers are able to receive a higher price for corn because it is in demand for both food and fuel uses.

Complementary goods are those that are produced secondary to the primary product. These are also called byproducts. For example, leather is a byproduct of the meat industry. The animals are used for meat, and the leather is sold as a complementary product to the shoe and clothing industry.

Perception of Future Prices:

Producers are motivated to maximize profits. If they anticipate a price increase for a good they supply in the future, they are likely to wait to supply goods to the market until the price rises. This is the opposite of the consumer reaction to a perceived future increase in prices. Consumer demand will increase before the price rises because the consumer wants to pay the lowest amount possible for the good or service to be as efficient as possible with her resources. Producers want to maximize profits, so they reduce supply for release to the market after the price increases.

Politics:

The politics of governments can have a direct impact on the supply of goods and services, including raw materials and labor. Governments will sometimes place embargoes (restrictions) on the import of goods from or export of goods to specific countries that have policies that our government does not support. For example, a country that violates human rights, as defined by the U.S. or United Nations may be subject to an embargo. If that country provides a vital raw material for a specific industry, that industry will be unable to supply as much of their final product as they would if the embargo was not in place.

Political pressures may also come from consumers. A highly publicized example is the blood diamonds, also called conflict diamonds, from Africa. The African diamond mining industry has been shown to be very violent. The profits of the African diamond trade have also been used to finance civil wars in Africa. As a result of the poor conditions the African diamond miners work in and the civil wars, consumers have begun boycotting diamonds from these mines, which have become known as blood diamonds to reflect the violence associated with them. The Canadian diamond industry has benefited from this consumer behavior because the working conditions of the mines in Canada are considered more humane than those in Africa.

Panning for diamonds in Sierra Leone

Availability of raw materials:

In some situations, raw materials required for a product become scarce. Scarcity of a raw material will reduce the amount of an end product that can be supplied by the producer. Conservation of raw materials is critical for ensuring the continuation of industries, such as logging. Many logging companies replant forests to ensure a continual supply of wood for future use.

As you have learned in this section, supply of a good is affected by a number of factors. Some of these factors are within the control of the producer, such as the amount of a product supplied to the market. Other factors are out of the control of the producer, such as shortages in raw materials and labor costs. The amount of goods supplied by the producers and the demand of the consumers are often in conflict. Suppliers are motivated to increase profit and consumers are motivated to save money.

Deforestation caused by logging

Concept Reinforcement:

1. List the key factors that affect supply.

2. Discuss how changes in technology and capacity affect the supply of a product to the market.

3. Describe how politics are able to affect the availability of goods and services, including raw materials.

Section 2.11 – Supply and Demand in the Global Economy

Section Objectives:

- Study supply and demand in the global economy

- Identify how changes in the cost of an input affect the supply curve

The global economy follows the same rules of supply and demand as a national economy. International trade involves import and export of goods and services around the world. Why is this appealing to producers and consumers? Remember that companies want to minimize the cost of production to maximize profit and consumers want to minimize the purchase price of the goods they purchase.

Global trade allows people and companies to purchase goods they need from places that are able to create them less expensively, thereby increasing the efficiency of resource use. In order for this to be the most effective, the importer or exporter must have something that is of value to the other party. For example, the U.S. produces a huge amount of food products, especially grain, which are exported all over the world in exchange for goods that are produced more cheaply overseas. Both countries benefit from the exchange by reducing the cost of goods to their producers and consumers.

Comparative advantage occurs when the opportunity cost for a nation to produce a good is lower than that of another nation. Absolute advantage occurs when a nation can produce a good more cheaply than another nation. These are two different concepts. Comparative advantage is the measure that should be used to determine whether a good should be exported. Why? Comparative advantage shows that even if a country does not have the absolute advantage in producing any product, it can still benefit by producing goods and services for which it has the lowest opportunity cost.

Global supply and demand are affected by a number of factors besides classical supply and demand. In a free market, the only factors that would affect the global market for products will be supply and demand. This assumes that there are no barriers to trade in place.

In reality, governments put barriers to trade in place in a number of ways. Tariffs and quotas are common barriers to trade put in place by governments. A tariff is a tax levied on an imported good to increase the price of the good to consumers so that it is competitive with similar goods that are produced domestically. This increases the cost to both the producer and the consumer. A quota is a limit on the amount of a good that can be imported or exported. For example, a government might limit the number of vehicles that can be imported from a country to help support domestic automakers by restricting competition. Other barriers to import or export include regulations regarding product content or quality, packing and shipping regulations, harbor and airport permits, and overly difficult customs procedures.

Customs is an authority charged with the collection of duties on imported goods and controlling the flow of goods into and out of a country.

The barriers to trade described above increase the cost of inputs used to produce a good or service. This is likely to result in a reduction in supply of the good or service to the consumer. If the barriers to international trade are reduced, the reduced cost of the inputs should result in an increase in supply.

The Relationships Between Price, Supply, and Demand

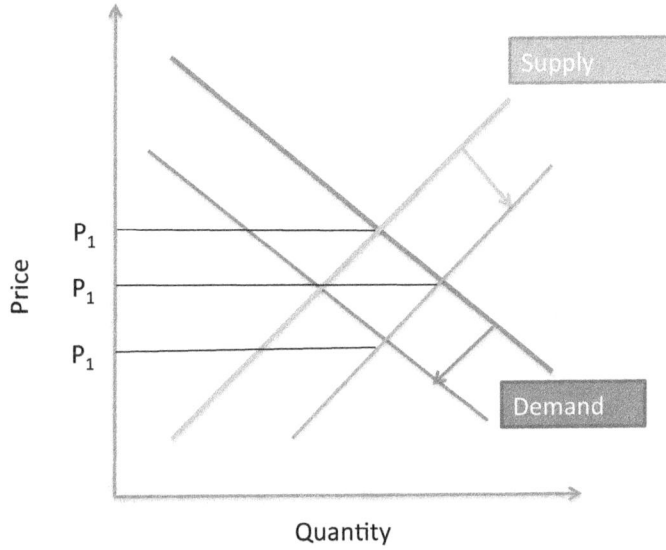

Concept Reinforcement:

1. Describe the global economy and how it is subject to the rules of supply and demand.

2. Discuss the effects of tariffs, quotas, and other factors on the supply of goods in an international economy.

3. Draw a supply curve shift from the following data points:

    $Price_1$=$4.00 per unit; $Supply_1$ = 500 units

    $Price_2$=$5.00 per unit; $Supply_2$ = 700 units

    $Price_1$=$4.00 per unit; $Supply_1$ = 500 units

    $Price_3$=$3.00 per unit; $Supply_3$ = 275 units

4. Combine the two curves into one summary graphs that shows the increase and decrease in supply.

Section 2.12 – Market Equilibrium and Disequilibrium

Section Objectives:

- Discuss why a company should increase output if the market price increases

- Compare a market in equilibrium with a market in disequilibrium

Market Balance

Markets tend to move toward equilibrium, meaning that supply meets, but does not exceed demand. This can also be stated as demand meeting supply, meaning that demand meets, but does not exceed, supply for a good or service.

A market that is not in equilibrium will either have too much supply for the demand (surplus) or too much demand for the available supply (shortage). This is caused disequilibrium, meaning that the market forces are out of balance in terms of supply and demand.

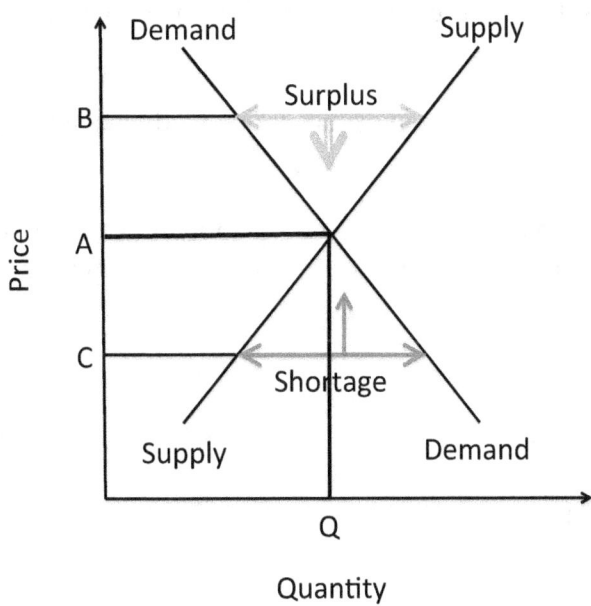

The chart above shows what happens when the market is in equilibrium and in disequilibrium. In this chart, the line marked "S" indicates supply and the line marked "D" represents demand. The point where the supply and demand curves cross represents at which point supply and demand are in balance. The area above the intersection of the supply and demand curves represents a surplus of goods on the market. This occurs because the producer is motivated to produce goods at as high a price as possible, which sometimes leads to overproduction of a good. The area below the intersection of the supply and demand curves represents a shortage of the good. In this instance, the demand for a good is higher than the available supply.

Both surplus and shortage situations are states of market disequilibrium, or imbalance. What should a company do if the market is out of balance? It depends on the imbalance that is present. If the demand for a product is higher than the available supply, this means that the company can choose to produce more goods at a higher price. Therefore, the company should increase production. Alternatively, if the supply is greater than demand, the company should consider reducing production of the good.

The market is constantly fluctuating between equilibrium and disequilibrium. The market constantly adjusts to changes in supply and demand.

So, what should a company do if market price for a product increases? In general, a company should increase production to increase supply of the product to the market. There may be some situations in which this is not possible (shortage of raw materials, regulatory restrictions, etc), but in general, the free market demands that an increased price should result in increased production.

Concept Reinforcement:

1. Describe what market equilibrium is and why it is the preferred state for the market.

2. Discuss how market disequilibrium occurs and what the results of this disequilibrium are.

3. Draw a supply and demand curve based on the following variables. Define the point at which the market is in equilibrium. Quantity is shown on the x-axis and price on the y-axis.

    $Q_1=500$; $P_1=\$7.00$

    $Q_2=750$; $P_2=\$5.00$

    $Q_3=1,000$; $P_3=\$3.00$

Section 2.13 – Shifts in Supply

Section Objectives:

- Discuss how supply and demand create a balance in the marketplace

- Discuss how a market reacts to a fall in supply by moving to a new equilibrium

Supply and demand are pressures that work together to create equilibrium in the market-place. When the supply and demand for a product are exactly the same, the market is in equilibrium. The market forces of supply and demand push the market to this point for every good and service available.

The situations that occur when a market is in disequilibrium, or out of balance, are surplus and shortage. A surplus means that there is more of a good available than the consumer is demanding. Alternatively, a shortage is the situation where demand is greater than supply.

A surplus of a good motivates the seller to reduce the price until the demand increases enough to balance out with the supply. A shortage of a good motivates the seller to increase price until the supply balances out with demand.

The example below shows the way a market reacts to overall shifts in supply or demand.

What happens when the supply of a good changes? How does that affect price? The chart below shows what happens when the supply for a good is reduced. The supply line shifts to the left, increasing the price the market will bear for that product when produced at that quantity. The intersection of the new supply line and the demand line moves to the left, as well, resulting in an increased price per unit for the good.

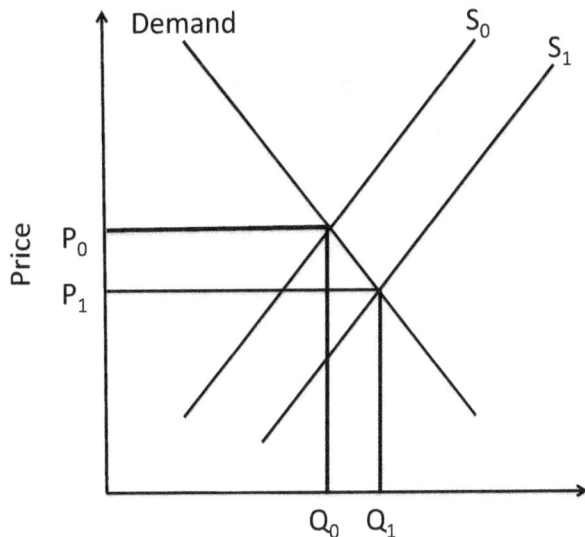

Effect of Changes in Supply

If the supply line shifts to the right, meaning that supply is increased, the price will decrease.

If supply and demand increase or decrease in relatively the same amount, the equilibrium point will remain at the same price.

Equal Changes in Supply and Demand

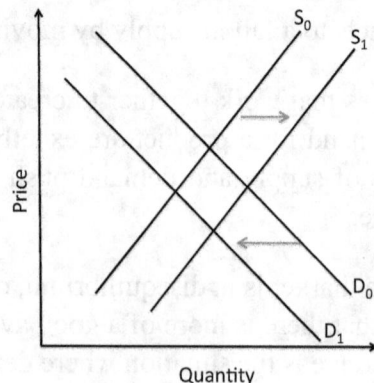

Let's look at another example. The Xbox™ gaming system was in very high demand when it was first released. As a result of this demand, the availability of goods at a given price was limited. As the company was able to increase production, it was able to provide additional units to the market at the same price point.

Concept Reinforcement:

1. Describe how the forces of supply and demand interact to move the market into balance, or equilibrium.

2. Discuss what happens when the supply curve shifts left while demand remains constant.

3. Describe what happens to price when both supply and demand change in the same direction in the same proportion.

Section 2.14 – Shifts in Demand

Section Objectives:

- Discuss how a market reacts to a shift in demand by moving to a new equilibrium

- Evaluate market reactions to change in demand and supply

Shifts in Demand

A shift in demand will have an effect on price if the supply of a good remains constant. For example, if the demand for tickets to a football playoff game increases, the price of each ticket is likely to increase. A stadium can only hold so many people, so the availability of tickets is limited. If the demand is greater than the supply, the price per unit (ticket) is likely to increase. In the graphical example below, the shift in the demand curve results in both an increased price per unit for the good and the amount supplied by the producer. The new equilibrium point is where the shifted demand and supply lines intersect.

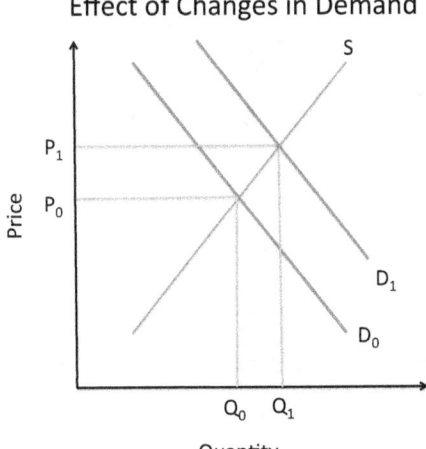

Effect of Changes in Demand

The opposite will occur if the demand curve shifts to the left. Both the supply of the good and the price of the good will decrease, resulting in a new equilibrium point and price. If the demand for the football playoff game tickets decreases, the price may decrease. This is most likely if the demand is less than the number of available tickets.

Market Reactions to Changes in Demand and Supply

The market will react in one of three ways to changes in demand and supply. The equilibrium point will increase, decrease, or simply shift to the left or the right.

An increase in the price per unit at the equilibrium point is a result of reduced supply for a level of demand, or an increased demand for a given level of supply.

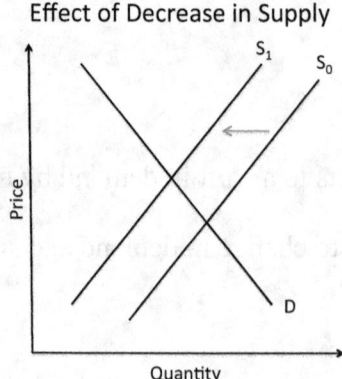

Effect of Decrease in Supply

A decrease in the price per unit at the equilibrium point is a result of an increased supply for a given level of demand, or a decreased demand for a given level of supply.

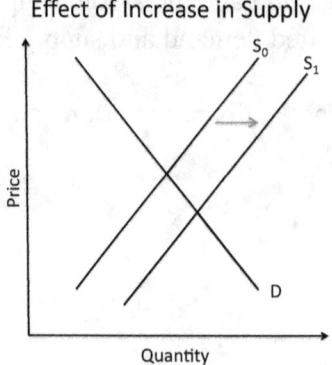

Effect of Increase in Supply

The price per unit of a good can stay the same if the supply and demand increase or decrease in proportion.

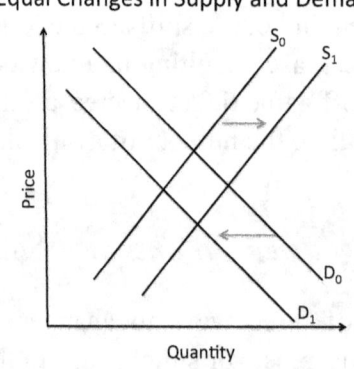

Equal Changes in Supply and Demand

The market is self-balancing. Shifts in overall demand or supply for a given product will result in a change in the equilibrium point (the point at which quantity and demand intersect), which also determines the price that the market will bear for the good or service.

Concept Reinforcement:

1. Describe how the equilibrium point and price for a product will change if there is an overall positive shift in demand while the supply remains constant.

2. Discuss what it means for the market to be at equilibrium.

3. How does the price point for a product remain the same if both supply and demand curves shift?

Section 2.15 – Determining Price and Quantity

Section Objectives:

- Determine price and quantity at points on a demand curve and on a supply curve.

- Describe the point of equilibrium between price and quantity.

Price is the amount of money a producer charges for a good or a service. Quantity is the amount of a good or service that is made available by a producer of a good or service.

Price and quantity are reflected on both demand and supply curves. As demand for a product increases, the price the producer can charge for the product also increases. As demand decreases, price also decreases. This is assuming that supply remains steady. This is called a direct relationship, meaning that as one variable increases, the other also increases.

If the supply of a product (quantity) available increases, the price tends to decrease. Likewise, if the supply decreases, price tends to increase. This is called an inverse relationship between the supply and the price. An inverse relationship occurs where as one variable increases, the other decreases.

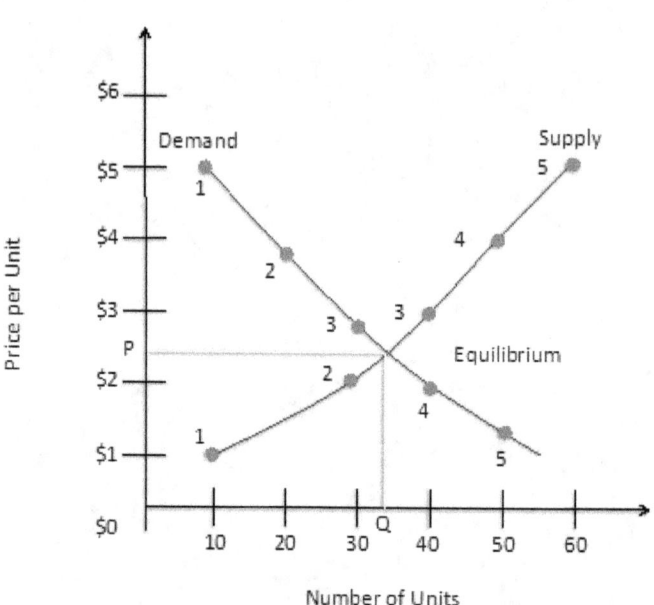

The price and quantity of a good or service may be determined from any point on the supply or demand curve. The chart above shows both supply and demand, as well as the equilibrium point where the two curves intersect.

Let's look at the left side of the graph first.

Determining price and quantity on the demand line is straightforward. In the chart above, look at the left hand point of the demand line. The point intersects with the price value of 5 and the quantity of 10. This means that 10 units of the product will be demanded at a value of 5.

The same concept applies to the supply line. If you look at the left-most point on the supply line, it is the intersection of a quantity of 10 and a value of 1. This means that at a price of 1 the producer will be willing to supply 10 units.

Do you see the difference between consumer demand and supplier willingness to produce the good?

Now let's look at the rightmost parts of the demand and supply curves. Again, we'll look at the demand curve first. Demand for the product increases as the price decreases. More than 50 units are demanded at the price point of 1.

The supply curve, or willingness of the producer to add to the supply, increases as the price increases. The rightmost point of the supply curve shows that the producer will be willing to supply 60 units at a price point of 5.

Any point on the supply curve will indicate the number of units a producer is willing to supply at a given price. The same concept applies to a demand curve. Each point on the demand curve indicates the number of units demanded at a specific price point.

So what does this all mean? Demand for the product at a price point of 5 is 10 units, which is far less than the supply the producer is willing to provide at that price. The difference is 50 units. If the producer supplies that maximum of 50 units, the price will be pushed down because demand does not support the price. Likewise, the quantity the producer is willing to supply (10 units) at a price pint of 1 is far less than the demand of about 52 at that price point. Again, this is a discrepancy of 42 units less supply demand. This will drive the price up.

The intersection of the supply and demand curves is called the equilibrium point. This is where supply and demand are in balance, meaning that the quantity supplied and the quantity demanded fall at the same price point.

Concept reinforcement:

1. Using the chart below, give the price and quantity for each point on the demand curve.

    Price: 1_____ 2_____ 3_____ 4_____ 5_____

    Quantity: 1_____ 2_____ 3_____ 4_____ 5_____

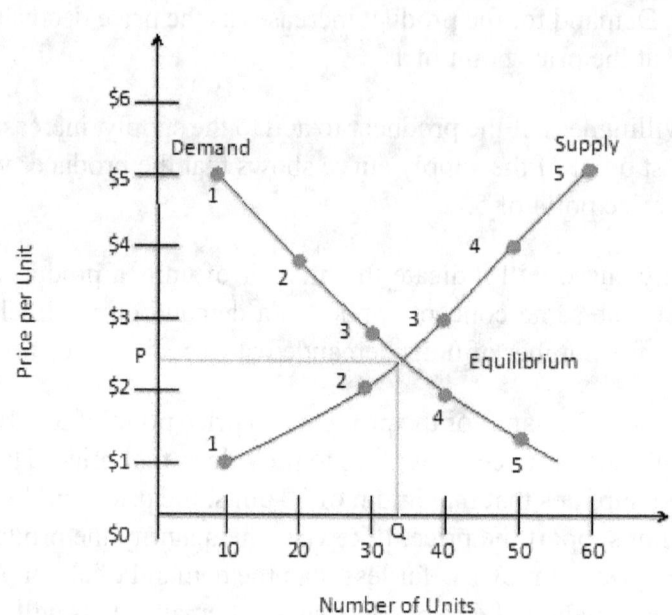

2. Using the same chart, give the price and quantity of each point on the supply curve.

    Price: 1_____ 2_____ 3_____ 4_____ 5_____

    Quantity: 1_____ 2_____ 3_____ 4_____ 5_____

3. Give the equilibrium price and quantity and describe how equilibrium is achieved.

    Equilibrium point: Price_____ Quantity_____

Unit Three

Section 3.1 – Key Economic Questions

Section Objectives:

- Discuss how people make decisions by thinking at the margin

- Describe the three key economic questions of what to produce, how to produce and who consumes what is produced

Thinking at the margin

> **Marginal Utility** is the increased or decreased satisfaction from an increase or decrease in the amount of a good or service consumed.

Consumers make choices every day based on the costs and benefits of the use of resources. People make choices about which foods to purchase, which clothing to buy, which place to live, and whether or not to drive a car. Each of these decisions is based on an individual cost/benefit analysis that is driven by the needs and wants of the person. Consumer use of a product is subject to diminishing marginal utility as more units of the product are used, just as producers face diminishing marginal returns as they increase their output. Consumers continue to gain by purchasing more of a product as long as the marginal utility (benefit) derived exceeds the cost of purchasing additional units.

Consumers will change their purchasing decisions based on the resources available (money, typically) and the product choices available. The first law of demand states that the amount of a product purchased is inversely related to its price. What does this mean? It means that the number of units of a product purchased increases as the price decreases. This occurs because the opportunity cost to the customer decreases as the price decreases, so the customer is more willing to spend resources on the product than he would at a higher price point. However, as more units of the product are purchased, the marginal utility (added benefit) of each unit to the consumer decreases. A person can only use so many units of a product. Once the marginal utility is lower than the price for a product, consumers are unlikely to purchase the product unless the price is decreased. For example, if you have a washing machine in your home already, the marginal utility of a second washing machine is usually very low, so you are unlikely to purchase one. This effect is dampened by the law of marginal utility, too. Again, how many units of a product can be absorbed by a market?

The tendency to substitute a relatively cheaper product for a more expensive product is called the substitution effect.

Another factor is the cost of a product relative to consumer income. The income of consumers tends to be constant. A reduction in the price of a product increases real income, which is the amount of goods and services the consumer is able to purchase. Consumers typically purchase the less expensive products because they can better afford to do so. This is called the income effect. An increase in the price of a good reduces real income, which discourages buying on the part of the consumer.

When these two effects (substitution and income) are combined, consumers will generally purchase less of a good. What happens when price increases? The opportunity cost of using the product rises when the price rises. What happens to marginal utility, however? Marginal utility per unit increases because the consumer is utilizing fewer units of the product. Remember that marginal utility is the additional benefit the consumer derives from the use of an additional unit of the product.

The key questions of production are influenced by the willingness of consumers to purchase specific products. These factors of production are the following:

- What should be produced?

- How should the goods be produced?

- Who will consume the goods produced?

All three of these concepts are driven by consumer demand. The companies who are producing goods and services must understand the demand for the goods they are producing. There must be a market for the products or there is no point in producing the goods. Once demand has been established, the next question is how the goods should be produced to maximize profit to the producer and marginal utility to the consumer. A major consideration of the decision to produce a good is who will consume the goods. An expensive product directed at a luxury consumer will have a different level of demand than an economy product directed at a budget-conscious consumer. Think about the vehicles that people drive. The majority of cars on the road are low to middle-priced vehicles. People purchase what they are able to afford to drive. The demand for luxury cars is much lower than the demand for the less expensive vehicles.

Due to a lower demand for luxury cars, manufacturers produce less
like the sports car above.

Consumers and companies think at the margin to maximize benefit and efficiency in the use of resources. In order to maximize benefit and efficiency, the manufacturers of products must consider what should be produced, how it should be produced, and who the end user for the product will be.

Concept Reinforcement:

1. Define marginal utility.

2. Describe how people make decisions to increase marginal utility of purchases.

3. Discuss how the key economic questions of production are influenced by consumers.

Section 3.2 – Free Market Economy

Section Objectives:

- Evaluate a circular flow of a free market economy

- Study the self-regulating nature of the marketplace

Free Market Economy

The free market economy is an economic system in which the forces of supply and demand set prices. No government intervention regarding price or production of goods and services exists. Producers decide what they will produce and consumers decide what they will purchase. This is different than a planned economy, in which the central government makes policy and decisions about production levels and prices.

In a free-market economy, money flows between businesses and consumers through product markets and factor markets. A product market is where a business sells goods and services to households. A factor market exists where households engaged in entrepreneurial activities sell labor, land, capital, and entrepreneurial ability, the factors of production, to businesses. Money can flow either through the consumers to the businesses or from the businesses to the consumers.

The free market is a self-regulating environment. Supply and demand are forces that act upon each other to regulate the market. If a consumer good or service is in high demand, the supply will increase to meet demand until it is no longer profitable for the company supplying the good or service to continue increasing production. For example, let's say that there is an increase in demand for retro products, such as lava lamps. Lava lamps are products that are specific to the 1970s and that enjoy occasional increases in demand as they come back into style. As the demand for lava lamps increases, the price will increase until the supply and demand for lava lamps equalizes. As the lamps go out of style, the demand for the product will decrease, likely resulting in both decreased supply and price for the product.

Inelasticity is a relative unresponsiveness in price as it relates to changes in supply or demand. Generally a good that individuals would buy regardless of price are considered inelastic.

The concept we just described applies to all products. Some products are very sensitive to changes in supply, demand, and price. These are typically products that are considered unnecessary. Other products are insensitive to price changes, meaning that people will purchase them regardless of price. Demand may decrease slightly, but not as much as for a product that is considered non-essential, such as a lava lamp.

Concept Reinforcement:

1. Describe the circular flow of a free market economy.

2. How does a free market economy regulate itself?

3. Give an example of free market economy self-regulation that was not presented in this section.

Section 3.3 – Factors that Influence Decisions

Section Objectives:

- Describe examples of public goods

- Study how the substitution effect and the income effect influence decisions

Public goods are things that everyone wants, but no one wants to pay for. Examples are clean air, a well-educated population, universal health care, and clean water. Markets and governments tend to be very inefficient at delivering public goods, such as education, clean air, and clean water. There are efforts underway in the U.S. to increase the efficiency of the delivery of public goods. These efforts, including tradable emission credits and school voucher programs, have met with limited success so far.

In microeconomics, an indifference curve is a tool used to show combinations of goods and services that consumer will find useful even though it doesn't matter which combination is available. Each combination is of equal value to the customer. In other words, any of the combinations that appear on the curve will provide equal utility and benefit. Each point on the curve represents the quantity of each good the consumer purchase based on a fixed income.

The chart below shows an indifference curve for two products. Any combination of Product A and Product B that falls on the curve will provide the same utility to the consumer.

Indifference Curve

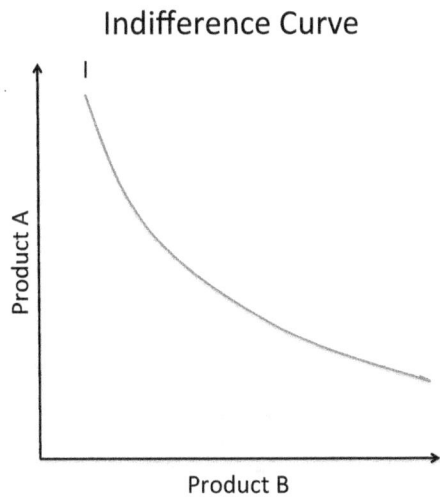

The substitution effect is the effect of changes in the relative price of a good on the level of consumption for that good. An increase in the price of one good causes a consumer to purchase more of the other good (substitution) because the first good has become relatively more expensive. The opposite also holds true. A decrease in the price of one good causes a consumer to purchase more of that good because it is relatively less expensive than the second good.

The income effect reflects the increase in real income of the consumer, either as a result of a price drop or an increase in wages. A drop in prices allows the consumer to purchase more goods, which is an increase in consumer purchasing power. Higher real income leads to an increase in demand for a normal good (a product for which demand increases as income increases and vice versa). Lower real income, resulting from an increase in prices or loss of wages, leads to a decrease in demand for a normal good.

The income effect has an interesting effect on inferior goods. Inferior goods are those for which demand decreases as real income increases. Examples of inferior goods are generic and non-name brand food products, instant noodles, and discount store clothing.

Concept Reinforcement:

1. Define public goods and give a couple of examples of public goods. Explain why public goods are difficult to deliver in an efficient manner.

2. Describe how the substitution affect and income effect interact to influence consumer purchasing decisions.

3. The income effect has different effects of normal goods and inferior goods. Describe the differences.

Section 3.4 – Consumer Choice and Resource Efficiency

Section Objectives:

- Distinguish between normal goods and inferior goods

- Discuss how a price-based system leads to a wider choice of goods and more efficient allocation of resources

Normal goods are goods for which demand increases when real income increases and decreases when real income decreases. Think about how you make spending decisions based upon the money you have available to you. If you are hungry and go to a restaurant to buy lunch, you will make different choices depending on the money available to you. If you have $5.00 for lunch, you will go to an inexpensive restaurant at which you will be able to purchase enough food to satisfy your hunger. The quality of the food is not likely to be high, but it will be sufficient to meet your needs. If, however, you have $30.00 to spend on lunch, you may go to a fine dining restaurant and order fresh broiled fish, salad and fruit, all of which are made of high quality, fresh ingredients.

Inferior goods are those goods for which demand decreases as real income increases and increases as real income decreases. Some of these goods show such consistent trends that they are used as reliable markers of the health of an economy. Instant noodles are one of these products. They are very inexpensive and are often used as a substitute for higher quality, more expensive foods.

Resource Allocation, Choice and Price

Adam Smith wrote about the invisible hand in his book "The Wealth of Nations." The fundamental idea behind the invisible hand is that market economies support spontaneous order, meaning that the market will naturally move to its most efficient structure based on each individual pursuing his own self-interests. In other words, people acting to help themselves ultimately contribute to the efficiency of the market. A totally free market is completely neutral. The producers who are most efficient in meeting the needs of the consumer will thrive. The producers are not efficient will either struggle or fail. The free market is flexible and adapts to changes in technology, resource availability, and society to reach the new point of maximum efficiency.

Freedom of choice is a key component of the free market. Producers are free to choose what to produce, how much to produce, the price they will charge, and the quality of the goods they produce. Consumers are free to choose whether to purchase goods or not, based on their available resources, needs and wants. Freedom of production and freedom of consumption are directly related to supply and demand of goods and services. Supply and demand meet at the equilibrium point for the product, which is where the producer is willing to supply as much of a good or service as the consumer demands.

Markets that are restricted by central government policies are unable to be as efficient as possible. Central government policies that affect resource allocation, production and distribution of products can lead to inefficiencies and disorder in the market. As an example, the former Soviet Union allocated a disproportionate amount of resources to the military and the central government set policy that the factories would produce specific goods. This resulted in the basic goods and services the general population needed, such as bread and shoes, being scarce, while the military and governmental elite had access to the majority of the resources of the country. A free market removes the administrative costs of managing a central government policy on production of a good or service. A free market also diminishes incentives to control the market because everyone receives maximum benefit at equilibrium.

Concept Reinforcement:

1. Define normal goods and give examples of how demand for normal goods changes with real income.

2. Define inferior goods and give examples of how demand for inferior goods changes with real income.

3. Describe how selfish individual behavior helps free market reach equilibrium, maximize consumer choice and ensure efficient resource allocation.

Section 3.5 – Price-Based Systems

Section Objectives:

- List the advantages of a price-based system

- Distinguish between a good that is normal and a good that is inferior

- Distinguish between a substitute good and a complementary good

A price-based system has the advantage of maximizing market efficiency. The system is efficient because the balance of market forces (supply and demand) determines the optimal price for the product. If a resource is limited, the producer is unable to supply as much of the good, so the price increases. Likewise, if resources become more available, supply increases and price drops, which typically generates an increase in demand.

Other advantages include development of a wide variety of goods and services to meet the varying needs of the consumers. A price-based system leads to companies offering discount items, middle-range items, and luxury items. The needs and wants of each individual are met.

Companies will sometimes try to set the price of a good higher than it would normally be, based on pure supply and demand, to increase the perceived value of the good. Common examples of this are luxury brands of clothing and accessories. The higher price of the good limits the number of people who are able to purchase it, often making it more desirable to those consumers who brand conscious. Think of what happens when a sports star promotes a particular brand or model of shoe. The fact that the sports star has allowed his/her name to be associated with the shoe increases the perceived value of the shoe to those who find value in celebrity.

Substitute and Complementary Goods

Substitute goods are those that can take the place of one another. For example, pizza is a substitute for a ham sandwich. The choices consumers make about which goods to purchase are highly influenced by the cost of the goods. This applies to both necessary and luxury goods. The demand for necessities, such as water, food, and energy, is highly influenced by the cost of the good or service. Consumers will begin to change their behavior to conserve resources as the resources become more scarce, thus more expensive to purchase. As an example, water is a scarce resource in the desert southwest. In order to conserve resources (financial and water), many people are moving away from having green grass lawns that require a lot of water to xeriscaping, which is a type of landscaping that does not require irrigation. In the desert, a xeriscaped lawn would have cactus and other desert plants instead of plants that require a lot of water.

Swedish gardeners who xeriscape use plants that are native to Sweden and are able to tolerate the extreme conditions found there.

Complementary goods are goods that are consumed with another good. For example, a hamburger and bun are complementary goods, as are pencils and erasers and bread and butter. If the demand for computers increases, for example, the demand for software will increase. Likewise, if the demand for salads decreases, the demand for salad dressings will probably also decrease.

Normal and Inferior Goods

Normal goods are goods for which demand increases when real income increases and decreases when real income decreases. There is a direct relationship between the increase in real income and the increase in demand for normal goods. As real income increases, the individual makes purchase choices that reflect his/her ability to purchase the 'finer' things in life. For example, our person may have an increase in real income that allows her to upgrade her kitchen appliances. She has a choice to make regarding the features she wants for each appliance. She can choose a basic model that is less expensive or a model with more features that costs more. Because our person has increased real income, she is likely to select appliances with more advanced features rather than just the basics. Another example of goods for which demand increases as real income increases is clothing. Think about the clothing poor people wear compared to those who are in the middle and upper economic groups. Poor people will maximize their resources by purchasing inexpensive clothes, often from resale shops. Those in the middle class may be more likely to purchase new clothes, but will often base purchase decisions on price more than quality of the goods. As people have more real income, they are able to purchase goods and services that have either real or perceived increases in quality or status. Think of the differences between a suit off the rack at a department store and a custom tailored suit. They both present a professional appearance, but vary significantly in price. A price based system allows people at all economic levels to make purchasing choices that are the best use of their resources.

Inferior goods are those goods for which demand decreases as real income increases and increases as real income decreases. The real income of many people decreased as a result of the rapid increase in gas prices in the mid-2000s. Real income decreased because people used a higher proportion of their resources to purchase transportation, in particular. As transportation costs increase, people will choose less expensive modes of transportation. Bus travel increases as real income decreases because the cost in dollars for traveling a certain distance is less than flying the same distance.

Concept Reinforcement:

1. Discuss two advantages of a price-based system.

2. List examples of normal and inferior goods and describe why the goods you listed are normal or inferior.

3. Define substitute and complementary goods and how the demand for each is impacted by a change in the original good.

Section 3.6 – Goods and Occupational Trends

Section Objective:

- Evaluate past and present occupational trends

Past and Present Occupational Trends

People are employed in occupations. Occupations include all of the jobs people do to earn money. The U.S. Department of Labor's Bureau of Labor Statistics publishes the "Occupational Outlook Handbook" every other year. The 2008-09 edition includes the following occupational categories: management, professional, service, sales, administrative, farming, construction, installation, production, transportation, and armed forces. The handbook provides detailed information about occupations within each of the occupational categories described above, including required education, pay ranges, current and anticipated demand for employees, and a number of other variables that are employment-related statistics.

Let's look at examples from each of the occupational categories.

Management: This group of occupations includes management, business and financial operations occupations. A few of the specific jobs included are administrative services managers, computer and information systems managers, education administrators, human resources, accountants, budget analysis, management analysts and top executives. This is a broad category that is present in all industries. Management positions typically require at least a four-year degree and often an advanced degree. As of July 2007, job applicants with four-year college degrees were receiving starting offers of $41,680 per year.

Professional: Professional occupations include many computer and mathematical jobs, architects, surveyors, cartographers, engineers, drafters, engineering technicians, life scientists, physical scientists, social scientists, science technicians, community and social services professionals, legal professionals, teachers, librarians, museum curators, artists and designers, entertainers, performers, athletes, media, communications, and medical professionals. Professional occupations can require anywhere from a high school (athletes and artists) to doctoral education. Wages in professional occupations range widely, from starving artists to highly-paid physicians and athletes. The estimated salary range for high school teachers in May 2007 was from $32,920 to $71,800, with a median salary of $49,420.

Service: Service occupations range from healthcare, protective services (corrections, police, fire, and security), food service, building and grounds maintenance, and personal care work. The educational requirements for service jobs tend to be lower than for management or professional occupations. High school diplomas may or may not be necessary for some of the occupations, such as grounds keeping or building maintenance. Other occupations require a two- or four-year degree or some other certification of skills. The May 2007 estimated range of hourly wages for fire fighters was from $10.35/hour to $32.83/hour.

Sales: Advertising, cashiers, clerks, product demonstrators, insurance agents, real estate brokers, retail sales people, travel agents, and securities traders are among the occupations included in this category. Many of these occupations require no formal training and pay low wages. Insurance, real estate, and financial sales occupations typically require some formal training and may require certification by an independent certification board. Again, most of the positions demand low wages, but others can result in high incomes, often as a result of sales-based commissions. The more product sold, the more money the salesperson earns. Insurance agent wages were estimated to range from $12.13 per hour to more than $54/hour as of May 2007.

Office and Administrative Support: Occupations in this category include financial clerks, information and record clerks, material (recording, scheduling, dispatch and distribution) occupations, and other office and administrative support positions. These jobs tend to demand low to middle-range wages and do not typically require any education beyond a high school education. The May 2007 hourly wages for executive secretaries and administrative assistants ranged from $12.53/hour to more than $28.50 per hour.

Farming, fishing and forestry: These occupations include agricultural workings, fishers, fishing vessel operators, forester, conservationists, and loggers. Some of these occupations require degrees (conservationist, forester), but most do not. These are physically-demanding occupations that often demand low to moderate wages. As an example, the highest paid fishing industry wage workers earn about $45,000.

Construction trades: This group of occupations includes the skilled trades, such as masons, carpenters, plumbers, and electricians, as well as a wide variety of construction-related occupations. Many of the skilled trades require workers to complete apprenticeships that can last up to five years and improve their skills through a variety of training programs. In May 2006, the hourly rate paid to electrical workers ranged from $17.15/hour to $31.90/hour.

Installation, maintenance and repair occupations: These include electrical, electronics, vehicle, mobile equipment, and other installation, maintenance, and repair occupations. In May 2007, the wages for auto mechanics ranged from about $9.25/hour to $27.72/hour.

Production: The production occupations include factory workers, assemblers, fabricators, food processors, metal and plastic workers, printers, textile, apparel, furnishing and other production-related occupations. Many of these occupations require specialized technical training, often obtained at vocational schools or through apprenticeship programs. The May 2007 wage range for machinists was from $10.42/hour to $25.83/hour.

Transportation and material moving: This group of occupations includes air transportation occupations, material moving occupations, motor vehicle operators, rail and water transportation. This group of occupations usually requires a high school diploma, but may also require additional technical training. For example, people who drive semi-trucks are trained at specialized truck-driving schools. The May 2007 hourly wage range for a semi driver was $11.24 to $26.24/hour.

Armed Forces: The armed forces include a wide range of occupations, with different educational and skill level requirements. The enlisted occupations require a high school diploma. The officer positions require a minimum of a bachelor's degree, and require advanced training as the officer is promoted to higher ranking positions. The monthly pay for the entry-level, enlisted personnel was $1,203.90 as of April 2007. The monthly pay for an entry-level officer was $2,469.30 at that same time.

The occupations available to people have changed dramatically as technology has changed. Think back to the 1800s. All of the basic occupations are the same as they are now. The technologies used to perform the duties of the various occupations have changed dramatically. Combustion engines, mass production, and computer technologies are three changes in technology that created new occupations. Combustion engines opened up occupations maintaining the engines (mechanics), building the engines (machinists and others), and upholstering the seats, as just a few examples. Mass production opened up a tremendous number of jobs working on the production lines. Computers have had an incredible impact on occupations. Almost every job a person can hold now requires some level of computer skills.

One result of the increased use of technology is a shift in the skill sets employees must have to be able to perform their duties. The computer industry has created a huge number of jobs programming software, maintaining hardware, developing user tools, creating and maintaining web sites, managing networks, and trouble-shooting systems, to name just a few. All of these jobs require technical education and skills that are typically gained through post-high school education. Computer skills are not just limited to the computer industry. Employees working in any technical profession (medical, graphic design, research and development, architecture, etc.) will have to have strong computer skills to perform their work.

FIGURE 1. U.S. industrial R&D employment: 1990–2001

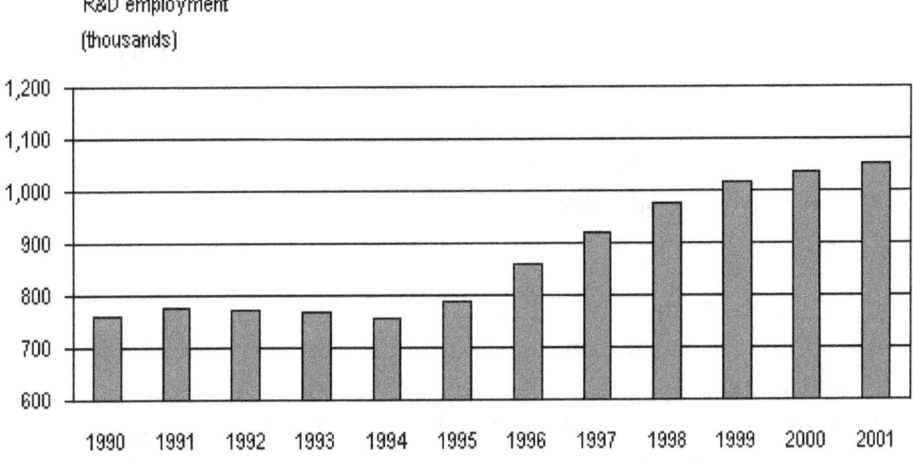

NOTE: R&D employment data are for full-time-equivalent employees.

SOURCE: National Science Foundation, Survey of Industrial R&D.

Concept Reinforcement:

1. List four of the major occupational groups and the characteristics of the jobs in those groups.

2. Describe how educational levels affect income potential.

3. Discuss how technological advances have changed the available occupations.

Section 3.7 – Labor Force Trends

Section Objectives:

- Identify how trends in the labor force are tracked

- Describe and explain trends in the wages and benefits paid to US workers

Labor Force Trends and How They are Tracked

The Bureau of Labor Statistics of the U.S. Government collects, analyzes and publishes data about the labor force in the U.S. The data collected include information on job title, responsibilities, salary, occupational category, educational requirements, demographics, geographic area, benefits, unemployment levels, new job creation, job loss, industry, productivity, safety, consumer spending, inflation, imports, exports and a number of other categories.

Each month the Current Employment Statistics (CES) group of the BLS surveys about 150,000 businesses and government agencies, which represent about 390,000 individual work sites. The survey collects detailed industry data on employment, hours and earnings on nonfarm payrolls for all of the state, the District of Columbia, Puerto Rico, the Virgin Islands, and over 300 metropolitan areas. Nonfarm payrolls are the payrolls for jobs that are not related to farming activities.

The CES group analyzes the collected data to understand employment trends based on geographic area, industry, worker demographics, etc. They publish a monthly report that summarizes information, as in the charts below, which are from "The Employment Situation: April 2008" that was published by BLS in May 2008. Chart 1 shows trends in the unemployment rate from May 2005 to April 2008. Chart 2 shows nonfarm employment for the same time frame.

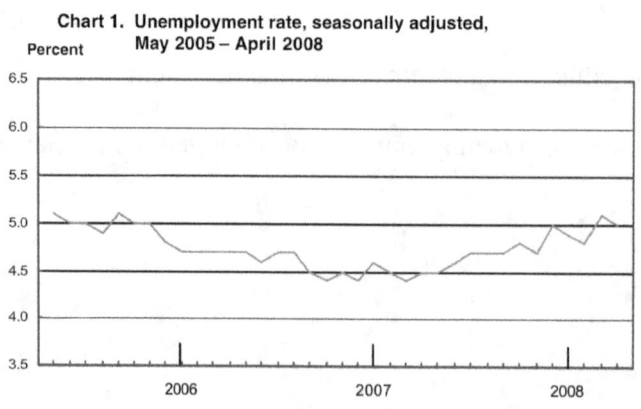

Chart 1. Unemployment rate, seasonally adjusted, May 2005 – April 2008

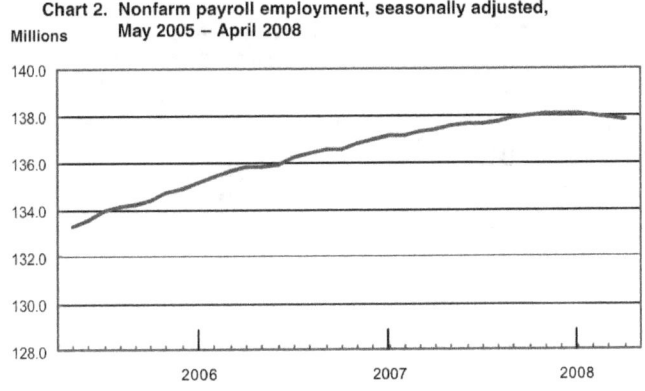

Chart 2. Nonfarm payroll employment, seasonally adjusted, May 2005 – April 2008

Trends in U.S. Worker Wages and Benefits

Employees work to both receive money (wages) and to have fringe benefits (health insurance, retirement, life insurance, dental insurance, vacation, sick leave, and disability insurance). Some employers provide more or less in the way of fringe benefits.

The charts below are from the Bureau of Labor Statistics and reflect the availability of specific benefits and the employee participation rate for each benefit. The employee participation rate is a measure of how many employees take advantage of the benefits offered by the employer. The chart below reflects benefits offered by private industry. It is important to understand the benefits available before accepting a position.

Essential chart

Chart 1. Access and participation rates of workers by selected benefits, private industry, March 2007

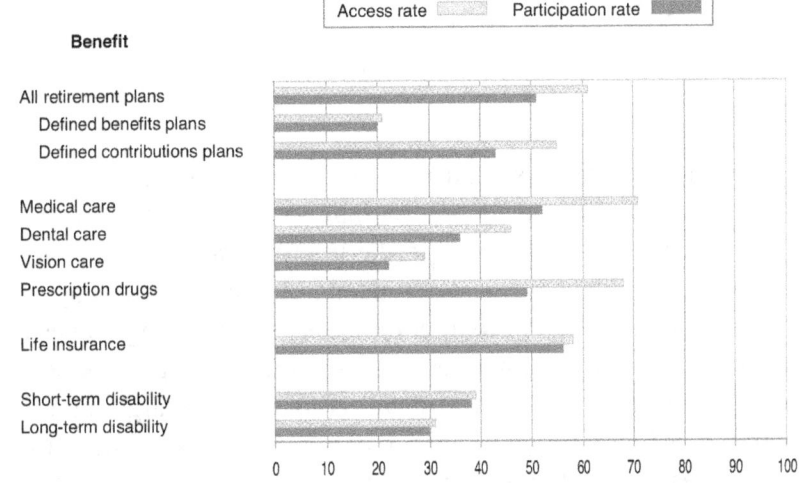

Note: The access rate represents the percent of employees offered the benefit and the participation rate represents the percent of employees that receive the benefit.

Fringe benefits are often expressed as a component of total compensation, which includes wages and fringe benefits. The chart below shows the value of benefits in relationship to wages. Notice that health insurance is rising rapidly, while other benefits are actually falling.

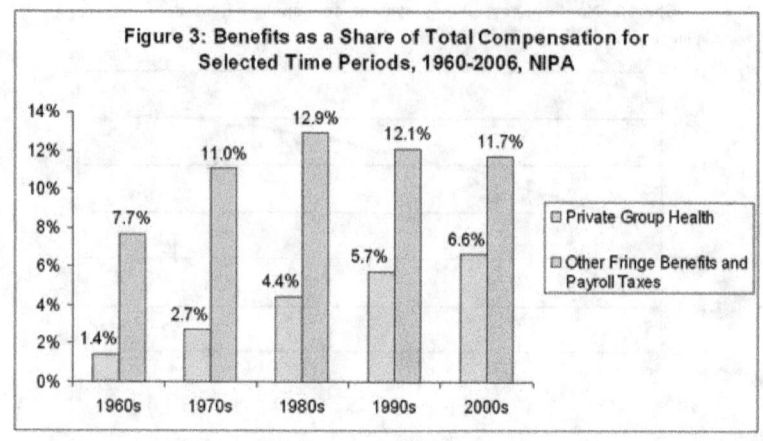

Figure 3: Benefits as a Share of Total Compensation for Selected Time Periods, 1960-2006, NIPA

Per capita personal income is a measure of income per capita (per person) in the country. The data for this and many other economic statistics are provided by the Bureau of Economic Analysis, which is part of the U.S. Department of Commerce.

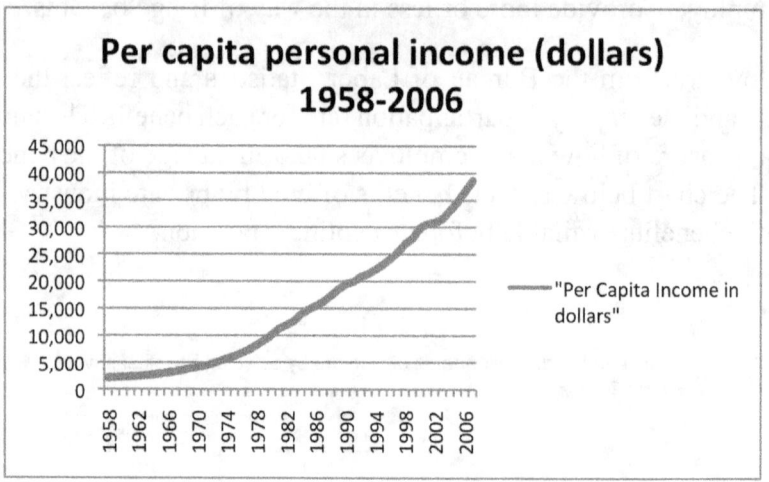

Source: Data from Bureau of Economic Analysis, regional economic accounts data.

The U.S. government tracks labor statistics for all components of the U.S. market, as well as internationally. These data are available for analysts to understand the labor market and economy from the local level all the way to the international level. These data are useful indicators of economic health as well as to understand how the economy of this country is changing and developing. Trends in total compensation, including wages and fringe benefits, have been increasing for U.S. workers. The components of fringe benefits are changing because of the rising cost of health care, which is taking a larger and larger portion of the fringe benefits. This increasing cost has led employers to assess the fringe benefits they offer and to sometimes change the mix of benefits to manage costs.

Concept Reinforcement:

1. Describe how labor force statistics are tracked and used.

2. Define the components of total compensation and describe how they are different.

Section 3.8 – The U.S. Labor Force

Section Objectives:

- Summarize how the U.S. labor force is changing

- Evaluate the relationship between supply and demand in the labor market

The Age Wave Theory of Harry Dent says that consumer spending peaks at age 50. As a result, the aging of the Baby Boom Generation will have a dramatic effect on economic activity, which peaked in 2012 in Europe and the United States.

The U.S. labor force is changing in a fundamental way. The baby boomers (people born between 1946 and 1964 – after World War II) have begun to retire, leaving more job openings than there are experienced people to fill them. In addition, the labor force participation rate, which is the proportion of the working-age population that is either working or actively looking for work, is declining in the population under age 55. The labor force participation rate is directly linked to the health of the economy. When the economy is strong and jobs are plentiful, more people join the labor force because they are able to find work. The opposite occurs, as well, when the economy is weak. The job market shrinks, making it more difficult for people to find work, which reduces the labor force participation rate. The chart below from the U.S. Government's Bureau of Labor Statistics shows general labor participation rates from 1948 to 2005.

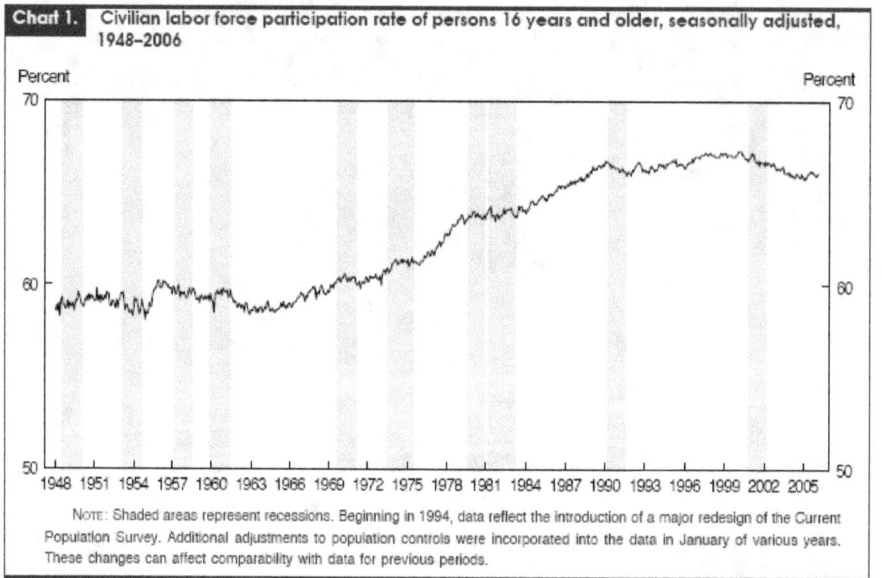

Source: Trends in Labor Force Participation in the United States. By Abraham Mosisa and Steven Hippie of the Division of Labor Force Statistics, Bureau of Labor Statistics.

Other changes in the labor force include declining participation by men and a rapid increase in women participating in the labor force after World War II. Fewer high school students are participating in the labor force because they are staying enrolled in school rather than dropping out to work. This is important for the future success of the country because so many careers now require a high level of education and technical skills at the entry level.

The chart below shows the trends in the labor force participation rate from 1948 to 2006.

Women have had the largest increase in participation since World War II, with the general population over 55 years of age increasing significantly since the early 1990s. The population between 16 and 24 years of age has a reduced participation rate as a result of the increased enrollment in school.

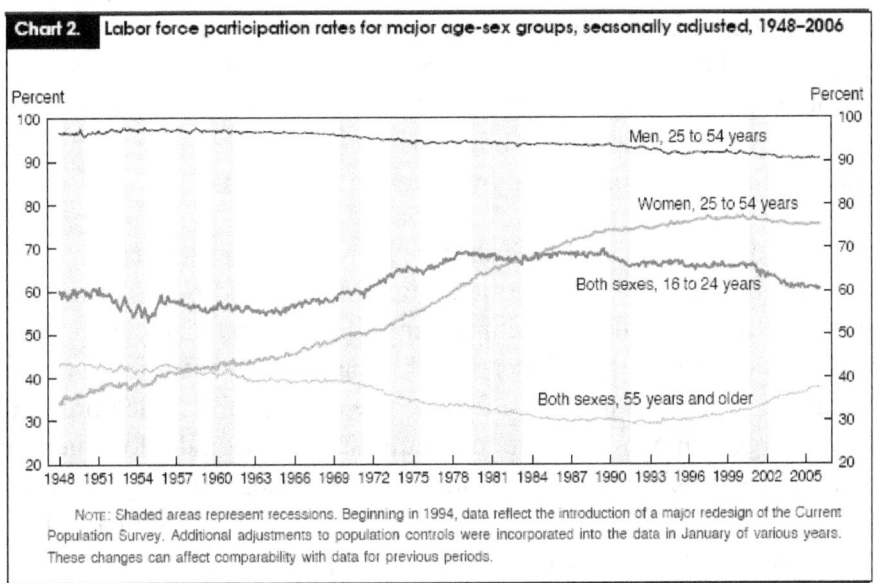

Chart 2. Labor force participation rates for major age-sex groups, seasonally adjusted, 1948–2006

NOTE: Shaded areas represent recessions. Beginning in 1994, data reflect the introduction of a major redesign of the Current Population Survey. Additional adjustments to population controls were incorporated into the data in January of various years. These changes can affect comparability with data for previous periods.

Source: Trends in Labor Force Participation in the United States. By Abraham Mosisa and Steven Hippie of the Division of Labor Force Statistics, Bureau of Labor Statistics.

Another important factor that is affecting the labor force is immigration. People immigrate to the U.S. for a number of reasons. Many young people come to the U.S. to attend school. Others wish to pursue careers that they are not able to in their home countries for various political, social or economic reasons. Still others wish to escape desperate economic situations in their home countries. America is still considered the land of opportunity.

The immigrant labor force is remaining at about the same percentage of the total U.S. labor force over time. This is very different from what is generally represented in politics and in the news. Immigrant labor plays a vital role in the U.S. economy. Some immigrants are willing to take whatever jobs they can get, which are often dirty, low-paying jobs that Americans don't want. Other immigrants bring high technical skill sets to the country in fields that contribute to the technology component of the U.S. economy. Computer science, biomedical research, and information technology are just a few fields that rely on the availability of skilled workers from other countries to work in the U.S.

Supply and Demand of Labor

As we discussed above, labor is a critical component of the U.S. economy. Just as with any other commodity, labor is subject to the forces of supply and demand. Think about the demand for unskilled labor, which includes jobs that do not require any specific education or technical training. Examples include laborers, dishwashers, field workers, and other similar jobs. Unskilled jobs do not typically have a high wage associated with them. Most unskilled workers are paid at the minimum wage or a little higher for their efforts. As the jobs demand higher levels of skill and education, the wages paid to the workers generally increase. This is not always the case, however. The value the market places on particular jobs will also affect the wages paid to the worker. There are certain professional jobs that are highly valued by society, but for which the pay scales are not consistent. Think about the difference between the wages an educator earns and the wages an attorney in private practice earns. The attorney is likely to earn several times more than the educator because of the financial value placed on legal services and education. Teachers are professionals who are working for the public good. Teachers are working to prepare each of you to join the U.S. economy as a productive member of the labor force. This contribution to the public good is of great value to the society, but is also subject to downward forces on compensation because teachers are usually paid by governmental funds.

A rapid increase in demand for a specific skill set increases the cost of labor to the employer because the employees are able to negotiate higher wages and benefits in order to maximize the benefit to the individual. The employer will benefit by hiring the individual, even at a higher rate, because the skill set is scarce. This happened in the information technology (IT) industry in the late 1990s and early 2000s. The demand for skilled programmers and other IT cause a large number of people to get training that would allow them to enter the field. As this large group of people was graduating and actually entering the work force, the changes in computing technology actually reduced the need for additional skilled workers, leading to a reduction in the compensation paid to IT professionals.

The forces affecting the labor supply (baby boomers, participation rate, and increases in the education required to perform jobs) directly affect the wages paid to the workers. Supply and demand apply just as much to labor as to any other raw material. When there is a surplus of labor, the price of the labor goes down. When there is a shortage, the price goes up until equilibrium is reached.

Concept Reinforcement:

1. Summarize the ongoing changes that are affecting the labor supply.

2. Discuss why you think immigration, even though the numbers have remained steady as a percent of the labor force, is such a contentious issue.

3. Describe how supply and demand apply to labor.

Section 3.9 – Factors Affecting Wages

Section Objectives:

- Identify other factors affecting wages, such as minimum wage and workplace safety laws

- Discuss how laws against wage discrimination affect wage levels

Supply and demand have a large impact on the wages paid to workers. An unskilled worker is likely to earn far less than a skilled worker. Likewise, a worker with a skill that is in high demand will be able to demand higher compensation than a worker with a skill that is in low demand.

There are several other factors that affect wages. These include the minimum wage, workplace safety laws, worker productivity, specialized skills, working conditions, location, union influence, mobility of labor, and race and sex discrimination.

Let's go through these one at a time.

The minimum wage is the absolute minimum hourly rate an employee may be paid for work. The minimum wage is set at the federal level, and sometimes raised by local or state governments. The goal of the minimum wage is to provide every worker with a living wage, meaning that all of life's necessities can be purchased with the wages paid. There is debate about whether this is actually the case. Jobs that pay the minimum wage are typically unskilled jobs that can be done by a wide variety of people. Whenever a proposal is made to increase the minimum wage, there is often pushback from businesses saying that they cannot afford to pay more wages to the workers for various reasons, including whether or not the business will remain open.

Workplace safety laws may affect wages negatively because of the actual costs of implementing safety regulations and the potential cost of a workplace injury. Companies are in business to make a profit. Every additional cost reduces the potential profit. Worker safety is a critical part of every production process. The cost of implementing safety regulations is a basic cost of doing business. It is possible for safety laws to become so stringent that companies, especially small companies, cannot afford to implement them. The balance of reasonable safety regulation and coping with the costs of supporting injured employees will have a downward pressure on wages. Workers may also be willing to reduce the amount of money they demand in wages if they are working in a safe environment.

Worker productivity is a reflection of how much work an employee is able to accomplish relative to others doing the same job. The higher the amount of work an employee is able to accomplish, the higher the revenues to the company, and the greater the profits. Companies will prefer highly productive workers to less productive workers and will be willing to pay a premium wage to the productive workers to retain them at the company.

Specialized skills increase the value of the individual worker to a company that requires the skills. For example, a highly skilled carpenter will be much more valuable to a construction company than someone who is just learning how to construct buildings. Likewise, a scientist who is skilled in manipulating cells will be much more valuable to a company that requires those skills than a scientist who is skilled in designing electronic devices.

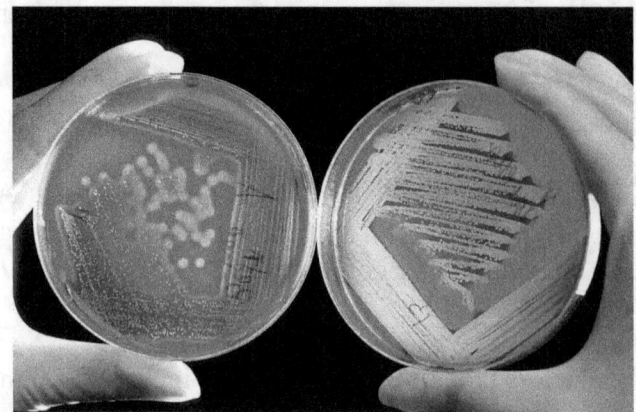

Working conditions will affect the employee's willingness to accept a specific wage. If an employee is going to be working on a strict schedule or in dangerous situations, for example, the employee will demand higher pay than she might in a work situation that is safe and flexible about schedule. An employee will often value the flexibility, safety or other employee-friendly characteristics of an employer more than higher pay.

Job location has a large influence on wages. A convenience store job in a big city with a high cost of living will pay more than the same job in a small town with a low cost of living. Mobility of labor is related to job location. If the labor force needed by a company is available locally, the wages will not be affected. However, if the labor force required by the business is located elsewhere, in other words people need to move to work at the company, this will influence wages. The company will need to compete for people in different markets, whose wages may be higher, and attract them to the company's location.

Unions have had a large influence on wages, both positive and negative. Unions originally formed to help workers earn a competitive wage and have safe working conditions. Unions and corporate managers negotiate specific terms of employment for the union members. Unions try to maximize the benefit to the workers and unions while corporate managers try to minimize labor costs while retaining workers. This has sometimes backfired on union members when management and the union were unable to reach an agreement on terms. A lack of agreement can lead to a strike, which means lost wages to the employee.

Wage discrimination often occurs in the context of race or sex discrimination. When discrimination exists, the people of the race or sex that is being discriminated against typically earn lower wages than the other employment groups. When discrimination results in a lawsuit, this increases the costs to the company and reduces profits. It also damages the reputation of the company accused of the discriminatory behavior. Unions and governmental legislation have also added to the cost of wage discrimination. Unions have formalized procedures in place to address employee complaints. The administrative costs of addressing these complaints can be significant because of the number of hours of employee, union representative and management effort required to address the problems. Additionally, if a company is found to have engaged in wage discrimination, the company is usually forced to review the wages of all the employees of the company for equity (fairness) and increase the wages of those whose wages are low. Governmental legislation mandates a minimum federal, and sometimes state or local, wage be paid to each employee. As the minimum wage increases, wages increase for all employees to ensure that all employees are being paid in an equitable manner.

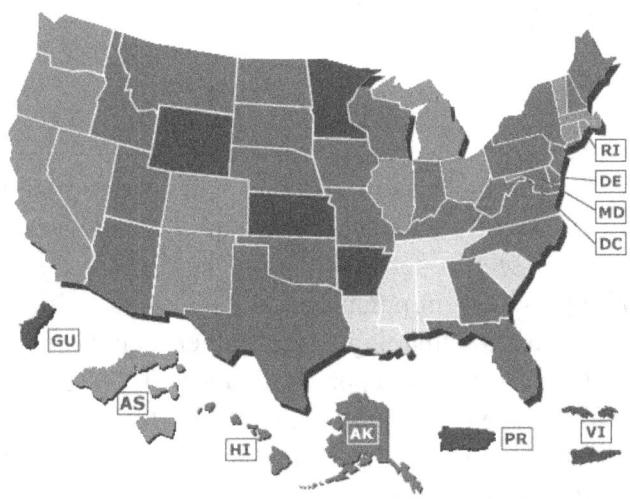

States with minimum wage rates higher than the Federal rate.

States with minimum wage rates the same as the Federal rate.

States with no minimum wage law.

States with minimum wage rates lower than the Federal rate.

American Samoa has special minimum wage rates.

Wages are influenced by a number of factors, some of which push wages up and some of which reduce wages. Some of these factors are affected by the employee, some by the government, some by unions, and some by employers.

Concept Reinforcement:

1. Discuss how unions have affected labor costs.

2. Describe how government regulations, such as minimum wage and workplace safety laws affect labor costs.

3. How does discrimination affect wages?

Section 3.10 – Skill Levels and Job Migration

Section Objectives:

- Study the connection between wages and skill levels

- Identify the effects of job migration

Wages and Skill Levels – What is the Connection?

The U.S. economy is gaining more and more jobs that require highly skilled employees to perform technical jobs. Highly technical jobs require employees with the appropriate technical training and skill sets to perform them. These skills are obtained by continuing education beyond high school in pursuit of Associate, Bachelor, Master and Doctoral degrees. The opportunity cost of attending school rather than working is compensated for by the higher wages typically earned upon graduation. The Bureau of Labor Statistics published the chart below in their Occupational Outlook Quarterly in the fall of 2006. This chart shows the relationship between educational level and average weekly earnings. The trend is that as you achieve a higher level of education, you also earn more money. This is not always the case, of course. Many other factors such as work ethic, job availability, and location will also affect your ability to earn money.

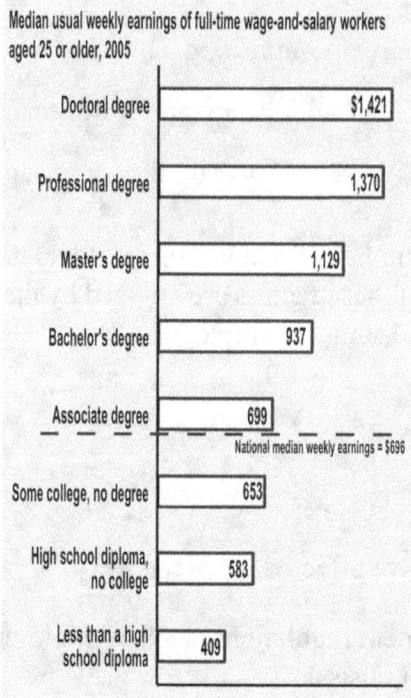

The chart above shows median weekly earnings for people at different levels. If you want to see what the weekly median earnings equate to for a year, simply multiply the weekly figure by 52 (weeks). For example, for those with less than a high school diploma, the average annual salary was 409 x 52 = $21,268. The national median income was $696 per week in 2005, which equates to annual earnings of $36,192. The average for a person holding a bachelor's degree in 2005 was $937 x 52 weeks, for an annual wage of $48,724. This is not to say that you will or will not earn any of these specific amounts. That will depend upon you.

There are other ways to gain skill levels, such as serving an apprenticeship to learn a trade. The trades include skilled professions such as carpenter, plumber, electrician, painter, and the other building trades. There are other types of trades, as well, such as shoe repair or seamstress.

Job migration is closely connected to wages. Employers are motivated to earn profit. One of the costs they work to carefully control in earning a profit is the cost of labor. If labor costs become too high in one area, companies may decide to move their operations else-where, taking the jobs with them (migration). There are many reasons companies move jobs from one place to another, including supply and demand for products and services, business conditions, labor markets, government policies, political reasons, competition, environmental conditions, local business costs, technological obsolescence, outsourcing, and higher productivity.

It is typically most efficient to manufacture products near the location that has the highest demand for the product or service. Transportation of goods from the factory to the retail store is getting increasingly expensive because of rapidly increasing fuel prices and increases in the costs of labor, and it is often important to be near the client when providing a service because of the time and money cost of travel.

Business conditions may motivate companies to move jobs elsewhere, especially if the move reduces the cost of production. Labor markets, governmental policy, local business costs, environmental conditions and politics can all affect business conditions and the decision to keep jobs in a location or move them to another location. If a company is in need of a pool of employees with a specific skill set, that company may choose to locate near other companies that require similar skill sets or near an educational institution that trains students in those skills. Another condition could be the availability of raw materials or access to a shipping system (rail, water).

Technological obsolescence (outdated technology) may result in conditions that allow the company to move out of the outdated facilities and relocate where the raw materials and highly skilled talent they need are located. This could even lead to outsourcing of work to other companies that are already set up to do specific processes with state of the art equipment. It is getting to the point where many companies simply outsource portions of their production process to other companies who are able to make the component at a lower cost. In many cases, jobs are outsourced to other countries, such as Mexico and India, which have lower employment costs.

Job migration typically has a negative economic effect on the area losing the jobs, but a positive effect on the community gaining the jobs. Those who lose jobs often face a very difficult transition because they have to learn a new skill set or move to retain their old jobs. This is part of the market balancing itself to produce goods and services at the most efficient quantity and price.

Concept Reinforcement:

1. Describe the general trend showing the relationship between educational level and wages.

2. Do you think it is possible to have too much education? What effect might highly specialized training have on job availability and wages?

3. Describe job migration and the various conditions that may lead to job migration within the U.S. and outside the U.S.

Section 3.11 – Job Stresses And Wage Differentials

Section Objectives:

- Study the connection between job stresses and wages

- Describe and compare earnings differences between men and women

- Describe net gain or loss of jobs

Job Stresses and Wages

Job stress is a part of life for everyone who works. The National Institute of Occupational Safety and Health (NIOSH) studies stress levels in the workplace. NIOSH did a large study in the 1990s to better understand the factors that lead to job stress. An interesting finding is that job stress is more closely linked with health problems than with financial or family problems. In fact, the NIOSH report on the 1990s study indicated that 40% of workers reported that their jobs were very or extremely stressful, and 75% of employees believe that workers have more stress now than they did a generation ago.

Job stress can lead to health problems, stress, behavioral problems, and even violence. Think about the source of the phrase "going postal." Job stress can result from insecurity about continued employment or working too many hours. Job stress results in health problems, such as migraines, back and neck pain, more frequently than financial or family problems.

Some high stress jobs demand a higher wage. For example, a person working third shift is paid a night differential for the stress and inconvenience of working at night. There are some jobs that actually pay hazardous duty pay, such as when military members are in a combat zone.

Gender Differences and Wages

The Bureau of Labor Statistics tracks demographic information on the labor force in the US. One of the demographic measures they track is the average earnings for men and women in different occupations. The table below shows the median weekly earnings for men, women and then both combined, as well as a measure of women's earnings as a percent of men's earnings. As you can see by looking through the chart, women earned between 62.6% and 95.8% of what men earned in 2006, depending upon the industry. These numbers have improved over time, although they are still not equally matched. In 1979, the median proportion was 62.5% of what men earned. In 1998, the proportion increased to 76.3% of what men earned. By 2007, the proportion increased to 80.8% of what men earned.

Why do you think there is such a disparity between what men and women earn, on average? Some fundamental factors include experience and education level. Women have been gaining traction in the business world by increasing their education achievements. In 1970, only about 1/10th of women in the work force had a four-year bachelor's degree. By 2007, this percentage had risen to 1/3rd of the women in the work force. An equally important statistic is the number of women who completed their high school educations. In 1970, 34% of women were high school dropouts. By 2006, the dropout rate was 8% for women.

Another factor that affects women's earning capacity is the decision of whether to have a family or not. Women traditionally shoulder most of the burden for child care and household chores, although that is changing as more men choose to either be stay-at-home dads or contribute more equally to the child care and household duties. The breaks in careers to allow for child birth and rearing impact the amount of experience a woman has at the same age as a man. If a woman takes two years to have children, then returns to work, she has two years less professional experience on her resume, which may put her at a disadvantage against others who did not take a break from work. Women also tend to take the burden of elder care when aging parents require assistance. This role can also lead to a break in service from a profession. This can put a woman at a disadvantage, especially in rapidly changing, highly technical fields.

The Glass Ceiling is a term used in economics to describe the situation that occurs when qualified applicants within an organization stop advancing on the career ladder due to some form of discrimination.

Table 19. **Median usual weekly earnings of full-time wage and salary workers by industry and sex, 2006 annual averages**

Industry	Both Sexes		Women		Men		Women's earnings as percent of men's
	Total Employed	Median Weekly Earnings	Total Employed	Median Weekly Earnings	Total Employed	Median Weekly Earnings	
Total, 16 years and over..........................	106,106	$671	46,358	$600	59,747	$743	80.8
Agriculture and related industries	911	437	175	378	735	449	84.2
Mining	615	912	73	780	542	935	83.4
Construction	8,262	646	688	622	7,574	649	95.8
Manufacturing	15,063	703	4,297	564	10,765	767	73.5
Durable goods	9,752	729	2,477	587	7,275	782	75.1
Nondurable goods	5,310	649	1,820	520	3,490	735	70.7
Wholesale and retail trade	14,868	578	5,917	484	8,951	647	74.8
Wholesale trade	3,821	724	1,072	612	2,749	775	79.0
Retail trade	11,047	520	4,845	460	6,202	599	76.8
Transportation and utilities	6,126	766	1,388	677	4,738	804	84.2
Transportation and warehousing	4,968	737	1,148	654	3,820	767	85.3
Utilities	1,158	933	240	761	918	978	77.8
Information	2,858	860	1,223	722	1,635	982	73.5
Financial activities	8,087	758	4,548	659	3,539	974	67.7
Finance and insurance	6,099	795	3,612	668	2,487	1,138	58.7
Real estate and rental and leasing	1,988	665	936	622	1,053	718	86.6
Professional and business services	10,197	753	4,198	649	5,999	862	75.3
Professional and technical services	6,032	997	2,652	769	3,380	1,229	62.6
Management, administrative, and waste services..	4,165	507	1,546	484	2,619	521	92.9
Education and health services	22,058	697	16,188	651	5,871	850	76.6
Educational services	9,528	768	6,375	739	3,154	879	84.1
Health care and social assistance	12,530	626	9,813	594	2,717	815	72.9
Leisure and hospitality	6,837	421	3,140	391	3,697	472	82.8
Arts, entertainment, and recreation	1,483	548	576	499	908	599	83.3
Acomodation and food services	5,353	400	2,564	372	2,789	430	86.5
Other services	4,090	568	1,814	465	2,276	668	69.6
Other services, except private households	3,692	597	1,453	501	2,239	673	74.4
Private households	398	363	361	352	36	(¹)	(¹)
Public administration..	6,134	811	2,710	707	3,424	913	77.4

¹ Data not shown where base is less than 50,000.

SOURCE: Current Population Survey, U.S. Department of Labor, U.S. Bureau of Labor Statistics

Net Gain and Loss of Jobs

The economy is a dynamic system. As companies are started or fail, jobs are created or lost. Job creation and loss also occur with expansion or contraction of an industry, changes in technology, development of new industries, and the decline of long-time industries. The government constantly monitors the number of jobs created or lost and reports these statistics on a regular basis. The numbers are often reported as raw numbers: x jobs were created and y were lost. Another way to look at the job creation/loss trend is to look at the net change in the number of jobs. The net change is the number of jobs added minus the number of jobs lost.

Let's say that the report for one quarter is a gain of 115,000 new jobs and a loss of 80,000 jobs. The net gain for the quarter is calculated as follows: $115,000 - 80,000 = 35,000$ net gain in jobs. The next quarter things look a little grimmer. The number of new jobs reported is 30,000 and the number of jobs lost is 45,000. How does this calculate out? $30,000 - 45,000 = -15,000$. This is a negative number, indicating a loss of 15,000 jobs in that quarter. Job creation and loss is a widely used number for assessing the health of the economy.

Concept Reinforcement:

1. Discuss some reasons why there is a disparity between the earnings of men and women.

2. Describe how the wage gap is becoming narrower. Do you think the wage gap will ever be totally closed? Why or why not?

3. Define how net gains or losses of jobs are used to assess the health of the economy.

4. Discuss the relationship between job stress and wages. Be sure to include comments on sources of job stress and how job stress sometimes leads to higher wages.

Section 3.12 – Karl Marx and His Economic Theories

Section Objective:

- Investigate Karl Marx's economic theories

Karl Marx – Economic Theories

Karl Heinrich Marx was born in 1818 in Trier, Prussia, and died on March 14, 1883 in London at age 64. Marx was a political economist and philosopher who is considered the father of communism. He was a student of history and came to believe that capitalism produces internal tensions that eventually lead to its destruction. He developed the concept of communism, which, in its ideal form, is a classless society in which everyone has their needs met and the government is run by the proletariat (the people). Marx authored the "Communist Manifesto," "Das Kapital" and the "Economic and Philosophical Manuscripts of 1844."

Marx was very interested in the relationship between people and the fundamental resource of their own labor power. He felt that giving up one's ability to transform the world (being paid for work) was the same as being alienated from one's own nature, resulting in a spiritual loss. He used the term commodity fetishism to describe this concept, which includes the idea that the things people produce seem to have life and movement of their own, to which humans adapt.

> Karl Marx's co-author of *The Communist Manifesto* was Frederick Engels. Engels was a Prussian-born social scientist whose first book was *The Condition of the Working Class in England in 1844*. He began working with Marx in Paris in 1844, a collaboration that continued throughout their lives.

Karl Marx

Marx continued to develop this concept and argued that commodity fetishism and the alienation of people from their own labor are the defining features of capitalism. Prior to capitalism rising in Europe, people were self-sufficient, meaning that they used their labor to produce the things they needed to survive. Marx argued that Europe moved to a capitalist society when labor became a commodity. The peasants were able to sell their labor as a commodity, and soon had to sell their labor because they no longer owned land, so they had to obtain work to survive. Marx called those who sell their labor the proletariat and those who buy the labor and control the resources required for production, are called capitalists, or the bourgeois.

Capitalists, according to Marxist thinking, take advantage of the difference between the labor market and the market for the product being manufactured. He called the difference between the sale price and the production cost per unit surplus value and argued that the surplus value had its origin in surplus labor. Marx defined surplus labor as the difference between what it costs to keep a worker alive and the amount of goods the worker can produce. He believed that the surplus value of labor is the source of profits, and that the rate of profit would fall as the economy grew under a capitalist market.

He considered the capitalists the most revolutionary class in history because they were always reinventing and improving the manufacturing processes and technologies. He was concerned that they would invest more in machines than in labor and would eventually be in crisis as a result of not investing in labor. He believed the cycle of growth, collapse and growth would result in the enrichment of the capitalists and the marginalization of the proletariat (the workers). As a result of this belief, he felt that the proletariat should take control of the means of production (factories, etc.) to protect the production system from the periods of crisis he felt the capitalists would cause to happen. Marx was willing to pursue the revolution required to transition countries from the capitalist society to rule by the proletariat using either peaceful or violent means.

While communism is a good idea from an academic perspective, it does not work well in application to society. Centralized socialist economies, as described by Marx, have proven to be far less efficient in producing the goods and services required by the people. In other words, they are less efficient at producing the greatest good for the greatest number than capitalist systems. Additionally, worker incomes (real income) have risen over time, meaning that workers are sharing in the growth of the economy and the profits of the company. The distribution of profit may not be equal, but it is there.

Concept Reinforcement:

1. Discuss Karl Marx's basic economic theory.

2. How does Marx's economic theory relate to capitalism?

3. Why has Marxist economic theory not succeeded?

Section 3.13 – The Decline Of The Labor Movement

Section Objectives:

- Identify why, historically, some American workers have joined labor unions.

- Evaluate reasons for the decline of the labor movement

The Decline of the Labor Movement

The economic conditions of the 1980s and 1990s led to a reduction in the power of organized labor (unions). Fewer people were members of the work force. In 1945, more than 33% of employees belonged to unions. By 1979, that percent fell to 24.1% and further declined to 13.9 percent by 1989.

Unions function by collecting dues from their members and using those resources to negotiate with management for increased wages and benefits. The reason people joined unions was to gain better wages and benefits, as well as job security and improved working conditions. The unions also work hard to maintain political influence, which they accomplish by contributing to political campaigns and working to encourage people to vote. The political power has declined less than union membership because of the relationships the unions have established with political parties and offices. This power is not directly related to membership levels.

The National Labor Relations Board rulings and court decisions about employees' rights to withhold the portion of their union dues used to influence political candidates reduced union influence. The unions therefore had fewer resources to use in their efforts to influence political campaigns.

Another influence that has reduced the power of unions is increased foreign and domestic competition. Management, which has the goal of maintaining the viability and profitability of the company, is less willing to give in to union demands for increased wages and benefits than they were in the past.

Management has become much more aggressive when opposing establishment of unions (organization of workers). Management became much more willing to employ strike breakers when unions went on strike in the 1980s and 1990s. Management would then retain the strike breakers as employees rather than rehiring the striking union workers. This reduced the effectiveness of the strike as a way of getting additional wages for the union members. It doesn't matter if you win the negotiation if you don't have a job. Part of the reason management changed its approach was President Reagan's 1981 decision to fire illegally striking air traffic controllers employed by the Federal Aviation Administration.

President Ronald Reagan making a statement to the press regarding the air traffic controllers strike in 1981.

Automation has been an ongoing challenge for unions and union members. As technology develops more efficient labor-saving devices to perform tasks previously performed by union workers, the need for workers has declined. Examples are robotics on production lines. Unions had some success to protect jobs and incomes against reductions in staffing due to automation. A few of these successes are free retraining, shorter work weeks to share the available work among employees, and guaranteed annual incomes.

The shift from manufacturing to service industry employment has been a challenge for labor unions. The service industry unions tend to be weaker and the service industry employees traditionally less willing to join a union. This demographic includes women, young people, temporary, and part-time workers. The service sector also has the largest number of new jobs created over the past several years. This combination has reduced the influence of unions.

Relocation of industry from the northeast to the southern and western parts of the U.S. has reduced union influence, as well, because the southern and western U.S. states have a weaker tradition of union membership and power than the northern or eastern parts of the U.S.

One of the biggest reasons for the unions' loss of influence is the extensive negative publicity about corruption in the Teamsters Union and others. Despite the unions' success in increasing working wages and benefits, and improving working conditions, younger workers do not feel they need a union to represent them. The independent-minded younger workers are not interested in belonging to an organization that they feel limits their independence in their work.

The economy of the late 1990s was so strong that the unemployment rate fell to 4.1%, a record low. This had a negative effect on union membership because the people who wanted jobs had them. Only the chronically unemployed and those between jobs were out of work.

Concept Reinforcement:

1. Describe why the state of the economy in the 1980s and 1990s had a negative effect on union membership.

2. Discuss how automation has affected union workers and what the unions have done to help the workers retain their jobs.

3. Why do people join unions?

Section 3.14 – The Labor Movement

Section Objectives:

- Trace the history of the labor movement in the United States

- Discuss how labor and management negotiate contracts

Organized labor has been part of American history since very early in American History. The first guilds (primitive unions) of craftsmen (carpenters, cabinet makers, cobblers, and other tradesmen) began to develop in cities along the Atlantic seaboard. These first guilds were often short-lived, but provided the basis for the modern unions. Strikes go back as far as the 1700s.

- 1794   New York   Printers

- 1796   New York   Cabinet Makers

- 1797   Philadelphia   Carpenters

- 1799   Philadelphia   Cordwainers (shoemakers)

As unions became more organized and gained membership through the beginning of the 19th century, strikes and negotiations to support improvement in wages and working conditions became more frequent. Unions began discussing joining each other into federations in the 1820s to gain strength and influence in their efforts to help reduce the working day from 12 to 10 hours.

The steam engine and increasing use of water to operate machinery were developing in the factory system beginning in the 1830s. The factory system developed rapidly through the 1800s, especially during the civil war. This system gained larger and larger shares of the production capacity of the U.S., which made some people very wealthy and left others in extreme poverty. The unions recognized the desperate conditions of their members and began to join together in federations. The National Labor Union formed in 1866 and eventually persuaded Congress to reduce the work day for Federal workers to 8 hours. This federation disappeared during the economic depression of 1873.

The Knights of Labor were formed in 1869 by Uriah Stephens and expanded quickly under the leadership of Terrance Powdery. The Knights welcomed anyone into their organization and were committed to a cooperative society. There were no barriers to membership based on skill level, race, or gender. The membership was soon at 750,000 workers. The disparity of skill sets led to fragmentation of the membership between the skilled and unskilled workers. The violence of the Haymarket Square riots contributed to negative publicity for the Knights, who were accused of throwing a bomb that killed police officers. This led to the eventual disbanding of the group.

Samuel Gompers founded the American Federation of Labor in 1886. Gompers moved to the U.S. as a child and worked in the cigar making trade. As a child, he worked as a reader, reading books, newspapers, poetry and magazines to fellow employees to break the monotony of their work. This provided him an education that allowed him to become leader of his local union and eventually of the National Cigar Makers Union. The American Federation of Labor (AFL) pushed for more effective union organization to protect workers from changes in the workplace resulting from introduction of automation, subdivision of labor, the use of women and children as labor and the lack of an apprentice system for the skilled trades. The AFL was a federation of unions that represented only skilled workers.

Initially, federal intervention in strikes was harsh. The 1894 Pullman Strike in Chicago resulted in 125,000 railroad workers engaging in a sympathy strike. The government swore in 3,400 special deputies and President Cleveland using federal forces to break the strike. The sympathy strike was ended by a federal court injunction and many of the railroad workers who participated in the strike were blacklisted. The injunction became the key legal weapon used against unions and their efforts to organize and take action in support of the workers.

President Theodore Roosevelt took a different approach to strike resolution in response to the 1902 strike of anthracite coal miners, who were part of the United Mine Workers union. Over 100,000 miners called a strike on May 12 of that year. The mines they worked, which were in Northeastern Pennsylvania, were closed all summer as a result of the strike. Negotiations were unsuccessful and the mine owners refused a request for arbitration, which would have used a third party to help negotiate and finalize the labor agreement. On October 16, President Roosevelt appointed a commission of mediation and arbitration. This commission was charged with developing new terms of employment for the workers. The miners returned to their jobs in 5 days, and 5 months later received a 10% wage increase and shorter work days. They did not, however, obtain the formal union recognition they wanted.

Unions have played a key role in improving safety of workspaces. The 1911 Triangle Shirtwaist Company fire in New York killed about 150 employees, most of which were young women. The workers were unable to escape from the building because the safety exits were locked shot. This was the driving force behind Frances Perkins' efforts to reform industrial safety and fire prevention measures.

Triangle Shirtwaist Company fire

Congress created the U.S. Department of Labor (DOL) at the urging of the AFL. The mandate of the DOL is to protect and extend the rights of wage earners. The Clayton Act of 1914 clarified that "the labor of a human being is not a commodity or article of commerce." This is crucial because it means that labor was not subject to the Sherman Act provisions that had been used in the past to prevent union organization. The Clayton Act legalized strikes, boycotts, and peaceful picketing, as well as limiting the use of injunctions in labor disputes.

Unions lost significant membership after World War I – about a million members between 1920-23. The National Association of Manufacturers, which was an anti-union group, used fears of communism to make people wary of unions, claiming that the trade unions were an un-American, illegal and infamous conspiracy. Yellow-dog contracts became common at this point. The Yellow-Dog contract was a requirement of employment for many workers, so they had to sign it, and it bound the workers to never joining a union. The manufacturers also developed employee representation plans or company unions, which did not typically help the workers at all.

The Committee for Industrial Organization (CIO) was created in 1935 by John L Lewis. The CIO was composed of about a dozen leaders of AFL unions, with the goal of continuing to develop industrial unions. Industrial unions are different in that they organize an entire industry regardless of skill set or skill level, so they represented unskilled workers. Lewis began to verbally attach his colleagues on the AFL Executive Council, which led to expulsion of the CIO unions from the AFL. The CIO reorganized into the Congress of Industrial Organizations in 1938. The CIO was incredibly successful in organizing large sectors of American industry and continued to gain membership.

During World War II, the AFL and CIO began to work together on some issues, while agreeing to disagree on others. Eventually, this cooperation led to a merger of the two labor groups, which occurred in 1955 when they became the AFL-CIO. This merger led to further organization of workers in areas and industries where the workers did not have labor representation or had resisted unions.

Since the 1960s, there has been a steady decline in union membership and influence. A number of factors contributed to this decline, including the desire of businesses to remain union-free, that new additions to the work force (women and teenagers) did not have loyalty to unions, and because union-produced goods became more expensive than other, equivalent products, because the unions were successful in representing their members. The technology shift that has occurred since the 1970s has made our economy less reliant on factory jobs and resulted in a more highly educated work force that tends to work in professional, white-collar jobs.

The unions worked hard to improve conditions and wages for working Americans, with great success. If negotiations with management did not result in an agreement, the unions would organize strikes, boycotts and protests to bring the situation of the worker to the attention of others and pressure corporate management to accede to the union demands for improved working conditions, wages, and benefits. In fact, unions were so successful in their work to improve worker conditions, the union-made products became substantially more expensive than comparable goods manufactured in a non-union shop. This cost difference resulted in loss of business, which led to a loss of jobs as companies had to scale back production.

Concept Reinforcement:

1. Describe the primary goals of unions.

2. Discuss why corporate management resisted union organization.

3. Describe how unions gained political influence and were able to help improve worker wages, benefits and conditions.

4. Why has the membership and influence of unions declined since the 1970s?

Section 3.15 – Impact of Labor Unions

Section Objectives:

- Evaluate the improvements in American working conditions

- Identify how a failure of collective bargaining can lead to a strike

Labor unions can be credited for significant improvements in American working conditions. Unions have been influential in shortening the work day, improving workplace safety, and improving wages and benefits. The National Labor Union persuaded the government to reduce the Federal work day to eight hours. The Knights of Labor represented any worker who wished to join them and had a membership of 750,000 workers in the late 1800s before they disbanded as a result of negative publicity about violence at the Haymarket Square riots. The AFL and CIO joined in 1955 and have been powerful unions organizing and representing workers in American industry. The AFL-CIO has been influential in improving working conditions, wages and benefits for members.

Improved working conditions include basic things such as temperature (heating and cooling), scheduled breaks and lunch times, increased wages and improved benefits packages, fire safety, ergonomics and general safety, job training, protection against unfair labor practices, and increased job security.

Labor Unions helped the push for child labor laws in order to protect children from exploitation and the dangers of poor working conditions

The unions and management negotiated improved working conditions through a process called collective bargaining. The collective bargaining process involves negotiation between union representatives, who represent the collective (the group of workers), and management, which represents the company. Collective bargaining includes the union making demands for certain improvements in wages, benefits, working conditions, etc., of management. Management evaluates the demands and decides whether to accept or reject them.

The management decision is then presented to the union representatives, who respond. This process continues until either agreement is reached or they are at a stalemate. If agreement is reached, production continues and business is uninterrupted. If the two sides are unable to come to an agreement on terms, the union may organize a strike, boycott or other action to pressure management into accepting the union demands.

Collective bargaining is affected by the economy in which it happens. If, for example, the product of the company has a strong and increasing demand, management is going to be more willing to accept significant increases in pay or other benefits. On the other hand, if the market for the product is weak, the company will not be willing to accept increases in labor costs. This is a result of the law of supply and demand. If there is high demand for the product, the equilibrium point for the value of labor will be higher because the company will still make profit even if they are paying more for labor. However, if demand for the product drops, demand for labor drops, and the company will make an economic decision to reject union demands. If the union representatives and management are unable to come to an agreement in this environment, the company is more likely to reduce production, resulting in job losses for the union members.

Concept Reinforcement:

1. Describe how working conditions in America have improved as a result of union efforts.

2. Define collective bargaining.

3. Discuss how collective bargaining is affected by market conditions.

Unit Four

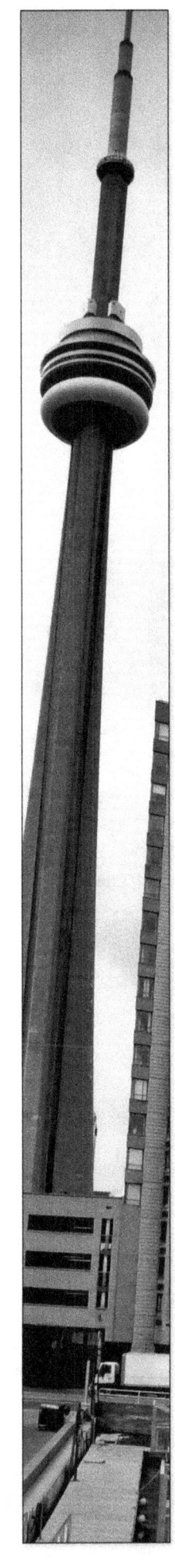

Section 4.1 – Scarcity and Opportunity Cost

Section Objectives:

- Discuss why economists say all resources are scarce

- Discuss the concept of opportunity cost

Scarce Resources

Scarcity drives economics. The more scarce a demanded resource is, the higher its value. If a resource is scarce, but there is no demand, the value does not increase. Scarcity is NOT the same as poverty. Scarcity affects all economic systems regardless of wealth. Poverty is a situation in which people cannot meet their basic needs of food, shelter and clothing. These are two different concepts. As an example, if only one of a certain model of luxury car is produced, it is a scarce good. The only people who will be able to consider purchasing it, however, are those with enough disposable income to allow them to choose to purchase the vehicle. Poverty means that the consumer is often choosing between necessities, such as when people choose between the medications they require to survive and the food they require to survive.

What resources are we discussing? We are discussing the raw materials, labor, and infrastructure required for production of goods and services. We are also discussing resources we all need to survive and thrive, such as clean air, clean water, healthy food, green spaces, leisure, and time. Economists consider all resources scarce because humans want more resources than are freely available from nature. Some of these limited resources are also called economic goods. The table below shows some desired economic goods and limited resources. This is by no means a comprehensive list of economic goods and limited resources, but it gives you an idea of the concept.

Economic Goods	Limited Resources
Clothing	Land
Food	Man-made physical resources, such as machines and buildings
Household goods, such as furniture, beds, dinner ware, rugs, etc.	Rivers, trees, oceans, minerals, and other natural resources
Education	Non-human animal resources for food and other uses (cattle, buffalo, chickens, fish, horses, etc.)
Clean, healthy environment (trees, lakes, parks, rivers, bike paths)	Technology resulting from physical and scientific advances
Recreation (vacations, hobbies)	Human resources (skills, talents, knowledge of individuals.

What happens when scarce resources meet unlimited human wants? The consumer has to make choices about which goods and services are critical for survival and which are luxury items. Choice is selecting from limited alternatives. Choice is affected by budget, culture, competition, cost of production, technology, etc. Choice also implies that if the consumer chooses one good or service, he will have to forego another good or service because of the limited budget available.

Opportunity Cost

Scarcity of resources leads to the concept of choice. Choice means people have to choose one option over another. Opportunity cost is the cost of lost opportunities. The choice to do one thing is also a choice to NOT do another thing. Opportunity cost is the highest valued option that is not selected because another option is chosen.

The value of time is a good example of opportunity cost. People have different perceptions of the value of time and money. Some people value their time very highly and some place a low value on time. For example, a female college student who wants to go home for the summer has to choose the mode of transportation that will get her home. The student does not have much discretionary income, so values her money highly. The student has no deadline by which she needs to be home, so she will value her time less highly than she might if she had a deadline to meet. When she does the research required to compare costs, she finds that the bus ticket to get her home will be \$75.00 and plane fare will be \$300.00. The bus ride will take her 12 hours and the plane trip will take her 3 hours. The cost per hour for the bus trip is \$75/12 hours = \$6.25/hour. The plane trip will cost \$300/3 hours = \$100/hour. The opportunity cost for this travel is time versus money. If the student values her time at \$6.25 per hour or less, she will take the bus. If she values her time at \$100 or more she will take the airplane. What about the gap in the middle – between \$6.25 and \$100 per hour? The opportunity cost will include the time and money invested in the travel, as well as many other variables, including personal preferences. Some people enjoy taking the bus and dislike airplanes, or value their money more than their time, even when the cost/hour of travel is higher than the value the person places on his time. The decision-making process is unique to each person and the circumstances in which the decision is made.

Concept Reinforcement:

1. Describe the difference between scarcity and poverty.

2. Explain why economists consider all resources to be scarce.

3. Discuss the concept of opportunity cost using an example different than the one presented in the text.

Section 4.2 – Economic Systems

Section Objectives:

- Compare the mixed economies of various nations along a continuum between centrally planned and free market systems

- Discuss the rise of mixed economic systems

Economic Systems

The economies of different countries all have unique characteristics and are usually a blend of different economic models. The extremes of the economic models are the centrally planned economy (total government control) and the free market economy (no government control).

Notice that no countries have purely free market or centrally planned economies. The free market requires some oversight to ensure consumer safety and fair economic practices on the part of producers and vendors of products. The centrally planned economy is not possible because of the wide variety of economic activity that humans engage in. Imagine trying to control the sale of goods between individuals. It is not possible. People will find a way to make trades for what they need if a centrally planned government does not provide it.

The economic system of a country is highly influenced by its past governments (socialist, communist, capitalist, etc.) and its current political situation. Most of the developed companies have some form of a free-market economy. The countries have individual differences because of variation in regulation and policy that affect the economy. The chart that follows shows the wide variety in the economic systems that have developed over time.

Economic Systems without a profit motive	Economic Systems with a profit motive
State Socialism: The state owns and manages all land, capital and means of productions to meet social goals.	**State Capitalism:** The state owns and controls land, capital and means of production to make profit.
Marxian Socialism: Consumer goods may be privately owned. The state controls all capital, land, and means of production.	**State Regulated Capitalism:** The state regulates industries, but does not own the land, capital or means of production.
Democratic Socialism: economy and society are run democratically to meet the needs of society, not for profit.	**Private Enterprise Capitalism:** Business and unions regulate industries with very little oversight by the state.
Utopian Socialism: Perfectly compatible cooperative communities.	**Free Enterprise Capitalism:** Nearly perfect competition with very little state regulation.
Communism: Everyone in society owns in and shares in the product of the land, capital, and means of production.	

Many of the eastern European countries have economies that are transforming from centrally planned communist/socialist economies into capitalist economies. As they transition through the state capitalism and state regulated capitalism toward free enterprise, the industries are moved from government ownership to private ownership and often result in a blended economy that reflects some of the former economic system combined with the new economic model. The success of individual countries in making this transition varies. The reasons for the variability are the current government, the ability and willingness of the people to adapt from the centrally planned economy to a free-market economy, and the resources the country has to use in making the transition. A country with abundant natural, technical, and human resources will probably be more successful in transitioning to a free market system than a country with limited resources.

Alternatively, countries can move from a free-market economy to a more restricted economic system. This occurs when the government imposes new regulations to ensure consumer safety, financial ethics, and address other concerns.

Certain portions of the economy may operate more freely than others. For example, drug companies are subject to extensive federal oversight regarding the development, production, and distribution of their products. This part of the economy operates less freely than, for example, the wheat market. Wheat is not subject to the same amount of oversight as the prescription drugs.

Note in the diagram of the various economies that some infer a profit motive and others do not have a profit motive. The centrally planned economies are typically described as communist or socialist economies, meaning that their primary goal is to provide for everyone at a basic level through government control of all economic activities. Profit is a secondary goal, if profit is important at all. Because profit is not a motivation, efficiency is less important, resulting in a market that is not naturally moving toward equilibrium and maximum efficiency.

Centrally planned economies have not reached their full potential because of human greed and politics. The profit-motivated economies have profit as a primary goal. In theory, each person is motivated by self-interest, but the result of all the self-interest is a benefit to the overall economy and society. Why is this? Each person wishes to maximize her wealth, which motivates her to provide a good or service that is in high demand, which satisfies the needs or wants of a large number of consumers. The market naturally moves toward equilibrium, meaning that supply and demand are in balance and the market is working as efficiently as possible for that good or service.

In summary, each country's economy is subject to different influences that result in an economy that is a mix of free enterprise and centrally planned economies. Even the U.S., which has a very free economy, has government influence in the form of financial regulations, import-export controls, industry-specific regulations, and consumer safety regulations. Centrally planned economies tend to be less efficient than free market economies because the motivation of the economy is different. Profit is not the key economic driver – providing for everyone is the key economic driver.

Concept Reinforcement:

1. Discuss the differences between a free market economy and a centrally planned economy.

2. Why does no country succeed in achieving a fully free economy or a fully centrally planned economy?

3. Describe how a country might transition from a centrally planned economy to a free market economy. Be sure to discuss some of the social and governmental influences that influence this process.

Section 4.3 – Centrally-Planned Economies

Section Objectives:

- Evaluate the centrally planned economy of the former Soviet Union

- Identify how a centrally planned economy is organized

- Describe the problems of a centrally planned economy

Centrally planned economies are often described using the political terms of socialism or communism. The primary differences between a centrally planned economy and a free market economy are who owns and controls the means of production and who determines resource allocation. A centrally planned economy includes a government that owns and controls the means of production (factories, natural resources, etc.) and also determines the allocation of resources to suit the goals of the government. An economy of this type represents the idea that society's economic affairs belong in the public, rather than the private, sector of the economy.

The physical resources in a socialist economy are owned by the state. Workers retain the right to sell their labor and gain the benefit of the wages they earn. Because the physical resources belong to the state, all of the profits resulting from the use of those resources go to the state. The state also makes the decisions about resource allocation and use in the economy.

A socialist economy has the following traits:

Property rights	Physical (nonhuman) resources are owned by the state.
Employment	Government or government-controlled cooperatives provide employment opportunities.
Investment	The central planners determine investment strategies that support the objectives they have established for the economy.
Allocation of goods and resources	The central planners allocate all goods and resources.
Income Distribution	The central planners determine income distribution to meet their goals of equality or some other income distribution pattern.

An example of a large centralized economy was that of the former Union of Soviet Socialist Republics (USSR). The USSR was a huge country that was a union of many eastern European countries and had a socialist government. The economy of the USSR is called a command economy, meaning that the central planning committee, called Gosplan, would draft both annual and long-range (5 years) economic plans, which would then be written into law by the Soviet Government. Gosplan economic plans impacted more than 200,000 different state-owned enterprises, setting production targets and allocating resources (raw materials, production capacity, labor, etc.) to each state enterprise. The success of the state enterprise in using the allocated resources to meet the production targets was evaluated and used as the basis for rewarding the enterprise.

A **collective** is a grouping of resources to achieve economic goals. Governments have moved to organize resources like small farms into groupings of larger **collective farms** worked by a group to increase production through economy of scale. In Israel a collective farm is called a **kibbutz**.

Often, the output of one state enterprise (steel, for example) was a raw material for another state enterprise (tank factory, for example). If the steel enterprise was unable to meet its production goals, it would directly impact the ability of the tank factory to meet its production goals. In a free market, the steel would increase in price until a new market equilibrium was reached. In a socialist economy, resources are allocated by law and the market does not have an impact on the allocation of resources. In the case of the USSR, the central committee focused resources on defense (military). Focusing on defense drained resources from the rest of the economy. The products of the industries required to produce the goods required by the Soviet military did not actually generate any income to the economy, reducing the ability of the Soviet economy to purchase goods and services from other countries and limiting it economic growth and health.

Another problem that could arise was the build-up of bottlenecks in the system. If production of a critical component was halted because of a natural disaster or some other disruptive event, it would cause a bottleneck at the next stage of production because the system did not allow the state enterprise to have alternate sources in place for emergency situations.

The managers of the production facilities were motivated by a combination of reward and punishment. If the production manager was able to meet all of the goals set by the central planning committee, he might receive a bonus and maybe even a promotion. If, however, he failed to meet the quota, he would probably be demoted even if he did his best to meet the goals set by the central planning committee. This led to an emphasis on quantity over quality. In addition to the obvious problem of the production of potential poor quality goods, the managers worked to get the central committee to set low production goals and falsify reports to show higher production than actually occurred to make the factory look good to the central committee.

The production of goods is one area where the economy of the USSR was inefficient. The wages workers earned were also inefficiently used. First, the wage discrepancies were significant, but not as large as the discrepancies in the U.S. The socialist goal was to provide for each according to his need and get from each according to his skill. In other words, each person would do whatever job he or she was able to do and each person would receive from government everything that he or she needed. In reality, there were wage discrepancies, ranging from twice to many times that of the basic laborer, depending upon the rank of the individual worker.

An interesting result of the wage discrepancies combined with the special privileges of the elite (easy access to cars, special stores that offered products unavailable to the average person, etc.) was that the elite had access to almost anything they wanted, but the common person was unable to get even the basics. The elite were insulated from the shortages of consumer goods because they were treated differently and allowed different access to the goods and services they wanted and needed. The shortages of consumer goods for the average person were a direct result of the production goals and resource allocation established by the central planning committee. Interestingly, the members of the central planning committee were counted among the elite members of society, so they did not often experience the shortages that most of the USSR citizens had to endure. A second interesting result of the central committee's resource allocation and goal setting was that there were surpluses of other products on the shelves of the same stores that had shortages of other goods. The surplus products may have been poorly made or too expensive, so the consumers did not purchase them.

In most cases, private enterprise was forbidden in the Soviet economy. There were a couple of exceptions, however. The private enterprise that was allowed was provision of personal services and some agricultural activities. Those who were allowed to moonlight in addition to their day jobs were professionals, such as teachers and physicians, and skilled laborers, such as tailors and painters. These people were allowed to sell their services directly to private individuals. The permitted agricultural activity was the establishment of collectives to grow agricultural products on private plots. Each person was allowed to use about an acre of land, on average, and all the goods grown on that land could be sold in the market at whatever price the market would bear. These were the only parts of the Soviet economy where the forces of the free market were active.

In summary, a centrally planned economy is a highly controlled economy in which the government owns and controls the means of production and allocates the resources required for production centrally instead of allowing the forces of the market to do so. This leads to a number of inefficiencies in the economy, which can result in shortages or surpluses of consumer goods. It can also lead to an emphasis on quantity over quality in production, bottlenecks in production, falsifying production reports, and pressure on the central committee to reduce production goals. Private enterprise was forbidden except in two instances: sale of professional services to individuals and agricultural collectives.

Concept Reinforcement:

1. Describe how a centrally planned economy is organized. Who makes the decisions? Who owns the resources?

2. Explain the problems encountered in centrally planned economies. What can happen in the production process? How are consumers affected?

3. Discuss the economy of the former USSR and explain how centralized planning and the focus on defense spending impacted all of the sectors of the economy.

Section 4.4 – Government Influence on Business Cycles

Section Objective:

- Discuss how the government tracks and seeks to influence business cycles

The government of every country monitors its economic activity and tries to influence business cycles to support economic growth and health. In the U.S., the primary agencies that monitor the economy are the Treasury, the Department of Commerce, the Federal Reserve, the Council of Economic Advisors, and state and local governments. The key data collection and analysis agencies are the Federal Reserve, Bureau of Economic Analysis, and Bureau of Labor Statistics. These three agencies collate, analyze, and publish statistics on the U.S. economy on a regular schedule. The statistics published by these agencies are further analyzed by various industries and used as a basis for planning future activities. Certain trends in the statistics are considered favorable or unfavorable for the economy.

Some of the most important measures are called key economic indicators. These include GDP growth (gross domestic product growth), unemployment, inflation, interest rate movements and cycles, the interest rate cycle, housing starts and sales, retail sales and auto sales. We will go through these one at a time.

GDP growth is the major indicator watched by economists. This statistic is reported monthly, but the quarterly numbers are watched most closely. The Bureau of Economic Analysis (BEA) generates quarterly reports that measure growth in real GDP. What does this mean? It means that the statistics from each quarter are directly comparable due to adjustments for seasonality. The quarterly numbers are also averaged over the three-month period, which provides a longer-term perspective on the short-term fluctuations in the market. Daily ups and downs have less impact over a longer period of time than a shorter one so trends become more apparent. GDP growth is compared to the growth rate from the same quarter of the previous year, as well as to the prior month in the current year. The average annual growth of GDP is three percent, so figures that show higher growth than that represent an economic expansion and figures lower than that may indicate an economic contraction.

Unemployment is strongly linked with economic expansion and contraction. As unemployment increases, economic contraction tends to occur. Conversely, as unemployment decreases, the economy is more likely to expand. Some of the specific measures related to unemployment are jobs lost, jobs created, and net job loss or gain.

Inflation is a major concern of all economists and those who want to maintain a healthy economy. The Fed responds to economic trends by tightening or loosening its economic policy. Increases in inflation that are out of the ordinary may cause the Fed to tighten its policy. The Consumer Price Index (CPI) and the Produce Price Index (PPI) are the two key measures of inflation. The rate of inflation is reflected by the CPI. The PPI is used as an indicator of future trends because it reflects increases in the costs of production, which are eventually passed on to the consumers.

Interest rate movements indicate business outlook because the cost of borrowing money is a big consideration in making an investment decision. Low costs encourage borrowing and high costs discourage borrowing. Key interest rates are the fed funds rate, the prime rate, and the fixed rate for a 30-year home mortgage.

The interest rate cycle is intimately linked with the business cycle. The business cycle includes recovery (low interest rates), expansion (rising rates that peak at the height of the expansion), and then contraction (falling interest rates). When money is cheap, people and businesses are more likely to borrow and when it is expensive, they are less likely to borrow.

Consumer confidence is reflected by the statistics on housing starts and sales and auto sales. Housing is a huge investment for any consumer, one of the biggest purchases most families make. The consumer must be confident of continued employment and ability to make the mortgage payments before committing to a purchase that will take 30 years to pay for. Retail sales, including car sales, are also a good indicator of consumer confidence. People spend more when they feel confident of their economic situation.

Governments attempt to influence business cycles using fiscal policy. Fiscal policy is the policy the government established and modifies in an effort to support economic growth. In order to establish fiscal policy, the government collects data on many different sectors of the U.S. and international economies. The data are then analyzed and interpreted by economists and other experts to understand how the economy is actually working.

Keep in mind that government spending in the U.S. is more than 25% of total spending. This means that government fiscal policy can affect the economy. If government spending increases, as it did during the Great Depression because of the government's programs to put people to work (The Tennessee Valley Authority, for example), the money flows through the economy as the workers make purchases with the wages they earn. If government spending decreases, the flow of money through the economy will slow down.

There are four key tools the government uses to affect the economy. The use of these tools is driven by fiscal policy. The tools include implementing taxes, raising or lowering taxes, borrowing money, or printing money.

The government is able to affect its revenue, which is the amount of money it has to spend, by implementing new taxes or changing existing taxes. Increases in taxes will provide the government more revenue, but may not stimulate the economy because increased taxes reduce the money available for the consumer and business to spend on goods and services. Reductions in tax, although they reduce the short-term revenue collected by the government, are often implemented to stimulate the economy because of the trade-off between short-term loss and long-term gains from the taxes paid for goods and services rather than in income tax.

The government may also raise funds by issuing bonds, which are a form of a loan from the consumer to the government. The consumer pays less than face value for the bond in return for being able to receive full face value when the bond matures and is redeemed.

Finally, printing more money obviously puts more money into the economy, but also has the potential of increasing the inflation rate because the dollar is worth relatively less than it was before the money was added to the economy.

Concept Reinforcement:

1. List the three agencies that collect and analyze economic data for the federal government and the key economic indicators reported.

2. Describe how key economic indicators are used to assess the health of the economy.

3. Explain how the government attempts to influence business cycles. Discuss a specific change in fiscal policy that the government might implement if the economy is contracting and a specific change that the government might implement during an expansion and describe how the change is expected to impact the economy.

Section 4.5 – Elasticity

Section Objectives:

- Discuss how firms use elasticity and revenues to make decisions

- Describe factors that affect elasticity

Elasticity describes the change in demand for a good or service that occurs in response to a change in price for the good or service. Another way to look at this is the degree to which a price change will impact demand. For some goods and services, a small price increase will significantly reduce demand. For others, which have a relatively inelastic demand, a price increase will have much less effect on demand.

Elasticity

There are three basic types of elasticity: unitary elasticity, elasticity, and inelasticity.

Unitary elasticity occurs when changes in demand resulting from a change in price for the good or service always result in the same revenues. The graph below shows unitary elasticity of demand for a good. Point A on the chart shows the starting price and demand for the product. Point A1 shows the increase in demand resulting from a price reduction and Point A2 shows the decrease in demand resulting from a price increase.

Price change	Price	Quantity	Revenue
Original (A)	$1.00	150	$150
Price decreases (A1)	$0.75	200	$150
Price increases (A2)	$2.00	75	$150

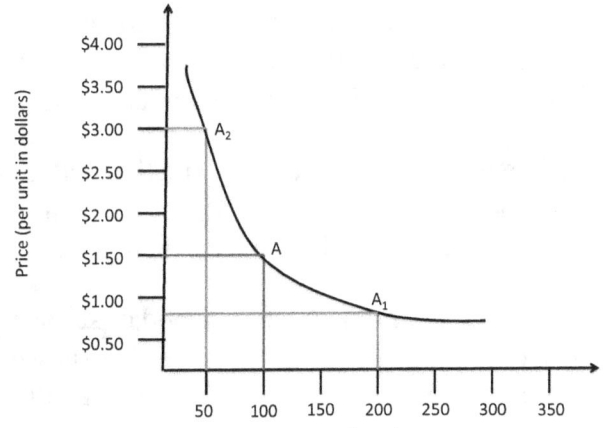

Elasticity occurs when price increases decrease demand or price decreases increase demand for a good or service. This is an inverse relationship, meaning that as one value increases, the other decreases and vice versa. Providers usually reduce prices to increase quantity, therefore increasing revenue. Keep in mind that the producer/seller of the good or service must recover the costs or producing the good or service and make profit, so the price is rarely less than the producer needs to recover costs. Occasionally, products will be designated as loss leaders, meaning that they are priced below cost to draw people to a retail location with the expectation that they will buy enough other products to recover the loss on the loss-leader product.

Infinite elasticity occurs when the price for a good or service remains the same regardless of how much of that good or service is used. Examples include monthly internet service charges, gym memberships, and telephone service packages that cost the same each month regardless of how much you use them. Infinite elasticity is shown as a straight horizontal line with price on the y axis and quantity on the x axis.

Inelasticity occurs when a reduction in price increases demand, but not to the point that would occur in unitary elasticity. Unity is the proportional change in quantity and revenue that occurs in unitary elasticity.

Price change	Price	Quantity	Revenue
Original (A)	$50	20	$1,000
Price decreases 50% (A1)	$25	50	$1,250
Price increases 50% (A2)	$75	5	$375

Perfect inelasticity is similar to infinite elasticity except that it shows that the quantity of a good or service demanded will not change regardless of price. This is shown as a vertical line with price on the y axis and quantity on the x axis.

How do firms use this information to make decisions?

A firm has to determine how to price its products based on both production costs and the supply/demand relationship for the product. Unitary elasticity does not occur in reality. It shows where the seller will be indifferent to different combinations of quantity and price. If the revenues are the same regardless of the package (A, A1, or A2), it does not matter to the seller/producer which combination of quantity and price is used.

Obviously, producers are in business to make a profit and they will maximize their revenue and profit by pricing their products at the level that will produce sales at that level. Producers take several things into consideration when pricing their products.

First, they have to recover the cost of production of a good or service. This includes recovering all physical plant and infrastructure costs, which are also known as sunk costs, as well as the costs of the raw material, labor, and overhead associated with the product.

Secondly, they will determine whether or not there are good substitutes available for their products. Gasoline, for example, has inelastic demand because people need to be able to fuel their vehicles to get to work, school, or wherever else they need to go. Demand may go down slightly with an increase in price, but there are no good substitutes, so demand will be there even as prices increase. The demand for products for which there are many substitutes, however, is much more sensitive to price changes. Let's look at jeans as an example. There are many different companies that make jeans. These companies also price their jeans at much different price points, depending upon the market they want to be in. Companies that have targeted people who purchase inexpensive jeans will provide a large supply at a low price point. The companies that target the luxury jeans market will provide a smaller supply at a higher price point.

Third, the short- and long-run demand for the good or service must be taken into consideration. Let's go back to the example of gasoline. What do you think will happen if the price goes so high that it is not worthwhile for a person to drive to a job because the transportation costs take up too much of the person's earnings? The person may find other modes of transportation that are less expensive (public transportation, walking, bicycling, car pooling) or the person may decide that it is not worth continuing to work in the job that requires the long commute. In this situation, it is possible that the individual would choose to quit working altogether, start his or her own business at home, or find a job closer to home, even if it pays less than the original job. The company wants to retain its customer base so it will monitor demand (sales) of the product and adjust its pricing strategy appropriately to ensure continued sales.

Fourth, the price of the product as a percentage of income is a key factor in its elasticity. The higher the price of a good or service is, the higher the elasticity of demand for that good or service. Let's think about vehicles, for example. We all see cars on the road that are old and beat up, but still serve the purpose of getting the driver from point a to point b. We also see luxury cars that cost many times more than the old cars and serve exactly the same purpose of getting the driver from one point to another. They are fancier and probably more powerful, but are still serving essentially the same function to the consumer. As the cost of a vehicle, as a percent of the consumer's income, increases, the demand for the vehicle will decrease. Likewise, the lower the percent of income a product consumes, the lower the elasticity. There is a big difference between a 10% price increase on a candy bar and a 10% price increase on a car as far as percentage of income is concerned.

Concept Reinforcement:

1. List the three primary forms of elasticity and discuss how they differ.

2. Describe the difference between infinitely elastic demand and perfectly inelastic demand.

3. Explain the four primary considerations of a company in making pricing decisions.

Section 4.6 – Production Costs and Profitability

Section Objectives:

- Evaluate the production costs of a firm

- Discuss how a firm decides to shut down an unprofitable business

Production costs are all of the costs a company incurs to produce a good or service. In general terms, the production costs include raw materials, capital equipment, infrastructure, labor, and overhead (administration, sales, marketing, transportation, etc.). These costs are evaluated in several different ways to assess the profitability of a firm.

Production costs include several categories: fixed, variable, direct, indirect, sunk, total, marginal, and average. We will go through these one at a time.

Fixed costs are those that the firm will incur regardless of the number of units of a good or service produced. An example of a fixed cost is the rent paid for the building.

Variable costs are those that the firm will incur more of less of depending upon the level of production. Examples are labor costs and raw materials costs.

Direct costs are those that can be directly attributed to a unit of a good or service. For example, if a widget requires 5 bolts, the cost of those bolts can be directly allocated to each widget produced.

Indirect costs are those that cannot be directly attributed to a unit of a good. Examples of these costs are maintenance, heat, lights, and administration.

Sunk costs are those that have been incurred based on past decisions. These are also called historical costs. These costs are real, but should have no direct influence on current decisions. The outcome of the past decision should provide information to help with current decision-making processes, but the costs are no longer relevant. For example, if a company invested in an expensive piece of equipment that did not provide the benefit expected, the money has already been spent. However, the outcome can be used to help with future decision-making processes to avoid such an unnecessary purchase from happening again.

The table below shows an example of the costs for a business to produce products in increments of 10 units. The first three of four columns represent quantity, fixed costs, and total costs.

Quantity	Fixed costs	Variable costs	Total costs	Marginal cost per unit	Average fixed cost	Average variable cost	Average total cost
0	$500	$0	$500	-	-	-	-
10	$500	$300	$800	$30.00	$50.00	$30.00	$80.00
20	$500	$575	$1,075	$27.50	$25.00	$28.75	$53.75
30	$500	$800	$1,300	$22.50	$16.67	$26.67	$43.33
40	$500	$1,000	$1,500	$20.00	$12.50	$25.00	$37.50
50	$500	$1,150	$1,650	$15.00	$10.00	$23.00	$33.00
60	$500	$1,275	$1,775	$12.50	$8.33	$21.25	$29.58
70	$500	$1,375	$1,875	$10.00	$7.14	$19.64	$26.79
80	$500	$1,425	$1,925	$5.00	$6.25	$17.81	$24.06
90	$500	$1,550	$2,050	$12.50	$5.56	$17.22	$22.78
100	$500	$1,700	$2,200	$15.00	$5.00	$17.00	$22.00
110	$500	$2,000	$2,500	$30.00	$4.55	$18.18	$22.73

Total costs are the sum of all of the costs of production of a good or service. Total costs are the sum of the fixed and variable costs. The equation that shows this relationship is: TC=VC + FC where TC = total costs, VC = variable costs, and FC = fixed costs for a specific number of units.

Marginal cost is the increase in total cost divided by the increase in the number of units. In our table above, the marginal cost is calculated by determining the difference in total costs between levels of production and dividing that by the increase in the number of units produced. In this example, we are increasing production by 10 units at a time, so that number is consistent.

The equation that shows this relationship is:

$MC = (TC_{new} - TC_{previous}) \div \Delta Q$, where MC = marginal cost of production, TC_{new} is the total cost at the new production level, $TC_{previous}$ is the total cost at the prior production level, and ΔQ is the change in the number of units. The symbol delta (Δ) stands for change in a variable. In this case, the change in production number is always 10 units.

As an example, if we look at the marginal cost of production between 20 and 30 units, the equation will be as follows:

MC = ($1,300–$1,075) ÷ 10 = $225 ÷ 10 = $22.50 per unit.

Average fixed cost is simply fixed costs divided by the quantity. If we look at the average fixed cost at 30 units of production, the equation will be AFC = FC ÷ Q, where AFC is average fixed costs, FC is fixed costs, and Q is quantity.

In this example, AFC = $500 ÷ 30 = $16.67 per unit.

Average variable cost follows the same principal. The equation or average variable cost is AVC = VC ÷ Q, where AVC is average variable costs, VC is variable costs, and Q is quantity. Let's look at another example from the table above – the average variable cost at a production level of 50 units.

AVC = $1,150 ÷ 50 = $23.00 per unit.

The last concept we will discuss in this section is average total cost. Average total cost combines both fixed and average costs of production to give the average cost of production per unit at a specific production level.

The equation that shows this is:

ATC = TC ÷ Q where ATC is average total cost, TC is total cost, and Q is quantity. Using our chart above, we will determine the average total cost per unit at a production level of 80 units.

ATC = $1,925 ÷ 80 = $24.06 per unit.

When does a company decide to close down a firm?

The rule of supply and demand states that the market reaches equilibrium at the point that the supply of a good or service is equal to the demand. At this point the producer maximizes sales and the consumer pays a fair price for the goods and services they purchase. If the producer reaches a point where the cost of producing the good or service is higher than the price the consumer will pay for it and there are no other opportunities for developing new products or modifying the product line to meet market demand, management of the company will probably decide to close the plant instead of continuing to product at a financial loss.

The United States Department of Labor has developed rapid response teams to assist workers who are suddenly out of work because businesses shut down. These teams are put into action when a company notifies the state or federal government that within 60 days, it will lay off 50 workers, if that number is equal to one-third of the workforce at one site, or if layoffs of more than 500 are going to occur.

Concept Reinforcement:

1. List the production costs of a firm and describe each.

2. Calculate the marginal cost, average fixed cost, average variable cost, and average total cost for the production levels below.

Quantity	Fixed costs	Variable costs	Total costs	Marginal cost per unit	Average fixed cost	Average variable cost	Average total cost
0	$1,000	$0	$1,000	-	-	-	-
25	$1,000	$400	$1,400				
50	$1,000	$775	$1,775				
75	$1,000	$1,100	$2,100				
100	$1,000	$1,300	$2,300				
150	$1,000	$1,450	$2,450				

Section 4.7 – Production Output

Section Objectives:

- Discuss how firms decide how much labor to hire to produce a certain level of output

- Study how a firm chooses to set output

Production level is an important decision for any firm to make. The number of units of each good produced affects the firm's profitability. The firm wants to maximize profitability, which means setting production at a level that will meet, but not exceed demand at market equilibrium. Market equilibrium is the price and quantity demanded that maximizes both profit and consumer interest in the product.

The business owner has to consider three things to maximize profitability. The first is the cost structure of the business. In other words, the fixed and variable costs required to produce goods and services at different levels of output. The second consideration is finding the right mix of fixed and variable inputs. It is sometimes a good decision to purchase capital equipment instead of hiring more people to improve efficiency. The third consideration is minimizing total costs by using the most efficient combination of inputs to produce the good provided by the company. This is measured in marginal product per dollar, both for fixed and variable inputs. Marginal product per dollar is the amount of additional output (product) produced by the last dollar spent on input. Costs are minimized where the marginal product per dollar for the variable inputs is equal to the marginal product per dollar for the fixed inputs. If the marginal cost (total of fixed and variable costs) of the last unit produced is greater than the price the good will demand on the market, the company loses money. On the other hand, if the marginal cost is lower than the price the market will bear for the product, the company is not maximizing profits because it is not producing enough units of the product. The company will make a profit as long as the marginal revenue (the money made by selling one more unit of the product) is greater than the marginal cost of producing that unit. Profit is maximized where marginal cost per unit is equal to the price per unit charged to the consumer. In reality, this is difficult to achieve because demand changes over time, meaning that the optimal price will change. Pricing strategies must consider both the internal costs and the external market.

Labor is a key component of production costs. The cost of labor varies dramatically with the skill, experience and education levels required to perform a task. In general, labor is divided into two groups: skilled and unskilled. Skilled workers have specialized training and expertise that demands higher wages than unskilled workers can demand. For example, a plumber (skilled trade) will earn more than a laborer who does not have a special skill set. Skilled workers have made the investment in additional training and education that makes them more valuable to companies. The number of skilled workers is less than the number of unskilled workers. Skilled workers tend to add more value to each unit of the company's product than unskilled workers, which is why they are able to earn more money.

Labor is a variable input. As such, the company will look at the marginal utility of adding staff to increase production. Let's look at an example to make the concept clear.

Units of Labor (days)	Total Product (output)	Marginal Product	Average Product
0	0	-	-
1	8	8	8
2	14	6	7
3	19	5	6.3
4	22	3	5.5
5	24	2	4.8

Marginal product is the output resulting from the addition of a unit of labor. Notice in the chart above that marginal product for one day of labor is eight, but it continues to reduce as more units of labor are added. This is because the total output does not increase in a linear manner to units of labor. If the relationship between total product and units of labor is linear, each additional unit of labor will result in a consistent increase in the total product output.

Average product is the total output divided by the units of labor. The goal is to maximize efficiency of production, which means maximizing the number of products produced per unit of labor (average product). As more people are hired, the fixed physical resources available for production are divided among more workers until the point where the fixed resources are unable to support the capacity of the labor force, so workers are unable to work at their full capacity.

The law of diminishing returns begins to take effect at this point. The law of diminishing returns states that as units of variable input, such as labor, are added to a production process with a fixed resource, the marginal return will increase to a point, and then decrease. The marginal product curve intersects the average product curve at its maximum.

Stages of Production

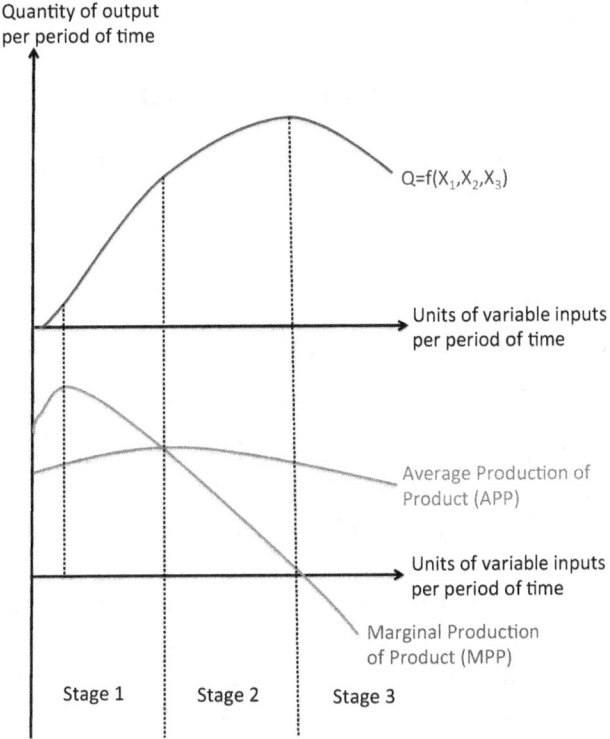

As with other variable inputs, the company will choose to set inputs at the point where marginal utility is maximized. With labor, this occurs at the height of the average production curve.

Concept Reinforcement:

1. Describe how a company decides the amount of labor required to produce its product.

2. List the three considerations for maximizing profitability and discuss how they interact.

3. Explain how a company sets output levels. What are some of the key considerations?

Section 4.8 – Maximizing Profits

Section Objectives:

- Identify how a company sets output at the best level for maximizing profits

- Discuss why and how firms respond to the rising or falling cost of inputs

Maximizing Profitability

There are three key considerations to maximizing profitability: cost structure, mix of inputs, and minimizing total costs.

The cost structure of a business includes both the fixed and variable inputs required to produce the good or service of the company. The product or service provided by the company will determine the mix of fixed and variable inputs required.

Determining the mix of fixed and variable costs is key to maximizing profitability. This should be reassessed over time as the company grows and the technology available to do the work changes. Some companies will have evenly mixed fixed and variable costs. Others will have high fixed costs and low variable costs. Others will have the opposite – high variable costs and low fixed costs. The mix of costs will depend on the type of business. A lawn service, for example, may have high variable costs (primarily labor) at the beginning. As the company grows, it may become practical to invest in equipment, such as riding mowers, leaf blowers, and other tools, to minimize the variable cost of labor. A person with a riding mower or a leaf blower will be able to produce more output than a couple of workers using manual tools such as a push mower or a rake.

Once the necessary fixed and variable inputs have been determined, the management of the company will determine the most efficient combination of these inputs to maximize profitability. Marginal product per dollar for fixed, variable and total inputs is used to determine the most efficient production combination.

Marginal product per dollar is the amount of additional output (product) produced by the last dollar spent on either a variable or fixed input. Costs are minimized where the marginal product per dollar for the variable inputs is equal to the marginal product per dollar for the fixed inputs.

Companies lost money when the marginal cost (total of fixed and variable costs) of the last unit produced is greater than the price the good will demand on the market. On the other hand, as long as the marginal cost of production is lower than the price at the market equilibrium, the company is not maximizing profits and should consider increasing production to market equilibrium. As long as the marginal revenue per unit is greater than the marginal cost per unit, the company is making a profit. Profit is maximized where marginal cost per unit is equal to the price per unit charged to the consumer.

It is important for companies to understand the market and their competition when setting prices and determining output levels. The thought process should include both short-term and long-term market analysis for product demand and the availability of inputs required to produce the company's good or service. External market forces (competition, demand, economy, availability of inputs) must be considered when deciding on production output.

What happens when the prices of inputs rise or fall?

The external market, particularly the availability of the inputs required for the business to produce its goods and services, has a huge influence on the decisions made regarding production and pricing levels.

The raw materials and other inputs required to produce the good or service of the company provide the basis of the price the company charges for the product. Of course, the price is also influenced by demand for the product. However, the company needs to charge more for the product than it costs to produce it, so the price point must be higher than the production cost in order for the company to make a profit.

The availability and price of the inputs are subject to the same laws of supply and demand as the final product. If the inputs become more scarce, assuming demand stays the same, the price demanded for the inputs will increase. Alternatively, if the inputs become more available, again assuming demand stays the same; the price demanded for the inputs will drop.

Since the price of the inputs is a key component of the price the company must charge to recover its costs, if the cost of the components increases, the company will have to raise its price to the consumer in order to continue to make the same level of profit. Again, if the cost of the inputs decreases, the company can choose to decrease its price and increase production to maximize profitability.

Concept Reinforcement:

1. List the three keys to maximizing profitability.

2. Describe how marginal product per dollar is used to maximize profitability.

3. Explain what happens when the price of the inputs required for production increase or decrease.

Section 4.9 – Maximizing Profits

Section Objectives:

- Describe the basic goal of a company as maximizing profits

- Evaluate the effect of price ceilings and price floors

The basic goal of every company is to maximize profits. People start businesses to make money, which only happens if the cost of the inputs is less than the price the product will demand on the market.

In a free market system, the market would dictate the costs of the inputs and the cost that the producer can demand for the product based on the supply provided. However, most economies have controls imposed by the government. Two of these controls are price floors and price ceilings.

Price floors are minimum prices for specific goods or services that are established by law. Likewise, price ceilings are maximum prices for specific goods or services that are also established by law. There are often unanticipated consequences (secondary effects) that result from the legislation of prices. These include shortages and surpluses.

Inflation leads to concerns about consumers being able to afford products because the value of the dollar is shrinking. One mistake that people who are worried about inflation make is thinking that the rising prices are the cause of inflation rather than an effect of inflation. Setting price ceilings by law creates a situation in which demand will be higher than supply, creating a shortage of the product. Market equilibrium occurs when supply and demand meet at a price and quantity point. If the price point is set at an artificially low point, the quantity the producer is willing to supply will be less than demand, which is what leads to the shortage. A price ceiling will keep prices down in the short run, but will eventually lead to an even worse shortage in the future because producers will redirect their production capacity to areas where they can maximize profits.

Another secondary effect of a price ceiling is a reduction in the quality of the goods produced. The producer will strive to maximize profits, whether a price ceiling is in place or not. If the price cannot increase, the quality will decrease in order to maintain profitability.

> **Deflation** is a decrease in the price of goods and services and takes place when the annual inflation rate falls below zero. **Deflation** results in an increase in the real value of money and is caused by a decrease in the money supply or available credit.

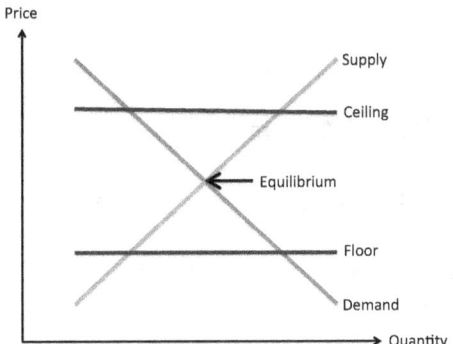

Price Floor and Ceiling

Price floors are established to keep the price of a good at a certain level above its equilibrium point. Because the price is above the equilibrium point, the suppliers will want to provide more than the consumers are willing to purchase. This leads to a surplus of products on the market. Examples of price floors are agricultural price supports and minimum wage legislation. The result of a price floor is that buyers will be more selective than if the price were allowed to set itself at the market equilibrium. Producers will have to compete based on quality and will have to be willing to offer other benefits to consumers, such as easier credit, price breaks on other products, or better customer service.

Concept Reinforcement:

1. Define price floor and state why a price floor might be established.

2. Define price ceiling and state why a price ceiling might be established.

3. What are the secondary effects of price ceilings and price floors?

Section 4.10 – Factors that Affect Price

Section Objectives:

- Describe cause-and-effect relationships

- Describe the determinants that create changes in price

Cause and effect relationships are those that require a specific event or condition to occur before the effect is seen. In the economic world, a price increase is a direct result (effect) of an increase in the cost of the inputs or an increase in demand. Likewise, a price decrease is a direct result of either a reduction in the cost of the inputs or a reduction in demand for the good or service provided by the company.

There are three criteria that must be met: temporal (time) precedence, establishment of a relationship, and a lack of plausible alternative explanations for the effect.

Time Precedence: In order for a cause and effect relationship to be established, the relationship between the events must be established temporally (in time). In other words, an increase in the cost of inputs to a production process at time point A will result in an increase in price of the final product to the consumer at time point B. Cyclical functions, such as inflation and unemployment, may both cause each other and be affected by each other. In other words, inflation can cause unemployment and unemployment can cause inflation.

Cyclical Functions

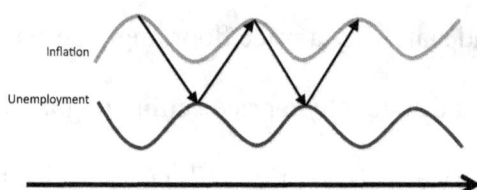

Establishment of a Relationship: Before you can establish a causal relationship, you have to first establish that a relationship of any sort exists. This is done by observation of both the cause and effect. If you observe that whenever X is present, Y is present, and when X is absent, Y is absent, you have established a relationship between X and Y. X (cause) must be present for Y (effect) to be present. A relationship (not necessarily causal) can be described as follows:

if X then Y

if not X then not Y.

No plausible alternative explanations: There may be other reasons (third variables) that explain the relationship. For example, you may think that you are in a microeconomics class because your teachers are trying to torture you. However, the desire to torture you would not be the cause of your enrollment in this course. The cause of your enrollment in microeconomics is actually that the course is a requirement for your graduation or that you chose to take the course because you are interested in the subject matter.

Changes in price are caused by a number of factors, including production costs, demand, supply, personal preferences, population, and the price of other goods (complements or substitutes).

1. ***Changes in production costs:*** Companies are in business to make a profit. The price of the good produced is based on the costs of the inputs required for production, as well as the demand for the good. If the cost of the inputs increases, the price the company charges to the consumer is likely to increase in order for the company to continue to earn a profit.

2. ***Demand:*** If demand for a product increases and supply remains the same, the price the market will bear for that product will increase. If demand decreases and supply remains constant, the price the market will bear for that product will decrease.

3. ***Supply:*** If supply of a product increases and demand remains constant, the price of the good will decrease. Likewise, if the supply of a product decreases and demand remains constant, the price of the good will increase.

4. ***Personal Preferences:*** Personal buying habits can be affected by social trends. For example, trends in the foods people purchase can change based on the perceived benefit or harm of each particular food. If the demand for a particular food product, for example soy increases and supply remains constant, the price demanded for that good will probably increase. If the demand for the product goes down and supply remains constant, the price of that good will probably decrease.

5. ***Population changes:*** Population increases or decreases affect consumption. More people will consume more products and fewer people will consume less.

6. ***The price of other goods:*** Substitute products and complementary products affect the price of products. A substitute product is a product that is easily substituted for another. For example, if the price of tuna suddenly increases so that it is higher than salmon, the demand for salmon will increase and the demand for tuna will decrease. Complementary products are goods or services that are used in conjunction with other products. For example, hot dogs and hot dog buns. If the price of hot dogs increases, demand for hot dogs will decrease, as will demand for the complementary product of hot dog buns.

Concept Reinforcement:

1. Describe cause and effect relationships.

2. List and discuss the three criteria for establishing cause and effect relationships.

3. Explain how cause and effect relationships change the price of goods.

Section 4.11 – Price and Profit

Section Objective:

- Identify the relationship between prices and the profit incentive

The profit incentive, also known as the profit motive, is the reason that companies are in business. Profit is the economic benefit gained by engaging in a specific activity. It is also the financial gain (the difference between price and cost of bringing the product to market) made by the producer.

Supply and demand, when at equilibrium, meet at the point where production is at the same level demanded by the market. This is the most efficient point of the market as far as price and quantity supplied are concerned.

Producers may be tempted to raise the price for a good or service to a point above the market equilibrium in an attempt to increase profits. They may also be tempted to produce goods of lower quality and charge the same price to increase profits. In a free market, these techniques will not work because the market will force the price to move to the equilibrium point where supply equals demand.

However, in a market that is not a completely free market, there may be other forces at play that can influence the price of a good or service. In an economy that has governmental restrictions, artificial controls on access to goods and services, finite resources or other forces that restrict free trade, there will be an opportunity for prices to be set at a point higher than the free market would bear.

A common example is the availability of tickets for sports events or concerts. A concert or sports venue will hold a limited number of people. If the demand for event tickets is greater than the capacity of the venue, the price of the tickets will be artificially inflated because of the demand for the tickets. Ticket scalpers take advantage of this economic trend to charge more than face value for tickets to high-demand events.

The chart below shows what happens when the demand is greater than or less than expected for an event. The middle line shows the expected demand at the face value for the event. The rightmost line (D_{high}) represents the price for a high-demand ticket and the leftmost line (D_{low}) represents the scalper's price for a ticket with less than anticipated demand. There are 10,000 tickets available. If the demand is greater than 10,000 tickets, the scalper's ticket price will increase to more than $40. If the demand is less than 10,000 tickets, the scalper will lose money because he will not be able to recover the money he invested in the tickets by purchasing them at the face value of $40. If demand is less than anticipated, the price the tickets will sell for will be less than face value.

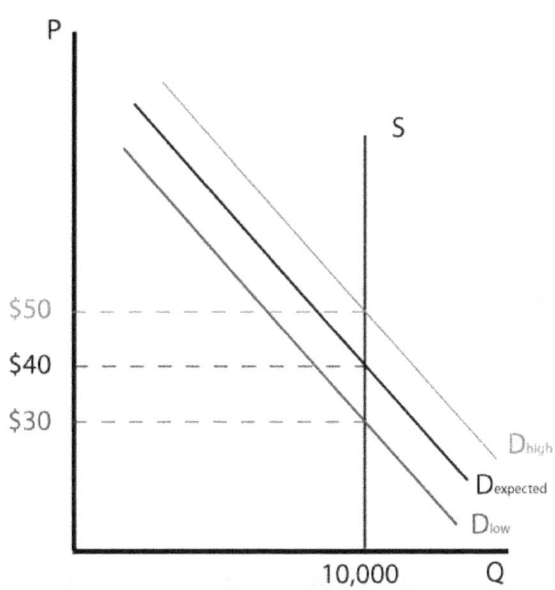

Concept Reinforcement:

1. Describe the profit motive.

2. Explain what a company may do to increase profitability.

3. How does a market that is not a free market allow prices to be set at levels that are not the most efficient based on supply and demand?

Section 4.12 – Total and Per Unit Costs of Production

Section Objectives:

Section Objectives:

- Construct per unit costs when given total costs and relevant output levels

- Construct total costs when given per unit costs and relevant output levels

Per unit costs are based on both fixed and variable costs of production. Fixed costs are those that the company incurs regardless of the level of production and variable costs are those that are dependent on the number of units produced.

We will go through some examples of how to determine per unit and total costs based on different information.

Total costs are based on the total fixed and variable costs of producing a good or service. Fixed costs include all of the costs the producer will incur regardless of the production level (number of units) of the company. These include building, equipment, heat, lights, and other overhead costs that remain the same regardless of production level. Variable costs are the additional costs incurred for each unit of production.

Let's look at how to calculate total costs first.

We will use the example of textbook production for this discussion. A textbook has several costs associated with it: the fixed costs of the publisher – buildings, printing presses, computers, etc. These costs are not going to change regardless of the number of textbooks published. For this scenario, we will say that the fixed costs for our publisher are $100,000. The variable costs associated with producing a textbook include author royalties (they may change depending upon the book and the author), editing costs, printing costs, artist and graphic design costs, shipping and marketing costs. For our situation, we'll say the variable costs are $35 per book.

The publisher wants to calculate total costs based on a number of different production levels. The table below shows the total costs based on different levels of production. Note that the total costs consist of the fixed costs plus the variable costs times the number of units produced. The equation for this calculation is: $TC = FC + (VC \times Q)$, where TC is total costs, FC is fixed costs, VC is variable costs per unit, and Q is quantity.

Fixed Costs	Variable Costs per unit	Quantity	Total Costs
$100,000	$35	0	$100,000
$100,000	$35	500	$117,500
$100,000	$35	1,000	$135,000
$100,000	$35	1,500	$152,500
$100,000	$35	2,000	$170,000
$100,000	$35	2,500	$187,500
$100,000	$35	3,000	$205,000
$100,000	$35	3,500	$222,500
$100,000	$35	4,000	$240,000
$100,000	$35	4,500	$257,500
$100,000	$35	5,000	$275,000

Let's use the same example to figure out per-unit costs. We have total costs per quantity of the books produced. In order to calculate the per-unit cost, we need to use the following equation: $UC = TC \div Q$, where UC is unit cost, TC is total cost, and Q is quantity. The table below shows the calculations.

Total Costs	Quantity Produced	Per unit cost
$100,000	1	$100,000
$117,500	500	$235
$135,000	1,000	$135
$152,500	1,500	$102
$170,000	2,000	$85
$187,500	2,500	$75
$205,000	3,000	$68
$222,500	3,500	$64
$240,000	4,000	$60
$257,500	4,500	$57
$275,000	5,000	$55

Notice how, even though the variable costs remain the same per unit, the total cost per unit decreases. This is because the fixed costs are being divided among a bigger number of units produced.

Concept Reinforcement:

1. Describe the difference between total costs and per unit costs.

2. State the equations used to calculate total costs and per unit costs.

3. Determine the per-unit and total costs given the following variables:

   - Fixed Costs = $75,000

   - Variable Costs = $12.00/unit

   - Quantity in increments of 50, from 0 to 500.

Section 4.13 – Types of Production Costs

Section Objective:

- Distinguish between the concepts of opportunity cost, marginal cost, and sunk cost

In addition to fixed and variable costs, there are other costs that contribute to the price of a good or service. These include opportunity cost, marginal cost, and sunk cost.

Opportunity cost is the cost the company incurs by choosing to produce one product rather than another. Opportunity cost is a result of scarcity of resources and the resulting need to make trade-offs when deciding which goods and services to acquire or produce. An example of an opportunity cost is when a student decides to pursue an advanced degree. A student with a bachelor's degree, which typically takes about four years to obtain, is ready to go out and get a professional job. Let's say this student is able to earn $40,000 per year with a bachelor's degree. Instead, the student decides to move on to graduate school and pursue a master's degree, which typically requires another two years of schooling. The opportunity cost of the student's decision to pursue additional schooling is the cost of tuition, fees, living expenses, as well as the lost earnings of the job the student did not take.

The costs included in an opportunity cost include:

> **Legacy costs** are expenses that businesses are obligated to pay based on earlier commitments to employees and pensioners. The most common **legacy costs** are healthcare commitments to retirees and other benefits that were agreed to in past contracts.

- Salary – year 1: $40,000

- Salary – year 2: $44,000 (10% increase for outstanding performance)

- Tuition & Fees – year 1: $20,000

- Tuition & Fees – year 2: $22,000 (10% inflation in tuition and fees)

- Living expenses – year 1: $15,000

- Living expenses – year 2: $18,000

Therefore, the total opportunity costs for obtaining the masters degree are: $40,000 + $44,000 + $20,000 + $22,000 + $15,000 + $18,000 = $159,000.

Is the opportunity cost worth the investment in the education? It depends on the salary the student will be able to earn upon graduation from the master's degree program. In most cases, the student will recover the cost of the education because he will have higher earnings over time than he would have with the bachelor's degree.

Marginal Cost is the change in total cost resulting from the production of each additional unit of a good or service. In most cases, the marginal cost per unit of product declines in the short term. In the long term, however, the marginal cost will increase because of the difficulty of using the same production capacity to produce more than the optimal number of units. As an example, if a factory is able to produce 2,000 widgets in a day at optimal production levels, but demand is 3,000 widgets per day, the company will work to meet the demand by increasing supply. The only way to increase supply is to try to increase the output from a fixed amount of production capacity. This often means adding workers who work another shift (night shift, for example) to increase the production capacity of the fixed plant. Factory workers who work second or third shift (afternoon/evening or night) are often paid a wage differential. This means they are paid more per hour for their time. This increases the variable costs per unit of production, therefore increasing the marginal cost of production.

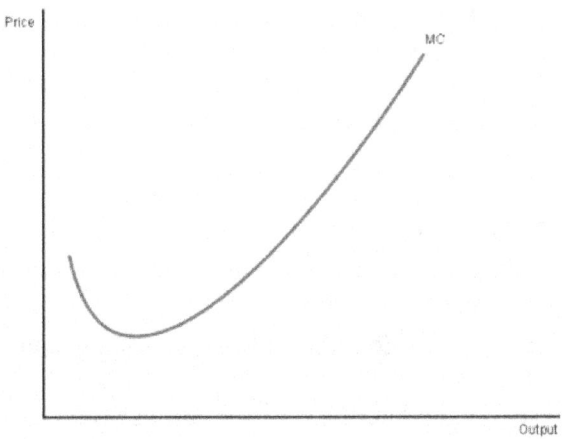

Sunk Costs are the costs associated with past decisions. These are also called historical costs. These costs do not have any influence on current decision-making except to provide knowledge that is relevant to making current decisions. Sunk costs are costs that have been incurred and the decision to incur the costs cannot be changed. This is why any decisions made by the company need to be made based the costs and benefits related to the current market conditions. An example of a sunk cost is a piece of manufacturing equipment that becomes obsolete (outdated). If the machine can produce products that are equal to or greater than the costs of running the machine, included sunk costs such as depreciation costs, the company should consider continuing to use the machine. If the costs become greater than the revenue generated, the company should consider disposing of the machine and upgrading to more efficient equipment.

Concept Reinforcement:

1. Define opportunity cost and give an example of an opportunity cost.

2. Define marginal cost and discuss how marginal cost can increase after a certain point in production.

3. Define sunk cost and explain why a sunk cost should not be considered in making current decisions.

Section 4.14 – Determining Resources

Section Objective:

- Given a diagram or a table, determine the best amount of a resource a profit-maximizing firm should hire

The total cost-total revenue method of determining maximum profit involves using total cost of production and total revenue to determine the profit-maximizing level of production.

We will discuss this using an example. In our example, the product is a coloring book. The anticipated demand (Q) is 50,000 copies of the book and the cost of the book (C) is calculated at $100,000 (fixed costs) plus $2.50 per copy variable costs (royalties and marginal costs of production). The price at a demand of 0 is $10.00 per unit.

The equations we will use to calculate the various curves are:

$P = 10-0.00004Q$, where 0.00004 is the reduction in per-unit cost for each unit of the product.

- $C = \$100,000 + \$2.5Q$

Our costs for production of 50,000 units will be calculated as follows:

- $C = \$100,000 + \$2.5 \ (50,000 \ \text{units})$

- $C = \$100,000 + \$125,000$

- $C = \$225,000$

Now let's calculate price per unit for a production run of 50,000 units.

- $P = \$10-0.00004 \ (50,000)$

- $P = \$10 - 2$

- $P = \$8.00$

The table of values for this product is below:

Price	Quantity
$10.00	0
$8.00	50,000
$6.00	100,000
$4.00	150,000
$2.00	200,000
$0.00	250,000

Price-Demand Curve

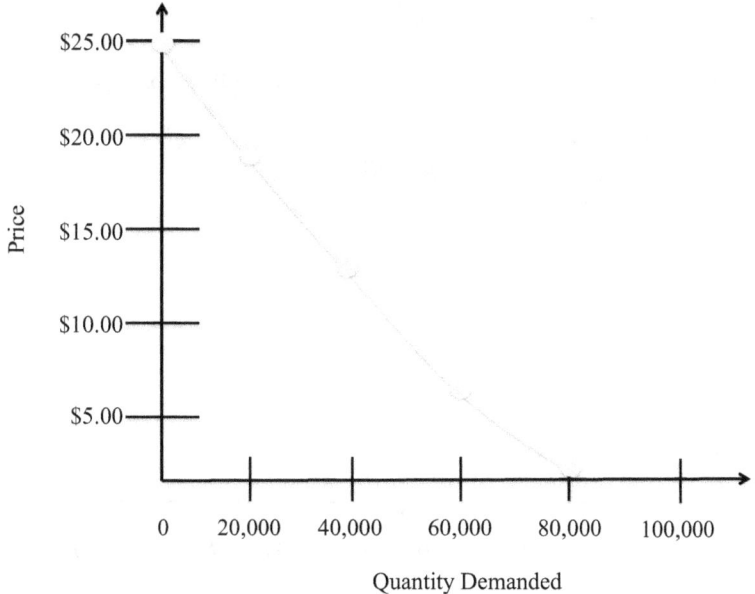

Quantity Demanded

As you can see from the price-demand curve above, the price is highest at zero supply ($10.00) and eventually drops to $0.00 when supply is large enough.

Now that we have the price-demand curve, we can determine the revenue at each point on the chart. This is calculated by using the equation $TR = P \times Q$ where TR is total revenue, P is price and Q is quantity. The table below shows the values.

Price	Quantity	Total Revenue
$10.00	0	$0
$8.00	50,000	$400,000
$6.00	100,000	$600,000
$4.00	150,000	$600,000
$2.00	200,000	$400,000
$0.00	250,000	$0

Next we will calculate total costs for production of the coloring book. The equation used for this is $TC = FC + (VC \times Q)$, where TC = total costs, FC = fixed costs, VC = variable costs, and Q = quantity.

Fixed Cost	Variable Cost	Quantity	Total Costs
$100,000	$2.50	0	$100,000
$100,000	$2.50	50,000	$225,000
$100,000	$2.50	100,000	$350,000
$100,000	$2.50	150,000	$475,000
$100,000	$2.50	200,000	$600,000
$100,000	$2.50	250,000	$725,000

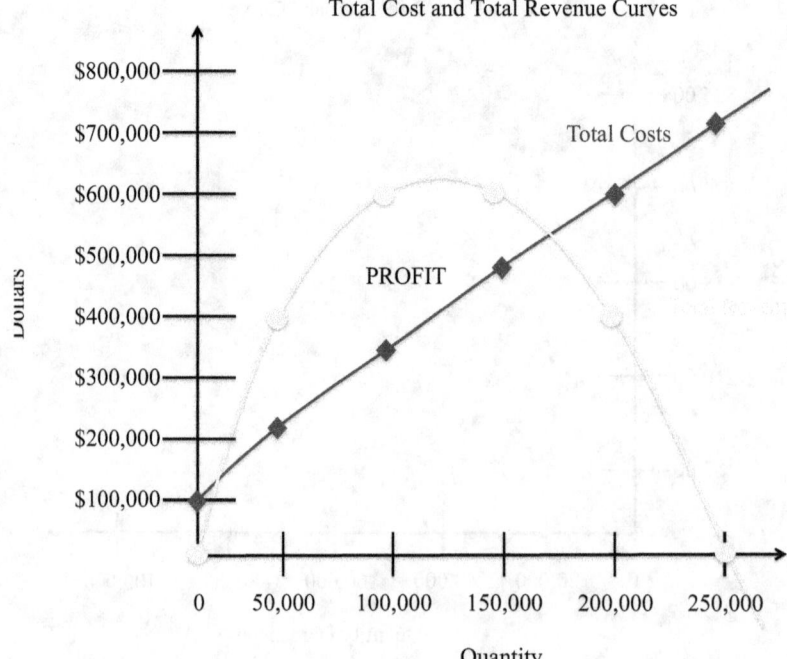

Total Cost and Total Revenue Curves

The area of the curve that falls under the total revenues curve and above the total costs curve is the area where the company will make a profit.

Now we will figure out total profit. Total profit is simply the difference between total revenue and total cost. The equation is TP = TR – TC, where TP is total profit, TR is total revenue, and TC is total cost.

Quantity	Total Revenue	Total Cost	Total Profit
0	$0	$100,000	-$100,000
50,000	$400,000	$225,000	$175,000
100,000	$600,000	$350,000	$250,000
150,000	$600,000	$475,000	$125,000
200,000	$400,000	$600,000	-$200,000
250,000	$0	$725,000	-$725,000

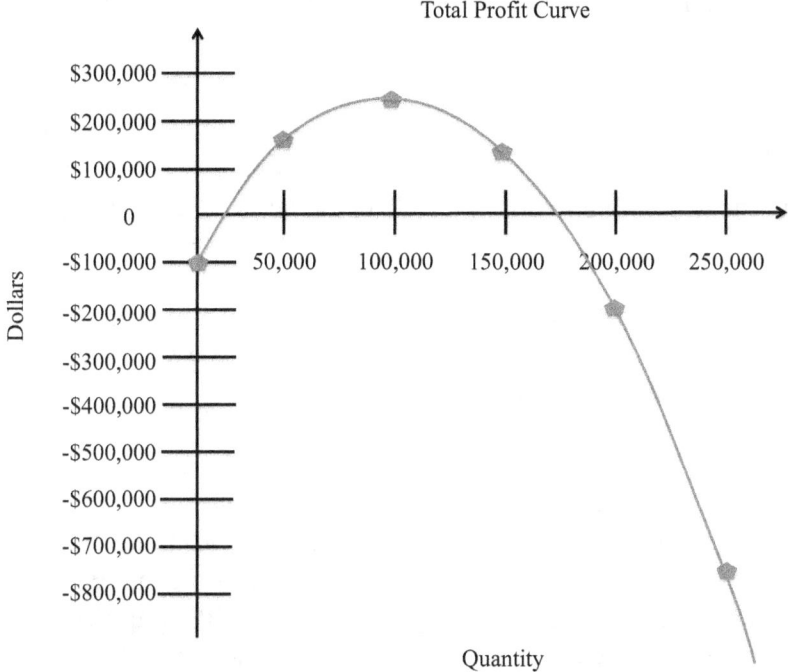

Total Profit Curve

Profit is maximized at a production quantity of 100,000 units, which results in a total profit of $250,000. Notice how the profit levels change based on the quantity produced. The company will make profit at production levels of 50,000, 100,000 and 150,000 units. The company begins to lose money when production is high enough that the price the market will support is lower than the cost of production.

Concept Reinforcement:

1. Describe how the profit incentive affects the price of a good or service.

2. Generate and plot the price demand curve for the following product:

   - The price at 0 demand is $25.00.

   - $P = 25 - 0.0003Q$.

   - Use increments of 20,000 from 0 to 80,000 units.

3. Generate and plot the total revenue, total costs, and total profit curves.

4. Identify the production level that maximizes profits.

Section 4.15 – Least-Cost Production Technology

Section Objective:

- Given a numerical example with prices, select the least-cost production technology for the firm

A firm that wants to maximize profit will also want to minimize production costs. When assessing production capacity and quantity, the firm will select the combination of technology and labor that will result in the least costs of production.

This is done by assessing the costs of production at different levels using different mixes of production inputs. The variables used to assess production level include explicit and implicit costs. Explicit costs are also known as expenditure costs and include the costs of purchasing additional input that is not already owned by the company. Explicit costs can include both fixed and variable costs. If a company needs to add equipment, buildings, or other costs of production that are not variable once they are acquired, these are additional explicit fixed costs. Explicit variable costs include additional labor and inputs of production. Implicit costs are those costs related to inputs already owned by the firm, as well as the opportunity cost of pursuing a particular production goal. The total cost of a production activity is explicit costs plus implicit costs.

Fixed and variable costs may be associated with both explicit and implicit costs. Fixed costs are those that do not change regardless of production level and variable costs are those that change with the production level of the good or service.

In general, a firm will employ additional units of labor, equipment and other factors of production as long as the marginal revenue product (the additional revenue of a firm resulting from use of one additional unit of a production input) is greater than the marginal cost (the additional cost to the firm of utilizing that additional input of production).

Let's look at an example of producing pots for houseplants. The product sale price is $5.00 per pot. The result of this analysis is that the marginal revenue product is maximized somewhere between nine and 10 units of labor. Adding the 10th unit of labor does not increase productivity or total revenue and brings marginal revenue product to zero. The additional unit of labor also increases production costs, making the staffing level of nine most efficient.

Units of labor	Total output	Marginal product	Product sale price	Total revenue	Marginal revenue product
0	0	-	$5	$0	-
1	50	50	$5	$250	$250
2	90	40	$5	$450	$200
3	125	35	$5	$625	$175
4	155	30	$5	$775	$150
5	180	25	$5	$900	$125
6	200	20	$5	$1,000	$100
7	215	15	$5	$1,075	$75
8	225	10	$5	$1,125	$50
9	230	5	$5	$1,150	$25
10	230	0	$5	$1,150	$0

The above example is simple. Let's see what happens when we add equipment into the problem. A new piece of equipment for forming and firing (baking) pots is available. The first unit of equipment is able to make 125 pots in a day with one laborer working at the machine, 200 pots with two laborers and 250 pots with three laborers. Each subsequent unit produces slightly less output per worker.

Let's look at the marginal revenue product for this new situation. Again, the marginal revenue product evens out between nine and 10 units of labor and between three and four machines. Until a new technology is developed or another cost variable changes the marginal revenue product, the company producing pots should consider producing at the number of workers and machines that results in a marginal revenue product of $0.

Units of labor	Number of machines	Total output	Marginal product	Product sale price	Total revenue	Marginal revenue product
0	1	0	-	$5	$0	-
1	1	125	125	$5	$625	$625
2	1	200	75	$5	$1,000	$375
3	1	250	50	$5	$1,250	$250
4	2	325	75	$5	$1,625	$375
5	2	400	75	$5	$2,000	$375
6	2	450	50	$5	$2,250	$250
7	3	490	40	$5	$2,450	$200
8	3	520	30	$5	$2,600	$150
9	3	545	25	$5	$2,725	$125
10	4	550	5	$5	$2,750	$25

Concept Reinforcement:

1. Define implicit and explicit costs and describe how they differ.

2. Describe how labor and equipment contribute to marginal revenue product.

3. Describe how marginal revenue product is calculated and how it is used to determine the levels of production inputs.

Unit Five

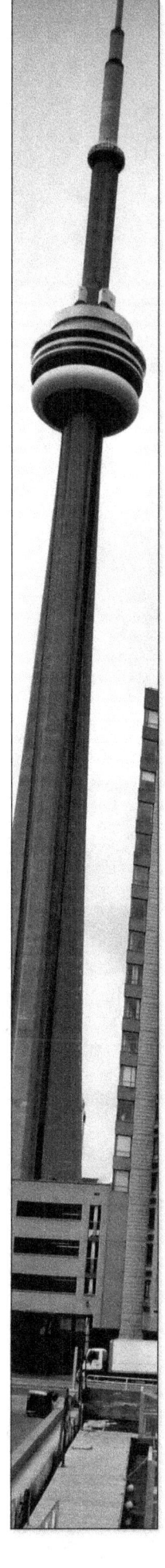

Section 5.1 – Market Economies

Section Objectives:

- Discuss the characteristics of traditional, command, and market economies and describe the societal values that influence them

- Discuss why the markets exist

A traditional economy has some unique characteristics. Resources are typically distributed through inheritance. For example, the children will receive shares of the parents' wealth based on the wishes and decisions of the parents. A traditional economy usually has a strong social network, is based on primitive methods and tools for doing work, such as subsistence farming, raising livestock and hunting. People in an economy like this are very self-sufficient, often making their own clothes and tools. Barter is used to exchange surplus crops or items the people make for other items that they need. Most countries have had traditional economies in the past that have been transformed to command, market or mixed economies. Traditional economies still exist in rural parts of Africa, Asia and South America.

A command economy is also known as a planned economy. In a command economy, the government determines what is produced, how much is produced, and often who will receive the goods. Command economies are associated socialism and communism, which are based on collective ownership of resources and means of production. This power falls with the state (government) making the central government of the country the central authority for planning the economic activities of the country.

A market economy is the result of consumers and producers deciding what they want to produce and purchase in the marketplace. Producers will produce as much of a good or service as they think will meet the demand from consumers. Supply and demand usually set the price that the market will bear in a market economy. Consumers vote with their dollars by purchasing the items they want at the price points they are willing to pay. Producers who are able to provide the goods and services at the price the consumer will pay will succeed. Those who are unable to do so are likely to fail in a market economy. In a market economy, the government has little or no role in regulating economic activity.

A mixed economy falls between a command economy and a market economy. In a mixed economy, which most developed countries have established, businesses are subject to both market forces (supply and demand) and governmental regulation (rules about import/export, safety, etc.).

Markets exist to provide a place where goods, services, and the factors of production (raw materials, labor, physical plant, and equipment) are traded (bought and sold). A market can be a physical place, such as a grocery store, or a market can also be much broader. When economists speak of a market, they are referring to all of the different mechanisms by which a particular good or service is traded. In the financial market, for example, trades may take place on the trading floor of a stock exchange, from a brokerage office, or over

The Heritage Foundation annually publishes the Index of Economic Freedom, ranking the freedom of the world's economies. For 2010, the United States was ranked number eight. The economies ahead of the U.S. include Canada, Ireland, Australia, and the number-one Hong Kong.

the Internet. Another way to look at a market is the potential pool of consumers who are interested in a product. Marketing groups use consumer demographics, data regarding the characteristics of consumers and their behavior, to predict markets for specific products and services. The tags you have seen used in stores for frequent buyer programs or discount programs are a common way to collect the demographic data that the companies use to assess the market for their products.

Concept Reinforcement:

1. Describe the characteristics of the three types of economies: traditional, command, and market.

2. Discuss the social values that underlie each type of economy.

3. Explain why markets exist.

Section 5.2 – Free Market Economy

Section Objectives:

- Describe the advantages of a free market economy

- Create a demand schedule for an individual and a market

A free market economy has three primary advantages over other economies: freedom to purchase and produce, pricing based on supply and demand, and, in theory, 100% efficiency in use of the factors of production to meet the needs of consumers.

- ***The freedom to purchase and produce.*** In a free market economy, consumers are free to decide what they want to purchase and how much they want to purchase as long as they are able to pay for the goods and services. Likewise, producers are free to use their factors of production (raw materials, labor, physical plant and equipment) to produce as much or as little of a good or service as they wish. This is very different than the traditional (subsistence) or command (centrally controlled) economies.

- ***Estimating Demand***. Producers try to estimate demand based on consumer behavior and past purchasing trends, trying to make the most efficient use of their factors of production. Consumers will purchase only those items they feel add enough value to their lives to be worth parting with the limited resource of money. When these two factors are in perfect balance, market equilibrium for that product is reached and this is the ideal price point for the product in that market. If the production level or price is too high, there will be a surplus of the product. Likewise, if the production level or price is too low, there will be a shortage.

- ***Efficient use of the factors of production***. If producers are 100% correct in their estimates of demand and price, they will be 100% efficient in their use of the factors of production because they will produce only enough to meet the demand of the consumer. No more and no less. This is not possible in the real world because the markets are constantly changing based on changes in the availability of resources, political changes, and other factors, such as natural disasters, that affect the economy.

Economists use a tool called a demand schedule to determine the demand curve for a product. The demand curve is a combination of price per unit the consumer is willing to pay and the quantity of the good supplied by the producer. Obviously these factors are inversely related. The higher the demand and the lower the supply, the higher the price of the good or service will be. Conversely, the lower the demand and the higher the supply, the lower the price of the good or service will be at market equilibrium.

Let's put together a demand schedule for a person for cheese. This person really likes cheese. Remember that a demand schedule has two components: price the consumer is willing to pay and the quantity the producer is willing to supply at that price point.

Price per pound of cheese	Pounds of cheese sold
$0.50	12
$1.00	10
$1.50	8
$2.00	6
$2.50	4
$3.00	2
$3.50	0

The demand schedule is shown graphically using a demand curve. The chart below shows the demand points plotted where price and supply meet. The line running through them represents the demand curve. In theory, the consumer will be indifferent to any combination of price and quantity on this curve.

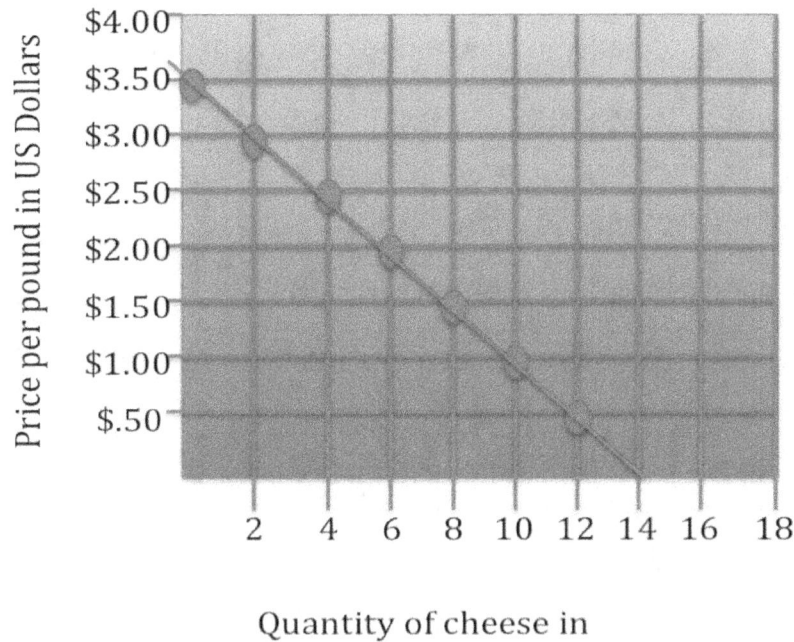

Quantity of cheese in pounds

Let's look at the market demand for cheese now. The market may have very different characteristics for what it will pay for a pound of cheese.

Price per pound of cheese	Pounds of cheese sold (in thousands)
$0.50	18
$1.00	15
$1.50	12
$2.00	10
$2.50	8
$3.00	6
$3.50	3
$4.00	0

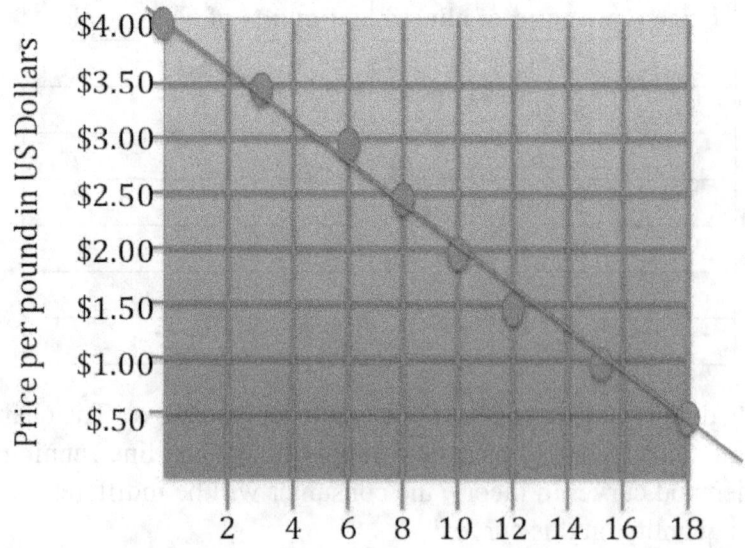

Quantity of cheese in thousands of pounds

Concept Reinforcement:

1. Explain the advantages of a free-market economy.

2. Describe why economists use a demand schedule.

3. Create a demand schedule for a good that you use. Describe how much of that good you are willing to purchase at different price points. Plot your demand schedule on a graph and create a demand curve.

Section 5.3 – Market Equilibrium

Section Objectives:

- Discuss how equilibrium is achieved in a market

- Interpret a circular flow model of a mixed economy

Market equilibrium for a product is established as a result of the forces of supply and demand. Producers decide how much of a good or service to supply based on the price they can demand and the potential profit. Consumers also decide how much they are willing to pay for a good or service based on the value they place it.

If producers supply more of a good or service than consumers are willing to purchase at the price demanded, there will be a surplus of the good or service. If, however, producers supply less of a good or service than consumers are willing to purchase at the price demanded, there will be a shortage of the good or service. Equilibrium is the point at which supply and demand are equal – producers are supplying the good or service at the level and price where consumers purchase all of the supply.

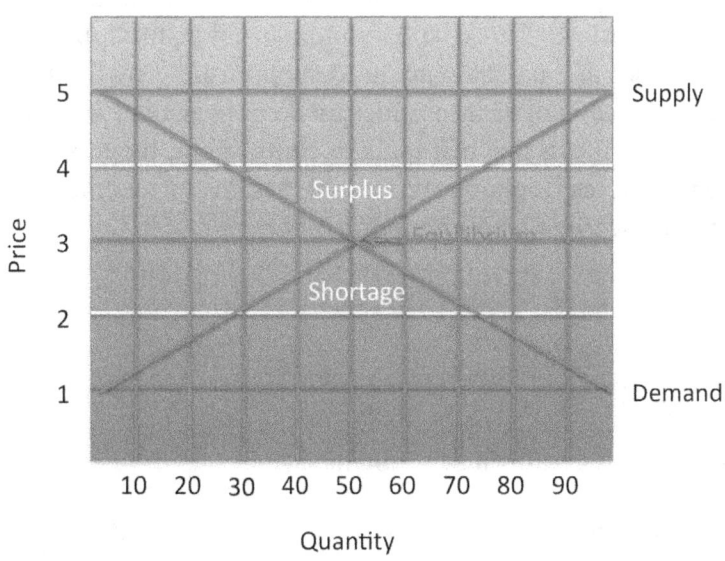

A shift in demand will move the equilibrium price point up (to the left on the demand curve) if demand increases and down (to the right on the demand curve) if demand decreases. Likewise, a shift in supply will move the equilibrium price point up (to the left on the supply curve) if supply is decreased, and down (to the right on the supply curve) if supply is increased.

The flow of resources toward equilibrium in a mixed economy can be shown using a circular flow model. The circular flow model includes flow of funds from households to product markets, as well as from businesses to households.

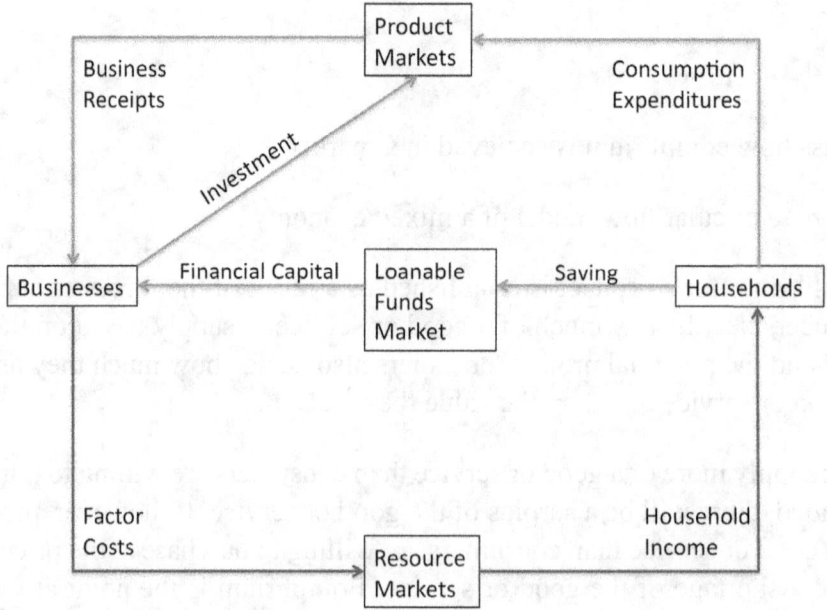

The basic concept of the circular flow model is that businesses pay employees, which moves money to the households, which then spend the money they have earned on goods produced by businesses. The graphic above also shows a second flow of money from households to businesses through the loanable funds market. Households save money in banks and other financial institutions. Those banks and financial institutions are then able to loan that money to businesses as financial capital to support the growth of the businesses, including investing financial capital in product markets to make more goods and services available to households. When this market is in equilibrium, the total of the consumption and investment expenditures (top loop) will equal the flow of income to the resource owners (businesses and households – bottom loop).

Concept Reinforcement:

1. Explain how market equilibrium is obtained.

2. Describe a circular flow economy.

3. Discuss how savings and investment affect the circular flow model of the economy.

Section 5.4 – Free Enterprise in the US

Section Objectives:

- Study the rise of free enterprise in the economy of the U.S.

- Identify the role of the government in the United States free enterprise system

The U.S. economy is based on the profit-seeking actions of English charter companies. Charter companies were groups of stockholders who wanted to find ways to make profit. Private individuals and companies would finance the charter companies, while the King of England would provide the project with a charter. The charter provided economic rights, and political and judicial authority to the charter company. When the colonies in North America did not turn a profit quickly enough, the charter companies turned their charters over to the settlers who chose to remain. This decision allowed the colonists to establish a new economy and the basic structures that would eventually become the United States of America.

The U.S. Constitution established the entirety of the U.S. as a common (unified) market. This means that all parts of the U.S are able to engage in unrestricted trade between states – that is interstate trade free of taxes and tariffs. The Constitution also granted the federal government the right to regulate commerce within the country and with other nations, establish uniform laws and standards to address bankruptcy, money creation and value, weights and measure, post offices, roads, patents and copyrights. The government went on to establish extensive infrastructure throughout the country in the form of roads, railroads, waterways, a national bank, the postal system, policies related to foreign trade, and over-sight of domestic production and trade activities. The oversight developed over time as safety, both for consumers and workers, became more important.

The end of slavery after the Civil War moved the country away from the cotton industry, which relied on slavery to remain profitable, to industrial economic activities, which were well established in the north. Industry thrived because of the demands of the war for goods required to support the troops.

The U.S. economy developed rapidly after the Civil War. The creativity of the U.S. people led to significant improvements in technology, which, combined with public and private investment, spurred economic growth. The incandescent light bulb, phonograph, telephone, automobile and airplanes are just a few inventions that have had a significant impact on the U.S. economy. While these technological advances were happening, the industrial infrastructure was being further developed, including coal, iron, copper, silver and lead mines and cement factories, which provided the raw materials required to build factories.

As industries were growing, people, such as Frederick W. Taylor and Henry Ford, were working on ways to improve the efficiency of people in doing their jobs. Taylor studied how people did their work and designed more efficient ways for them to accomplish the same work in less time. Ford implemented mass production when he developed the moving assembly line for producing automobiles. Each worker had one job to do before the car moved to the next worker.

The second half of the 19th century (1800s) saw the rise of tycoons, such as Rockefeller (oil), Gould (railroads), Ford (automobiles), Morgan (banking) and Carnegie (steel). These tycoons gained influence over the government, which continues to this day in the form of lobbying by special interests who try to influence laws to benefit their industries.

Corporations appeared in the 20th century as the economy matured. Business leaders were no longer tycoons, but highly paid and skilled managers who led corporations. The increasing influence of corporations also led to the organization of labor into unions. Business leaders in the 20th century and today do not control government, however they will try to influence governmental activities to benefit their companies.

The current mixed economy of the U.S. (free enterprise and government regulation) is highly successful and has consistently been the strongest economy in the world. The increased global competition from other growing economies, in particular the European Union and China, may change this in the future.

Government involvement in the American economy has grown over time. Initially, government was not heavily involved in the private sector, with the exception of transportation, and adopted a laissez-faire approach to the economy. This means that the government is not involved in the economy except to maintain law and order. This began to change in the late 1800s when farmers, small business owners and labor groups began to ask the government for assistance in maintaining free enterprise and competition in the economy. The Progressives, as they were called, favored government regulation of business practices to fight corruption in the public sector, and ensure competition and free enterprise.

The economic **theory of creative destruction** holds that economic growth is propelled by innovative entrepreneurs whose new technologies and products destroy the value of established companies. This process regenerates the economy by creating new sectors and eliminating old and less productive sectors.

The Interstate Commerce Act was passed into law in 1887 to regulate railroads, and the Sherman Antitrust Act was enacted in 1890 to prevent large companies from having a monopoly, controlling a single industry. Presidents Theodore Roosevelt and Woodrow Wilson, who were sympathetic to the views of the Progressives, enforced these laws. They also created new agencies, such as the Interstate Commerce Commission, the Food and Drug Administration, and the Federal Trade Commission to ensure safety and fairness in the marketplace.

The Great Depression of the 1930s brought some of the biggest changes to government involvement in the American economy. The New Deal, implemented by President Franklin Roosevelt, was an economic stimulus program that was used to provide jobs and building infrastructure (dams, roadways, etc.) for those who were unable to find work.

The New Deal was very important in defining our modern economy. This legislation established minimum standards for wages and hours worked, expansion of labor unions, extended federal authority in banking, agriculture and public welfare, the Securities and Exchange Commission (stock market regulatory agency), the Federal Deposit Insurance Corporation (FDIC), and the Social Security system. The New Deal legislation has led to almost every item that is sold in the U.S. being subject to government regulation. These regulations include safety regulations, clear pricing, and truth in advertising.

The 1970s saw increasing deregulation of industries that had been heavily regulated by the federal government. These included transportation and communications. Deregulation was implemented in an attempt to increase the variety of services offered to consumers, as well as reduce the prices of those services. Deregulation met with varying levels of success.

Environmental regulation is an example of government intervention in the economy for a social purpose. Several laws were enacted to control pollution, including the Clean Air Act (1963), the Clean Water Act (1972) and the Safe Drinking Water Act (1974). The environmental protection agency (EPA) was establishing in 1970 to manage and implement programs to protect the environment. This organization sets and enforces pollution limits.

Congress had created about 100 federal regulatory agencies by the 1990s. These agencies are structured so they are isolated from the President, so theoretically they should not be subject to political pressures. The agencies are run by independent boards, which are appointed by the president and confirmed by the Senate. The board members represent both primary political parties and serve terms of five to seven years. Congress funds and oversees the activities of the agencies.

Concept Reinforcement:

1. Explain how the U.S. Constitution established the basis for the current mixed economy in the U.S.

2. Describe how the federal government's role in the economy has changed.

3. Discuss the difference between government intervention in the economy for economic and social reasons.

Section 5.5 – Role of the Entrepreneur

Section Objectives:

- Study the role of an entrepreneur in the economy

- Identify prices and output in a perfectly competitive market

Entrepreneurs are people who organize and manage organizations, particularly businesses, and who are willing to take risks and bring significant initiative to the project. The word entrepreneur is based on the old French word "entreprende," which means "to undertake." Entrepreneurs decide which projects to undertake and how they should be conducted. If an entrepreneur is successful, these entrepreneurial activities will increase the value of the resources used to produce the good or service provided by the entrepreneur, resulting in a profit to the company.

Entrepreneurs are present in all levels of the American economy, from the biggest companies to single person businesses. Most people think of entrepreneurs as small business owners, but entrepreneurs can be found in all types of businesses. The primary characteristics of entrepreneurs are that they organize and manage businesses, are willing to take risks, and bring initiative to a project. These traits are found in leaders in every organization.

In a capitalist economy, entrepreneurs organize the factors of production to provide the goods and services demanded by consumers in exchange for making a profit. Entrepreneurs, especially those in small enterprises, are able to be nimble in their response to changing economic conditions and demands.

Ideally, a free market will be perfectly competitive. This means it will operate without any interference, particularly from the government or other agencies that provide regulation and oversight. In reality, markets are not completely free; therefore, perfect competition is not possible.

In a free market with conditions of perfect competition, supply and demand will determine both output and price. The company will supply only as much of a good or service as the consumer will purchase at a specific price – no more or less. Since the consumer wants to pay the lowest price possible for a good and the producer wants to maximize profit, equilibrium will be reached at the point where demand is satisfied at a given price. The producer must demand a price that will recover the costs of production as well as providing a profit. This means that a minimum price must be demanded. In general, the lower the price of a good or service, the higher the demand will be. However, the price cannot fall below the production cost or the producer will not be willing to supply the product.

Concept Reinforcement:

1. Describe an entrepreneur.

2. Explain the role of the entrepreneur in the American economy.

3. Identify how prices and output are determined in a perfectly competitive market.

Section 5.6 – Perfectly Competitive Market

Section Objectives:

- Identify the four conditions that are in place in a perfectly competitive market

- List three common barriers that prevent firms from entering a market

Four conditions must be present for a market to be perfectly competitive. We will discuss these one at a time.

There are many small suppliers that are each small enough that they are unable to influence the price for the overall market by changing the supply (increasing or decreasing the amount of goods available). This does not occur in the real world because companies are large and small. Large companies have economies of scale that make it possible for them to produce goods at a lower cost than a small firm.

The output of each firm must be identical. This does not meet the needs of the consumers who want variety in the products they purchase. Each consumer has different needs and priorities for the products they purchase.

The market is always in equilibrium. If the market is always in equilibrium, the supply and demand will always maximize benefit for both the consumer and the supplier. The market, in reality, is always changing due to changes in technology and the availability of alternative products. Consumers have perfect information about the prices being charged by all sellers. This will result in consumers moving away from a producer that demands a higher price for a product than other producers demand.

Competition is based only on price. In reality, consumers are influenced by more than price. Consumers demand quality, reliability, honesty, convenience and good service, and are willing to pay more for a good or service provided by a business that provides these attributes.

Under pure competition, firms face a perfectly elastic demand curve. This means that the firms must accept the price the consumer is willing to pay. Firms will expand production as long as the additional output adds more to revenues than to production costs.

There are three primary barriers to entry: legal barriers, economies of scale, and control over an essential resource.

Legal barriers to entry include licensing and patents. Licensing is a process of obtaining permission from a government to enter into a specific occupation or business. For example, licenses are often required for barber shops, beauty salons, taxi cabs, drugstores, and funeral homes. Patents are a second legal barrier to entry that allow the owner of the patent to prevent other people from using it for a period of time. In the U.S., patents are limited to 17 years. The patent owner may allow others to use the technology before the patent expires in 17 years, but usually requires payment of a fee to allow the other parties to use the technology.

Economies of scale are important in certain industries. Economies of scale occur when the production capacity of a company grows to a point that the per-unit cost of production is lower than that of a smaller company. Economies of scale often occur in the purchase of raw materials. Companies incur a lower per unit cost when they purchase raw materials in a large quantity because the provider of the raw materials will give them a quantity discount.

Control of an essential resource is a large barrier to entry. For example, if a company controls all of the sapphire mines in the world, no one else will be able to enter the market unless a new mine is discovered.

Concept Reinforcement:

1. List the four conditions that are in place in a perfectly competitive market.

2. Explain why these conditions are not possible to meet in the real world.

3. Describe two barriers to entry that companies face.

Section 5.7 – Monopolies

Section Objectives:

- Identify characteristics and give examples of monopoly

- Identify how monopolies are formed, including government monopolies

Monopolies occur when a single person or company controls the supply of a good or service for which there is no effective substitute and for which there are high barriers to entry. Monopolies are often natural monopolies, which occur when one supplier controls all or most of a resource. A natural monopoly can also occur when a supplier can meet demand at a lower cost than a group of competitors could. Natural monopolies include the De Beers diamond company, power generation, and a single standard of technology for an industry (operating systems).

A monopoly usually limits the supply of the goods it provides, which moves the supply curve to the left, raising prices, which does not benefit the consumer. This situation is called forced equilibrium. Forced equilibrium means that consumers are paying a price that is higher than equilibrium for a below-market total quantity of the product.

Examples of monopolies that once existed, but have been broken up, are the telephone system, power generation, and air travel. Breaking monopolies may or may not have benefits to the consumers. In the telephone industry, the breaking up of Ma Bell resulted in lower prices and increased innovation, both of which have benefited consumers. The energy industry, however, has shown different trends. Prices of energy continue to increase despite attempts to break the power generation monopolies. In 2008, gas companies were making record profits even though there was theoretically a shortage of gasoline and prices rose to about $4.00/gallon.

Government monopolies are typically coercive monopolies, meaning they are forced upon the market. A government monopoly occurs when the government is the sole provider of a good or service and prohibits competition by law. Examples of government monopolies in different places are the postal service, railroads, public utilities, alcohol sales, and police forces. In the U.S., the postal service is a monopoly that was granted to one organization. The USPS is not a government organization, but is the sole provider of postal services to Americans.

Concept Reinforcement:

1. Define the term monopoly.

2. List some characteristics of a monopoly.

3. Explain how a government monopoly is formed.

Section 5.8 – Monopolistic Competition

Section Objectives:

- Discuss how a firm with a monopoly sets output and price and why companies practice price discrimination

- Identify characteristics and give examples of monopolistic competition

Monopolists, like other capitalist companies, are in business to maximize profits. Monopolists that want to maximize profits will increase production until marginal revenue equals marginal cost. Marginal revenue is the revenue earned for each additional unit produced. Marginal cost is the additional cost for each additional unit produced. A profit-maximizing monopolist will increase production to a point where price is greater than marginal cost. Monopolists must consider the demand for their products when establishing a price. If a monopolist increases the price too much, the demand will decrease to a point that they are making less profit than if they had allowed the price to remain lower.

Let's look at an example. The market equilibrium price for a product is $12/unit at a demand of 100 units. At this level of production, the cost of production per unit is $8. This maximizes revenues for the firm. Revenues are calculated by multiplying price per unit by demand. In this case, we take $12 x 100 units = $1,200. The production cost for 100 units is $800. The profit to the company is $400.

If we increase the price to $20/unit, the demand will fall to 40 units and production price per unit increases to $11. What does this do to profits? Revenue is $20/unit x 40 units = $800. Costs of production are $11/unit x 40 units = $440. Profit is then $800–$440 = $360. This is less than the $400 that would be generated at the equilibrium price and supply. For a purely profit-driven monopolist, the $400 profit level is preferred.

Price discrimination occurs when a provider decides to set different price points for different markets or consumers. Providers decide to engage in price discrimination to increase revenues and profits. Three conditions must be met for price discrimination to be beneficial to the producer. First, the demand curve must slope downward, which occurs in monopolistic situations. Second, the provider must have at least two distinct groups of consumers to which the products are sold. The price elasticities of these consumer groups must be different and the groups must be easily separated. Third, the provider must be able to restrict the consumers to whom they sell the goods at a lower cost from reselling them to the consumers they are charging a higher cost.

Monopolistic competition is common. Monopolistic competition occurs when companies offer goods and services that are different than the products produced by other companies, but are also not perfect substitutes for the products produced by the other companies. In this type of imperfect competition, producers may act like monopolists, ignoring the price of competition, in the short term.

A market that is monopolistically competitive has the following traits:

1. Barriers to entry and exit are low or non-existent.

2. Producers have control of price. They do not consider the prices of similar products offered by competitors.

3. The market has many producers and many consumers.

4. No single company controls the market price of the goods and services offered.

5. Consumers perceive non-price differences between the products provided by different producers (quality, brand, etc.).

Concept Reinforcement:

1. Describe how a monopoly establishes production and price levels.

2. Define price discrimination and explain why companies engage in price discrimination.

3. Explain monopolistic competition.

Section 5.9 – Oligopoly

Section Objectives:

- Identify characteristics and give examples of oligopoly

- Discuss how firms compete without lowering prices

Oligopoly is a market where a few producers share the market, but no single producer controls the market (price or supply of the product). Oligopolies occur when there are high barriers to entry, high fixed costs, and the need for a large production capacity to reach an efficient level of production. Another characteristic of an oligopoly is that marginal costs continue to decrease as larger quantities are produced. The producers who share the market act in a way that they do NOT undercut the prices of the other producers. Profit is maximized in the long run by maintaining the prices at a certain level.

Cartels are a form of oligopoly, where members agree to limit the supply of a good in order to increase the price they can demand for it. A prime example is the oil cartel (OPEC). Cartel members work together to reduce competition and maximize profits to the cartel members.

As we mentioned, oligopolies do not compete on price. They compete more on public perception, advertising, and perceived benefits to consumers. Cereals, shampoos, and other packaged goods are examples of oligopolies. The products are essentially the same, as are the prices. But, the companies invest in significant marketing and advertising activities to differentiate them from one another.

Let's look at an example of an oligopoly – shampoo. There are hundreds of shampoos on the market. They all do basically the same thing – clean your hair. In order to gain market share, they have to make themselves special to the consumer. The companies do this by understanding what consumers value in a shampoo: bouncy hair, shine, body, color enhancement, dandruff control, etc. Characteristics such as dandruff control do require special formulations to treat this mild medical condition. The same occurs with color enhancement – the shampoo must actually do something to improve the color of the hair. The other characteristics (bounce, shine, body) will result from almost any shampoo because they are related to the health and cleanliness of the hair. People who are healthy tend to have shiny hair. People who are not healthy are more likely to have dull hair. Even within the more specialized areas of dandruff control or color enhancement, there are many substantially identical products that are competing for market share.

How do shampoo companies compete in this highly competitive market? They try to associate their brand name with a desirable hair quality (bounce, shine, dandruff free, etc.) and have that association be strong enough to induce consumers to purchase their products. Another way that shampoo companies differentiate themselves is establish themselves as a luxury product available only at salons. Again, the products are essentially the same as those in the store, but may have perceived benefits that consumers are willing to pay more money for.

Concept Reinforcement:

1. Define the term oligopoly.

2. Describe an oligopoly that has a strong influence on the U.S. economy.

3. Explain how oligopolies compete without reducing prices.

Section 5.10 – Monopoly and Oligopoly

Section Objectives:

- Study how firms in a monopolistically competitive market set output

- Evaluate the development of monopolistic competition and oligopoly

Monopolistic competition is a mix of perfect competition and monopoly. This is a more realistic representation of the market than either perfect competition or monopoly. Examples of monopolistic competition occur in the automobile, restaurant and cheese businesses, just to name a few. Any market where a variety of products that are slightly different are competing for consumers is monopolistic competition.

Monopolistic competition occurs when four specific economic conditions are in place:

- All firms in the market produce similar products that are NOT perfect substitutes for one another. This differs from perfect competition in that there is variation among the products offered by the suppliers. They are similar, but not the same.

- All firms are able to enter the market if the profits are attractive enough. Barriers to entry and exit are low, so firms are able to engage in production and supply of a good with relative ease.

- All firms maximize profits. Profits are maximized based on production factors, demand, and price.

- All firms have the ability to influence the market (market power), therefore are not price-takers. Firms are able to increase or decrease production to influence price, or increase or decrease price to influence demand, therefore production.

Another characteristic of monopolistic competition is that production does not occur at the lowest possible cost. This means that the companies in the market are likely to have excess production capacity.

Monopolistic competition is subject to consumer demand, which is expressed in two ways: love of variety and ideal variety.

The love of variety approach assumes that each consumer will demand different varieties of the same project. For example, restaurants use this consumer trait to provide a wide variety of meals for consumers. A person may decide to eat a Mexican meal one day, an American meal the next, and a Chinese meal the next.

The ideal variety approach is that each product consists of a number of characteristics, which can be selected by each consumer based on her individual preferences. A prime example is a car purchase. Thousands of a particular model of car are on the road, but the options selected for each car differentiate them from one another based on individual consumer preference.

Oligo-, as in **oligopoloy**, is a Greek word meaning "just a few." When combined with a suffix like *opoly*, it creates a word that means "control by just a few." Other prefixes derived from the Greek that you should know are *mono*, meaning "one," *poly* ("more than one" or "many"), *homo* ("the same"), and *hetero* ("different").

185

The companies in a monopolistic competition market will set production based on anticipated demand and with a goal of maximizing profits.

Monopolistic competition and oligopolies occur when the market is not able to support perfect competition. Monopolistic competition allows companies to choose the product they supply to the market and set price based on factors such as consumer demand and differentiation of the product from other suppliers. Some companies may choose to target the high-end market for the product and others will target the consumers who are not willing to pay as much for the good or service being provided. Let's look at the example of cheese. There are companies, with large production capacity, that take advantage of their factors of production to produce a large volume of a product of consistent quality. This cheese will be good, but not exceptional. Small cheese makers are able to focus on more specialized, expensive cheeses because they can target the market of cheese connoisseurs, who are willing to pay substantially more for high quality cheese. Small cheese makers are not likely to form an oligopoly, but the large cheese makers may do so. If they work together, the large cheese makers will be able to support each other's prices and compete based on differentiation based on advertising, marketing and public perception.

Oligopolies form when a few firms control the market. They are able to maintain prices above the market equilibrium level by engaging in collusion, sharing markets, and working together to restrict access to the goods and services they offer to the market. Firms may also work together to create stable market conditions for a product, reducing the risks of developing those product markets.

Concept Reinforcement:

1. List the four conditions that must exist for monopolistic competition to develop.

2. Explain how firms in a monopolistically competitive market set output.

3. Describe how monopolistic competition and oligopoly develop.

Section 5.11 – Markets and Prices

Section Objective:

- Review the connection between markets and prices

Markets are places where goods and services, as well as the factors of production (raw materials, labor, plant, equipment) are bought and sold. Markets may be better thought of as mechanisms by which these activities occur because markets are not necessarily physical places like grocery stores or farmers markets.

Markets may be described for specific products. For example, if a company is selling musical instruments, the market it is targeting is the group of people and businesses who are likely to purchase instruments. Likewise, the market for luxury automobiles is limited to those who can afford to purchase them. The market for this book is people interested in microeconomics.

Companies also target specific populations. For example, the baby boomers (people born after soldiers returned from World War II), are a large part of the American population. This group is affluent (has money) and is targeted by many companies. The companies try to determine what products the baby boomers will purchase and develop those products at a level of quality and price that will be attractive to this population. For example, companies that sell leisure activities (trips, sports, etc) have targeted the baby boomers by appealing to their active lifestyles. The retirees of today are not content to stay home. They are active, sometimes even pursuing new careers.

The prices of goods supplied will be influenced by the market being targeted. For example, a company that is targeting a population that is low-income will develop and produce goods that are inexpensive and meet the needs of the low-income consumer. That same company may also target high or middle-income populations. Each of these markets will demand a different product that will sell at a different price point.

A good example of this is jewelry. It is possible to get cheap jewelry, high quality jewelry, and then fine jewelry. Cheap jewelry is usually made of base metals or plastics with glass in place of stones. High quality jewelry may be made of base metals that are coated with gold or silver and use higher quality crystal in place of stones. It may also be made of semi-precious stones, silver, beads, and other less expensive jewelry components. Fine jewelry, on the other hand, is made of precious metals (gold, platinum, titanium) and gemstones (diamonds, emeralds, sapphires, etc). Which market do you think the jewelry makers will target for each of these categories of jewelry. They will target low-income populations with the inexpensive jewelry. Middle-income populations will be the target for the high quality jewelry and the high-income populations will be the target for the fine jewelry. There are even different marketing strategies for fine jewelry, especially for wedding rings. Fine jewelers will develop product lines that are less expensive for low or middle-income people to use as wedding rings.

Remember back to supply and demand. The larger a market for a product, the higher the demand is likely to be for that product. Price can be influenced by the producer, which may decide to restrict or expand the amount of a good or service provided. Likewise, consumers influence price by voting with their dollars. Producers will continue to produce goods that the consumers purchase. They will not produce goods if consumers do not purchase them. Market equilibrium is reached when the amount produced is the amount purchased, which occurs at a specific price.

Concept Reinforcement:

1. Describe markets.

2. Explain how producers of goods target specific markets.

3. Discuss how price and market are connected.

Section 5.12 – Sole Proprietorships

Section Objectives:

- Evaluate the advantages and disadvantages of a sole proprietorship

- Discuss the characteristics of sole proprietorships

A sole proprietorship is a form of small business that is owned by a single person and is NOT registered with the state as either a limited liability company (LLC) or a corporation. Examples of sole proprietorships are freelance writers, photographers, salespeople working on commission, independent contractors, or artists or craftsmen who take jobs on a contract basis. An advantage to a sole proprietorship is that they are very easy to set up and usually do not require payment of any fees or completion of any special forms. This is a good business structure for an individual who is starting a business that has three attributes: it will remain small, does not have great exposure to liability, and does not justify the expenses of incorporation.

Owners of a sole proprietorship are responsible for complying with local registration, business license and permit laws, as well as paying both income tax and business debts. One of the disadvantages of a sole proprietorship is that the business owner is held personally responsible for all business-related obligations. This means that if the business is unable to pay a debt, the creditor can come after the business owner's personal possessions, including a house, car, or other assets that could be liquidated to pay the debt.

A sole proprietor can hire any number of employees or independent contractors. The sole proprietor is not considered an employee because there is no legal distinction between the owner and the business.

Taxes remain relatively simple in a sole proprietorship. This is because the business is not legally separate from the business owner. As a result, the sole proprietor simply reports all income on the 1040 individual tax return with a schedule C attached to it to report the activities of the sole proprietorship. This avoids what some consider a double tax, which occurs when a business owner and a business both pay taxes on the same dollar amount of income. One of the disadvantages is that the business owner has to withhold and pay all income taxes, a self-employment tax that consists of contributions to Social Security and Medicare, and estimated taxes throughout the year. An employer usually withholds the income, Medicare and Social Security taxes. However, since a sole proprietor is not an employee, it falls to the individual to be responsible for these taxes.

Advantages to sole proprietorships are the following:

- Easy to establish.

- The owner makes all the decisions.

- Minimal startup costs.

- Taxes are reports on the owner's individual income tax forms.

- Owner manages and controls all aspects of the company.

- No reporting requirements.

- Business does not file or pay taxes.

- No fees.

Disadvantages to sole proprietorships include:

- The owner faces unlimited personal liability.

- Difficult to raise investment capital.

- Lack of continuity if the owner dies or becomes disabled.

- Owner can spend unlimited time responding to business needs.

Concept Reinforcement:

1. Define sole proprietorship.

2. Explain situations in which a sole proprietorship may be appropriate.

3. Discuss the advantages and disadvantages of a sole proprietorship.

Section 5.13 – Partnerships and Incorporation

Section Objectives:

- Evaluate the advantages and disadvantages of partnerships

- Compare and contrast the different types of partnerships

A partnership occurs when two or more people are co-owners of a business. The owners share the risks, responsibilities and rewards of the business. This arrangement is usually established before the partners go into business so the responsibilities of each are clear at the outset of the business venture. Each person involved as a partner contributes money, property, labor or skill. Each partner also expects to share in the profits and losses of the business. Partnerships consist of two or more persons. However, "persons" can include individuals, groups of individuals, companies, and corporations.

Partnerships are not required to file papers with the state to become a corporation or limited liability company (LLC). There are two types of partnerships: general and limited. General partnerships are the most common structure, in which all partners have a role in managing the business. Limited partnerships occur when one of the partners (the general partner) is responsible for running the business and the limited partners are simply passive investors.

Business partners have the same level of personal liability as sole proprietors. The owners of a partnership are personally liable for all business debts incurred by the firm, meaning that creditors may come after personal assets, including homes, cars and other real property to settle a debt. In a general partnership, all partners are based on their share of ownership. In a limited partnership, the general partner carries personal liability while the limited partners usually are only risking the investment they made in the firm. Common examples of partnerships are law, medical and accounting firms.

Partners have both joint authority and joint liability. Any individual partner is typically able to bind the company to a contract for the purchase of goods or some other business deal. There are a few limits on the ability of a partner to bind the company to a contract. A primary limit is that one partner is unable to bind the entire business to a sale of all the assets of the partnership. Joint liability, on the other hand, means that an individual partner can be sued for the full amount of any business debt. If this happens, the individual partner may have to sue the other partners for their shares of the debt.

From a tax perspective, a partnership has to file an annual information return to the IRS. The annual information return includes information on the income, deductions, gains, and losses of the operation. The partnership does not, however, pay income tax, because it is considered a pass-through entity. Profits or losses of the partnership are passed through to its partners, who then include these profits or losses on their individual tax returns. As with sole proprietorships, partners are not considered employees and are required to make quarterly estimated tax payments to the IRS each year.

One disadvantage to a partnership is that if one of the partners wants to leave the organization, the partnership is probably going to be dissolved. This means that all partners must fulfill any remaining business obligations, pay off all debts, and split any assets and profits among the partners. This can be avoided by including a buy-sell (buyout) agreement when the partnership is first established. A buyout agreement will allow the business to continue operations as usual if one of the partners becomes incapacitated or decides to leave the business.

Concept Reinforcement:

1. Describe a partnership.

2. Discuss the advantages and disadvantages of partnerships.

3. Compare and contrast the two types of partnerships.

Section 5.14 – Corporations

Section Objectives:

- Evaluate the advantages and disadvantages of incorporation

- Identify the role of multinational corporations

- Discuss the characteristics of corporations

A corporation is the most common legal structure for businesses in the U.S. Corporations have several characteristics that distinguish them from sole proprietorships and partnerships.

- Corporations are separate entities from the owners of the corporations. This provides protection to the individuals who own shares of the company.

- Corporations issue stocks, or shares of ownership, to the owners. The stocks are easily transferable.

- The owners of the corporation (stockholders) have limited liability for the company's activities. The owners are not personally liable if the company is sued.

- The company is considered a going concern, meaning that it will continue to operate indefinitely. This requires the company to be able to generate enough income/assets to continue its operations.

- Incorporation provides companies flexibility in how they manage their ownership structure.

- There may be some tax advantages to corporations.

There are three types of corporations: the standard for-profit corporation, the limited liability corporation (LLC), and the non-profit corporation.

Corporations and limited liability corporations are slightly different from a tax perspective. Both corporations and LLCs limit the liability of the owners regarding business debts. Corporations pay taxes and the owners pay income tax only on the money they draw from the corporation. This money can be drawn in the form of salaries, bonuses and dividends. The owners of LLCs, however, pay their taxes in a similar manner to partnerships. The owners report their business income on their personal tax returns.

Non-profit corporations are formed to carry out charitable, education, religious, literary or scientific work. Non-profit corporations are able to raise funds by requesting donations from individuals and companies, as well as applying for grant money from public and private sources. Non-profits are usually considered tax-exempt and are not taxed as long as their income is related to their non-profit purpose. This is to encourage them to continue to engage in activities that benefit society. However, non-profit corporations can be taxed on unrelated business income. This is called an unrelated business income tax (UBIT).

Multinational corporations (MNCs) conduct business in two or more countries. Multinational corporations are also called transnational corporations, or TNCS. These entities are often very large, with budgets that are more than those of some countries. MNCs have significant influence on both local and international economies and play a key role in developing a global economy.

Samel Palmisano, CEO of IBM Corporation, coined the term "globally integrated enterprise" in 2006. He used this term to describe a business enterprise that goes beyond the multinational corporation. This has implications that are both social and economic. The shift to a globally integrated enterprise has taken two forms: production location and producer. In the past, producers have chosen to produce goods near the place they will be sold. This limited who could produce the goods to those who were in the area. The globally integrated enterprise, however, is able to pull together resources (skills, production capacity, infrastructure, etc.) from around the world to produce its goods and services. Think about computer companies. Many technical support aspects of the computer industry are outsourced to India or other places where there is skilled labor that is less expensive than that in the U.S. This can be looked at as a modular approach to business. The individual pieces all work independently and can be reorganized to meet changing business needs. The globally integrated enterprise is based on collaboration and outsources much of its activity to service companies that specialize in sales support, back-office administration, and other services required to run a global company.

An important result of the globally integrated enterprise is the movement of corporate activities to developing countries, which is raising the standard of living for workers in those areas.

There are four primary challenges facing these companies:

- Access to highly educated and skilled workers who have collaborative management skills;

- Appropriate management of intellectual property (patented goods and services) to allow collaboration and innovation;

- Establishment of corporate governance structures that inspire and maintain the trust of all entities involved; and

- Significant changes in organizational culture, primarily movement from a short-term profit perspective to a long-term vision that embraces real earnings (not prospective earnings) and innovation.

Concept Reinforcement:

1. Discuss the advantages and disadvantages of incorporation.

2. Explain the characteristics of corporations.

3. Describe the role of multinational corporations and how the corporations are changing.

Section 5.15 – Cooperative Organizations and Franchises

Section Objectives:

- Describe the different types of cooperative organizations

- Study how a business franchise works

Cooperative Organizations

Cooperative organizations are businesses that are owned and democratically controlled by their members. The board of directors for a cooperative is elected from within the membership. Examples are agricultural cooperatives, food cooperatives, and credit unions. Co-ops can range from very small operations to multinational companies.

Co-ops follow seven fundamental principles: voluntary and open membership, democratic member control, member economic participation, autonomy and independence, education training and information, cooperation among cooperatives, and concern for the community.

Cooperative organizations have several unique characteristics:

- Members are the people who use and buy the goods and services provided by the cooperative.

- The board of directors of the cooperative is elected from within the membership.

- The cooperative returns surplus revenues to members. The surplus revenue is returned based on the members' use of the cooperative, not the members' ownership share.

- Cooperatives are motivated by service, not profit. The service cooperatives provide is typically access to affordable and high-quality goods and services.

- Cooperatives exist only to serve their members.

- Cooperatives pay taxes on income that is kept within the cooperatives for investment or operational reserves. The surplus revenue received by members is included in individual income taxes.

There are four primary types of cooperatives: consumer, producer, worker, and purchasing/shared services cooperatives. Consumer cooperatives are owned by the purchasers of the goods and services of the cooperative. Produce cooperatives are often seen in agricultural situations. Farmers group together to gain bargaining power with buyers and combine resources to market and brand their products. Worker cooperatives are owned and governed by employees of a business. Examples include employee-owned grocery stores and taxi-

The Stora Kopparberg mine in Sweden is considered to be the first corporation. The mine produced copper ore from around A.D. 1000 until 1992. Beginning in 1347, a charter was written that gave free miners shares of the operation in proportion to their ownership in the copper smelters. This is the structure used by modern joint stock companies.

cab companies. Purchasing/Shared services cooperatives are groups of small businesses, municipalities and other entities to enhance purchasing power, lower costs, and improve competitiveness.

Franchises

A franchise is another form of legal arrangement, called a franchise agreement, between a franchisee and a franchisor. A franchisor owns the trademark or trade name and provides support to the franchisee, who uses the trademark or trade name and expands the business with the support of the franchisor. The franchisee pays fees to the franchisor to use the trademark/trade name and obtain the support of the franchisor in developing the business.

There are two primary types of franchises: those that distribute products and business format franchises.

- Product distribution franchises occur when the franchisee simply sells the product of the franchisor. Common examples are car dealers and gas stations.

- Business format franchises are the most common franchise you see in the U.S. In addition to using the trademark, product, service, and trade-name of the franchisor, the franchisee also uses the complete method required to run the business. This includes use of marketing and operating plans and manuals. Business format franchises are found in service, restaurants (including fast food), grocery stores, building and construction, retail, automotive, maintenance, and lodging.

A franchisee may be granted the right to operate one franchise (single-unit franchise) or multiple franchises (multi-unit franchise).

Concept Reinforcement:

1. Describe a cooperative business and its unique characteristics.

2. List and describe the four primary types of cooperative businesses.

3. Explain a franchise and describe the two primary types of franchises.

Unit Six

Section 6.1 – Free Enterprise and Constitutional Protections

Section Objective:

- Identify the tradition of free enterprise in the United States and the constitutional protections that underlie it

Free enterprise in the U.S. can be traced back to the original colonies, before the country was established. Many of the original settlers arrived in the colonies as part of charter companies to engage in profit-seeking trade on behalf of British companies. A group of individuals or businesses would group together to form a charter company to engage in trade in the New World. The charter companies sometimes also furthered the goals of England. The King of England would provide a charter for the project, which would give the company economic rights, as well as political and judicial authority.

The charter companies went into business with a goal of making a quick profit from the New World. It did not prove easy to reach this goal. In many cases, charter companies would turn over their charters to the local settlers, who used them as the basis for developing the infrastructure of a new country.

The American Revolution was based on both political and economic issues. It was triggered in 1775 when British soldiers clashed with local militia as the British tried to capture an arms depot in Concord, Massachusetts. The result was an eight-year conflict that resulted in the establishment of the United States of America.

The U.S. Constitution, which was adopted in 1787, outlined the basic economic structure of this country. The Constitution established the entire country, from east to west and north to south, as a unified, or common, market. Interstate commerce is not subject to taxes or tariffs. The Constitution also establishes the right of the federal government to regulate commerce both within the country and with foreign nations. Other rights provided to the federal government are:

- Establishment of uniform bankruptcy laws.

- Creation of money.

- Regulation of the value of money.

- Fix standards of weights and measures.

- Establish post offices.

- Establish roads.

- Fix rules governing patents and copyrights.

The federal government has used its powers to enact laws to regulate and provide services related to transportation, monopolies, banking, agriculture, public welfare, employment, Medicare, food stamps, educational initiatives, and other areas of the economy. The government has also established more than 100 agencies to monitor and regulate the various sectors of the economy. These agencies enforce consumer safety, worker safety, employment, banking, transportation, and other aspects of the economy that benefit from oversight.

Concept Reinforcement:

1. Describe the foundations of free enterprise in the U.S.

2. List the constitutional protections to free trade.

3. Explain how the federal government has used these protections to support the U.S. economy.

Section 6.2 – Market Failures

Section Objective:

- Evaluate market failures

Market failure occurs when the system fails to meet the ideal allocative efficiency that can by hypothesized with models. In this situation, potential gains exist that have not been realized. In other words, market failure occurs when the costs of goods and services do not reflect the real costs of production and consumption of those goods. Yet another way to look at this is that market failure occurs when a market left to itself does not allocate resources efficiently.

Market failure is not necessarily negative. Sometimes the costs of a perfectly efficient market are higher than the benefit of that perfectly efficient market to the consumer. If it costs $5.00 per unit to reach ideal efficiency in a market, but the consumer is only willing to pay $2.00 more per unit, the cost of reaching perfect efficiency is more than it is worth to reach that goal

There are four primary causes of market failure: abuse of market power, externalities, public goods, and incomplete or asymmetric information.

Abuse of market power occurs when a single buyer or seller of a good or service is able to significantly influence prices or output. These situations, called monopolies, can be addressed through establishment of antitrust regulations to prevent the development of monopolies.

Externalities occur when the impact of an economic activity (production, etc.) on outsiders is not taken into account. Regulations are often used to manage negative externalities, such as pollution. The Clean Air Act is an example of legislation being used to reduce a negative externality. Property rights can also be used to force the market to consider the welfare of everyone who is affected by the externality.

Public goods, those that are provided to everyone regardless of ability to pay, are not subject to the forces of supply and demand. They are provided regardless of the market's willingness to pay. The funds used to pay for public goods are acquired through taxation. Defense, for example, is a public good that is paid for by taxes and benefits everyone regardless of their ability to pay the taxes used to provide the good.

Asymmetric information can cause market failure. This occurs when incomplete or biased information is provided to the consumer by the producer/provider. Most producers are interested in retaining customers and are motivated to provide complete and correct information about a product. However, when the good is purchased infrequently or has potentially severe harmful effects, the consumer may not have enough expertise to make an informed decision about the product and the information provided by the producer. Claims that exaggerate the effectiveness of medications are clear examples of asymmetric information.

Concept Reinforcement:

1. Describe a market failure.

2. Explain why market failure is not necessarily negative.

3. Discuss how monopolies contribute to market failure.

Section 6.3 – Sources of Market Failure

Section Objective:

- Describe and give examples of each of the major sources of market failure

The four sources of market failure are externalities, public goods, incomplete or asymmetric information, and monopoly (abuse of market power).

Externalities are present when production and exchange affect the welfare of non-consenting secondary parties. Externalities may be positive or negative. External costs occur when the welfare of the secondary parties is negatively affected. Examples of negative costs include air pollution, noise pollution, junkyards, litterbugs, muggers, and others who adversely affect the secondary parties. External benefits occur when spillover effects benefit the secondary parties. Examples of external benefits include flower gardens, parks, and golf courses. When external costs and benefits are present, consumers and producers will not receive the proper signals, which results in market failure (inability to meet maximum efficiency).

Public goods are goods that are available to all if they are available to one. Joint consumption of the goods means that it is impossible to separate the non-payers from the payers for the public goods. There are a few examples of pure public goods. These are national defense, the legal system, the money system, individual rights, and the quality and management of the air, rivers and waterways. Near public goods are those that are jointly consumed even though nonpaying consumers can be excluded. Cable television is an example of a near public good, as are national parks, interstate highways, and movies. Additional consumption of near public goods, once they are produced, is costless to society. This then begs the question of whether they should be provided at no cost to society. In order for these near public goods to be provided at no cost, taxes will be increased. Is this in the best interests of the society? That is a matter of debate.

Asymmetric or incomplete information often results in dissatisfied customers. This is a negative effect for producers if the customers are dissatisfied with the good or service provided. In the case of products that are purchased repeatedly, consumers are able to use trial and error to find the products that work best for them, and suppliers are highly motivated to promote customer satisfaction. However, when the goods are difficult to evaluate because they are infrequently purchased or purchased from multiple suppliers, or have potentially serious and lasting harmful effects, trial and error is not a satisfactory means of determining quality. For example, soap is something that is purchased repeatedly. Companies advertise the qualities of their soaps and consumers are able to pick and choose the soaps that best meet their needs. On the other hand, automobile purchases are typically infrequent and most consumers do not have the technical expertise to truly evaluate the quality of the vehicle. If the consumer receives bad information and is unhappy with the car, the consumer is unsatisfied and the company has lost a future customer.

Monopolies induce market failure because they are not motivated to be as efficient as possible. Monopolists do not have competition because they control the market. Therefore, inefficiencies will occur due to the lack of competition. Examples of monopolistic inefficiencies are public utilities and the telephone companies before they were deregulated.

Concept Reinforcement:

1. List the four causes of market failure.

2. Provide some examples of market failures.

3. Describe how poor information can lead to a market failure.

Section 6.4 – Government Allocation of Resources

Section Objectives:

- Evaluate how the government allocates some resources by managing externalities

- The government is able to respond to externalities in three ways, establishment of property rights, regulation and taxation.

Establishment of property rights is the first tool used by the government to improve the efficiency of resource allocation when externalities are present. There are situations in which property rights can be clearly defined. For example, the granting of property rights to ranchers and homesteaders improved the efficiency of land utilization in the 1800s. This is more difficult to do with air and water rights. The air and water rights of property owners often overlap. For example, people living near a factory may experience negative effects from the air pollution emitted by the factory. Likewise, if the factory is on a river, the landowners downstream from the river may experience negative effects from emissions of the factory into the water. Property owners are able to go to court to enforce their property rights (clean air or water and/or compensation for abuse of the air or water). They must be able to prove three things: 1) the extent of the damage caused by the pollution, 2) that the pollutant actually caused the damage, and 3) the identity of the company or person whose emissions caused the damage. When it is not possible to establish property rights, the government may decide to manage resources by charging user fees, or establish regulations that have significant fines associated with breaking them.

Taxation. The resource management approach is used when the government decides to charge, or tax, companies that engage in activities that may harm the environment. This can be done by assessing the minimal costs of production for the company when no pollution controls are in place, as well as the negative costs to the secondary parties who are affected by the pollution (neighbors, those who share waterways, and those who are affected by emissions). The costs to the secondary parties can be difficult to assess, but the governmental agencies are required to estimate the environmental damage. The per unit damage costs to the neighbors can be assessed against the company generating the pollution, theoretically reducing the motivation for the company to pollute. Again, the theory behind this is that as long as the costs of cleaning up operations to reduce emissions is less than the tax paid, the company will opt for reducing emissions and maximizing profit. Some people consider this approach to be a license to pollute for the companies that would incur a cost higher than the tax to clean up emissions. On the other hand, the companies with lower costs of controlling emissions will opt to implement cleaner production processes rather than pay the taxes.

Regulation is an allocation of government resources to establish regulations that control negative externalities, such as air pollution and water pollution. The government has established agencies to monitor the long and short-term environmental impact of production activities. The Clean Air Act, the Clean Water Act and other regulations have been enacted to address these externalities. The agency primarily responsible for enforcing these regulations is the Environmental Protection Agency. The EPA works with government and industry to develop strategies and incentives for reducing pollution. Other government agencies oversee public safety (police forces, Food and Drug Administration), provide for national defense (the armed forces), and support research and development activities for future economic growth (National Institutes of Health, National Science Foundation, Department of Defense, Department of Energy, etc.).

Continuing to use pollution as an example, regulators typically establish a maximum emission standard that all companies must meet. If the company is unable to meet the standard, they are required to stop production until they are able to meet the standard. This is perceived as an inefficient method of reducing pollution because of the variation in cost for each of the producers to meet the standard and will impose a high cost on society in the form of increased prices.

One question that should always be asked is whether the government should try to control externalities. First, sometimes the inefficiency is small. Therefore the cost of increasing efficiency is more than the benefit to society. Second, the market often finds a relatively efficient way of dealing with externalities. Externalities represent potential gain. If the potential gain is sufficient, someone in the market will work to improve efficiencies to capitalize on the gain. Third, governmental action to correct one externality may impose a different externality on a different party.

Concept Reinforcement:

1. List the three ways the government can manage externalities.

2. Describe how property rights are used to manage externalities.

3. Discuss the difference between regulatory and taxation approaches to managing externalities.

Section 6.5 – Government Redistribution of Income

Section Objective:

- Identify the main programs through which the government redistributes income

The government redistributes income from the well-to-do segments of the population to segments of the population that require assistance. In the U.S., this process occurs in several ways.

A redistribution of income in a market economy facilitated by a government agency is called a **transfer payment**. In the United States, transfer payments include programs such as social security, food stamps, and veterans' benefits.

Welfare is a primary tool used by the government to redistribute income to those in need. Individuals who are employed are taxed and part of that tax is used to pay for social welfare programs. Social welfare programs include welfare, some social security payments, and Medicaid. Welfare and Medicaid programs are designed to provide basic levels of income and health care to people in need. Some social security payments are made to individuals who are disabled and unable to work and to children of parents who died to help support them until they are 18 years old. Food stamps are another form of social welfare used to ensure that people in need are able to acquire nutritious food.

Unemployment insurance is a social welfare program designed to assist people who are temporarily unemployed for reasons that are out of their control. Unemployment will provide a certain level of benefits for a short time while the individual is seeking other employment. This is also used to help individuals who are in seasonal jobs while they are laid off during the off-season.

Taxes are also an effective way to redistribute income. Marginal tax rates (tax rates that are lower at lower incomes and increase as income increases) are very effective in redistributing income because those who earn less money pay less tax as a percentage of income than those who make more money. The Earned Income Tax Credit is a second tax tool that provides a tax benefit to those with lower incomes, allowing them to retain more of their income.

As with everything else, there are differing opinions about the effectiveness of income redistribution. Arthur Okun postulated in the 1970s that government policies that reduce income equality by redistributing income will lead to reductions in economic production. The wealthy will react to having their resources taken away by using their resources in a manner that was less productive. One of the drivers of economic growth and prosperity is risk taking. If those who are willing to take the risk do not see a large reward, they are less likely to take the risk to innovate new products and services. This can lead to economic slow downs. The challenge to the government policy makers is to find the appropriate balance between income redistribution to help those who really need assistance while still encouraging production and economic growth. Okun was willing to see a reduction in efficiency in order to achieve greater equality.

Charles Murray, on the other hand, argues that the social welfare programs of the U.S. have increased poverty. His argument is that if government payments for poverty are attractive enough, it becomes more common. His views are controversial. Long-term studies of government income redistribution programs will show whether or not they are effective.

Concept Reinforcement:

1. Explain why governments redistribute income.

2. Describe the primary ways the U.S. government redistributes income.

3. Discuss some of the benefits and drawbacks to income redistribution.

Section 6.6 – US Political Debate on Poverty

Section Objective:

- Summarize the United States political debate on ways to fight poverty

Poverty is often raised in the news and by charities raising funds for their programs. What is poverty? Poverty is a state of being poor. What does it mean to be poor? If you are poor, you are unable to provide for your material needs or comforts, such as food, shelter and clothing.

Think about this definition. Conditions that may be considered poverty in the U.S. may be considered a high standard of living in other places. For example, almost all Americans have access to clean water, indoor plumbing, decent food and clothing, access to health care, and education. Many Americans who have access to these resources are considered poor by American standards. However, in a 3rd world nation, a family with access to these same resources will be considered well off. Poverty is relative. Often income inequality rather than actual destitution creates poverty in an economy. Poverty is perceived relative to the accepted and average standard of living.

Given the relative nature of poverty, it is logical that there is a political debate in the U.S. about how to fight poverty.

In January 1964, President Lyndon Johnson gave a speech in which he declared a "War on Poverty." With a poverty rate at nearly 20% at that time, Johnson pushed Congress to pass legislation to improve the lives of the poor. As a result, the Office of Economic Opportunity was created as well as the Head Start pre-school program and the Jobs Corps.

One of the challenges facing American politicians and the public is how the U.S. defines poverty. The current U.S. poverty standard is based on one measure of income deprivation based on lifestyles of the 1950s. In the 1950s, housing costs required a smaller percentage of the household budget, one worker could support most families, and childcare costs were negligible. The definition of poverty in the U.S. is at the core of the debate.

Liberal and conservative groups have different, conflicting views on poverty that are based on different definitions of poverty. Liberals tend to believe that more resources are required to alleviate poverty. Conservatives, on the other hand, tend to argue that more resources are unnecessary and that social welfare programs should provide temporary assistance rather than long-term support.

Different groups use different statistical measures for poverty. Different statistical measures make different assumptions about the populations and collect data in different ways, so they are not usually comparable. Measures can be absolute (they are the same regardless of context) or relative, meaning that they can be perceived differently depending upon what they are being compared to. Based on the different statistics used, some groups feel poverty is overstated and others feel it is understated. This lack of consensus about the level of poverty makes it difficult to develop programs that will be effective in alleviating poverty.

Keep in mind that poverty is relative. Many people who are considered poor in the U.S. would be considered well-off in developing countries. Poverty is, in part, perceived in relationship to the accepted standard of living for the culture.

Concept Reinforcement:

1. Define the term poverty.

2. Explain why poverty is a relative concept.

3. Describe the U.S. debate on poverty.

Section 6.7 – Government Intervention to Control Prices

Section Objective:

- Describe how the government sometimes intervenes in markets to control prices

The government sometimes intervenes in markets to control prices. These interventions include sales tax, rent controls, and the minimum wage.

Supply and demand, in a completely free market, will work together to set the equilibrium price for a good or service. However, when the government intervenes to artificially raise or lower the price so that it is not equilibrium, it changes supply and demand. If the price is artificially lowered, the supply will not meet the demand and if the price is artificially raised, the supply will exceed the demand.

Let's look at the interventions a government can make one at a time.

Sales tax is a tax that is levied on purchases and is based on the amount of a good or service purchased. Most states and many cities use sales tax to raise revenue to fund their operations. Sales taxes are based on a small percentage of the purchase. In Wisconsin, for example, the state sales tax is 5% on most purchases (except groceries). The city of Madison, however, levies an additional 0.5% sales tax on purchases (except groceries) to fund city activities. Sales taxes are different than the taxes levied on specific goods, such as gasoline (gas tax), and cigarettes and alcohol (sin taxes).

The general effect of a sales tax is to raise the price of a good or service, which will affect the demand for products that are taxed by reducing the amount the producers are willing to supply at the higher price. The increased price caused by a sales tax will reduce demand for a good or service. For example, when gasoline is in short supply, taxes may be raised to reduce demand. Likewise, increasing sin taxes on cigarettes and alcohol makes these products more expensive, which will reduce demand. A real life example of raising taxes occurred in New York City in 2002 when Mayor Bloomberg raised the cigarette tax to the point where a pack of cigarettes cost about $7.00. He did this in an attempt to make smoking so expensive that people would choose to quit rather than pay the high price of the cigarettes.

The graphic below shows the shift in supply caused by an increase in price due to a sales tax.

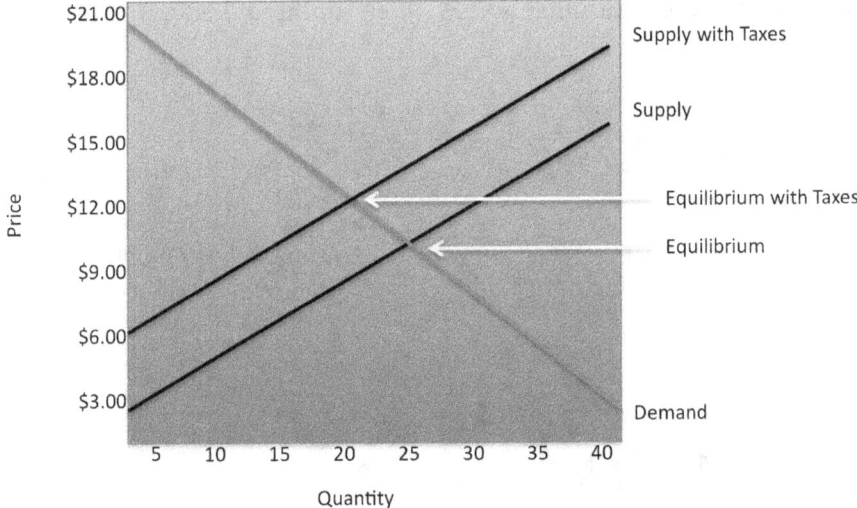

Rent controls and minimum wage standards are opposite sides of the same issue. Rent controls set a maximum price, also called a price ceiling. Minimum wage, on the other hand, sets a minimum price, which is also called a price floor.

Rent controls are established in some communities to keep housing affordable for those who work in the community but would not otherwise be able to afford to live there. The general effect of a price control is to keep the price below the market. In the case of rent, rent control will keep the price of rent for the controlled buildings below the market rate. This creates a high demand for the rent-controlled apartments and houses. Notice the difference between supply and demand for the rent controlled apartments in the graphic below.

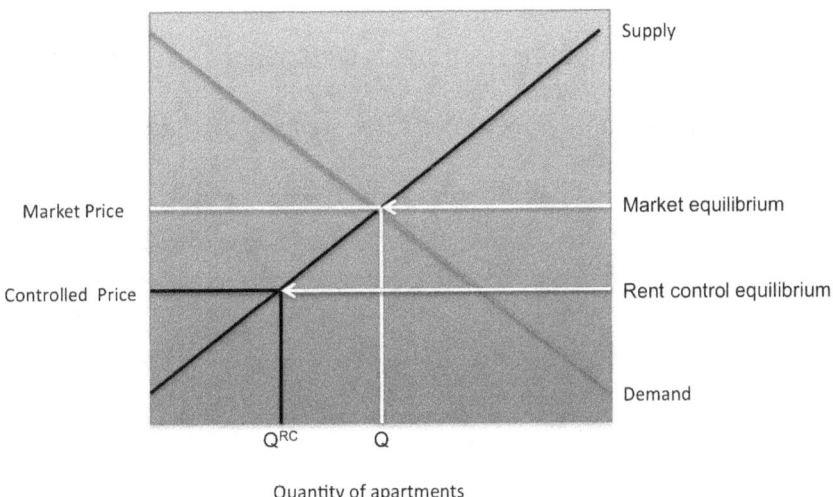

Minimum wage sets a floor on the price of labor. The primary goal of the minimum wage is to help workers earn a living wage, or enough money to support themselves without being in poverty. The minimum wage keeps a single person just above the minimum poverty threshold, which is a measure established each year by the federal government. The minimum wage, however, will not maintain a family with two or more people above the minimum wage if there is just one breadwinner (or worker).

As with rent controls, the minimum wage affects the supply and demand for labor. If the minimum wage is set above the wage that would be paid at market equilibrium, a minimum wage will generate unemployment, or a surplus of labor. The graphic below shows this relationship. Notice that at the controlled hourly wage (minimum wage), the demand is less than the available labor supply.

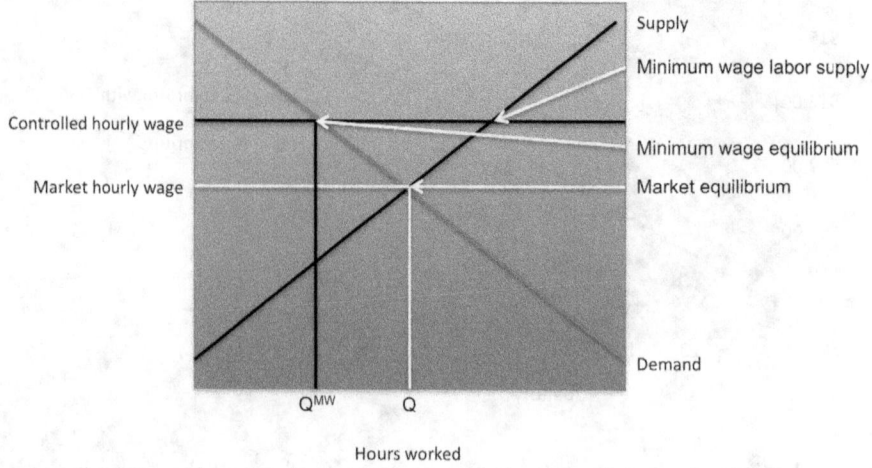

In summary, government interventions in price will distort supply and demand. If the price for a good or service is set below market, as in rent controls, a shortage will result. Likewise, if the price for a good or service is set above market, a surplus will result.

Concept Reinforcement:

1. Explain how sales taxes affect supply and demand.

2. Explain how establishment of price ceilings affects supply and demand.

3. Explain how establishment of price floors affects supply and demand.

Section 6.8 – Deregulation

Section Objective:

- Define deregulation and list its effect on several industries

Government regulation of economic activities has grown over time. Each time the government decides to regulate an economic activity, resources must be allocated for the purposes of regulation and enforcement of the regulations. Government regulation also increases the production costs of the supplier because the supplier must comply with the regulations, in addition to proving to the government that they have complied. This involves changes in production facilities, as well as additional administrative staff to manage the reporting process. The end result of regulation is an increase cost to the consumer for the good or service being provided.

Deregulation of an industry occurs when the government decides that the costs of regulation are higher than the benefit of the regulation. In the 1970s, dissatisfaction with traditional regulations grew, resulting in moves toward deregulation. This led to deregulation in the ground (trucking) and air (airline) transportation systems.

The railroad and trucking industries were regulated by the Interstate Commerce Commission (ICC). The ICC was established in 1887 and expanded to include the trucking industry in 1935 because of the competition the trucking industry brought to the railroads. The ICC had three primary roles in the transportation industry. First, the ICC limited the number of shippers engaged in interstate commerce by requiring licenses. Established shippers were given the opportunity to block the entry of a new shipper into the business if there was evidence that the new shipper was unnecessary or harmful. Secondly, the ICC regulated shipping rates and allowed the trucking and rail industries to establish bureaus to fix prices. If a shipper wanted to charge prices below the fixed prices, approval had to be granted by the ICC, which would take several months and effectively discouraged price competition. The third role of the ICC was to restrict the products that carriers could transport, their routes, and the number of cities they could serve along a route. The ICC also prohibited carriers from using price reductions to ensure a cargo for the return trip. This resulted in wasted mileage and trucks that were empty about 40% of the time. Deregulation allowed companies to use any rail or road route they chose and freely set rates for their services. The ICC was eventually disbanded by Congress in 1996.

Deregulation of the airline industry followed a similar pattern to the truck and rail transportation industries. The airline industries were regulated by the Civil Aeronautics Board, which imposed a monopolistic structure on the airline industry. As with the ICC, the CAB blocked competitive entry into the industry and competitive pricing. The CAB did not allow a new carrier access to a single long distance route, also called a trunk route, for the forty years between 1938 and 1978. If a carrier wanted to reduce prices, approval had to be requested from the CAB. The CAB would convene a hearing to give the carrier's competition an opportunity to state why the proposed rate reduction was unfair or would harm their operations. In the late 1970s, the CAB relaxed its regulatory policies because of excessive fares, half empty planes and a too uniform product offering. Under the new policies, the airlines could raise prices by as much as 10% and reduce them by as much as 70%. All they had to do was notify the CAB 45 days in advance of the price change. Congress passed the Airline Deregulation Act in 1978. This act reduced restrictions on entry of new carriers into the industry as well as on price competition. Deregulation results in a wider offering of services (charters, low priced night fares, seasonal discounts, etc.) and increased entry of new carriers into the market, leading to stronger competition and better value for the consumers.

The Reagan administration decided in the early 1980s that regulation of domestic crude oil was counterproductive, so deregulated the industry. After an initial increase of 5-10 cents per gallon, the prices of gas and fuel oil dropped, over about 12 months, to levels below where they had been prior to deregulation.

The telecommunications industry was dominated by American Telephone and Telegraph (AT&T) through the 1980s. AT&T was divided into regional subsidiaries that were regulated monopolies. The baby bells, as they were known, were given exclusive rights to operate in their regions. The Federal Communications Commission (FCC) set rates for interstate calls (calls between states) and states set rates for local and intrastate (within the state) calls. AT&T was considered a natural monopoly because the assumption was made that competition would require setting up multiple sets of telephone wires to cover the same areas. In other words, each company would have to set up its own infrastructure to serve each area. The 1970s saw rapid changes in the technology available for telecommunications and independent companies claimed that they could compete with AT&T if the monopoly would allow them to connect to its network. Telecommunications deregulation occurred in two phases. The first occurred in 1984 when a court decision forced AT&T to separate from its regional subsidiaries (the baby bells), which opened up competition to new companies. This competition was vigorous, resulting in lower prices and improved service to customers. The second phase occurred in 1996 when Congress passed the Telecommunications Act of 1996. This law encouraged competition in the local telephone industry by allowing long-distance carriers, cable television, and other start-up companies to compete for local telephone business. Regional monopolies were required to allow competitors to link with their networks. This was encouraged by also allowing the regional monopolies to enter the long-distance market once they new competition was established within their regions. This act also allowed Internet service providers to establish themselves and provide household access to the Internet. In the case of the telephone industry, deregulation was bringing higher, rather than lower, prices to residential and rural telephone users. This occurred because their service was no longer subsidized by businesses and urban customers.

Concept Reinforcement:

1. Describe the costs of government regulation on the cost of goods and services.

2. Explain why deregulation of an industry occurs.

3. Discuss the results of deregulation on supply, demand and price for a good or service.

Section 6.9 – Banned and Regulated Market Practices

Section Objective:

- List three market practices that the government regulates or bans to protect competition

There are some market practices that are detrimental to a competitive market by preventing unfair trade practices and monopolies. These include collusion and price agreements, predatory pricing, exclusive contracts, and reciprocal agreements.

Collusion occurs when competitors agree to engage in behavior that will provide them an unfair advantage in the marketplace through deceit, fraud or deception. Examples include wage fixing, price fixing, kickbacks, and misrepresenting the relationship between the colluding parties be presenting the parties as independent of one another. Wage fixing occurs when an industry works together to restrict the wages of employees. Price fixing occurs when an industry colludes to inflate the price of their goods and services. Kickbacks are undocumented payments for engaging in a certain behavior that results in an unfair competitive advantage to the payer. Misrepresentation occurs when companies that colluded to set prices present themselves as unrelated competitors, not disclosing the relationship established to set prices.

Predatory pricing occurs when a large firm that is able to take a financial loss temporarily reduces the price of its good or service to a level below the cost of production in certain areas. This is done to damage competitors or eliminate competition altogether. Once the competitors withdraw from the market, the firm that engaged in predatory pricing is essentially a monopoly and uses its monopoly power to raise prices.

Exclusive contracts, also known as dealerships, occur when a distributor (supplier) of a product prohibits retailers from selling competing products from other producers. Under the Clayton Act, exclusive contracts are illegal when they lessen competition. An exclusive contract may occur when an established company, with a variety of product lines, wishes to limit the entry of a potential competitor that offers a related, but more narrow, product line.

Reciprocal agreements occur when sellers of products are required to purchase another product, usually from the buyer, as a condition of sale. For example, if a car company uses a specific trucking company to ship their cars to dealerships, a reciprocal agreement will occur if the car company requires the trucking company to use trucks made by the car maker in order to get the shipping contract.

The business practices described above all use market power rather than better performance to gain an unfair advantage on their competition.

Concept Reinforcement:

1. Explain why the government regulates or prohibits certain market practices.

2. Describe the difference between collusion, exclusive contracts and reciprocal agreements.

3. Discuss predatory pricing and how it is used to stifle competition.

Section 6.10 – Government Regulation

Section Objective:

- Examine the benefits of government regulation

Government regulation has resulted in many benefits to both society and the market, and is generally divided into economic regulation and social regulation.

Economic regulation is generally targeted at controlling prices. Government regulation of the economy is usually enacted to protect consumers, small businesses, and destructive competition between companies of any size.

Social regulations are enacted to protect people and the environment, and encourage socially desirable behaviors. Examples include emissions controls, tax incentives for providing certain benefits, and product safety regulations.

The trends in government regulation swing between the laissez-faire environment of little government regulation to what some consider over-regulation. In general terms, conservatives tend to prefer minimal governmental regulation because it encourages an efficient market and liberals are more likely to encourage regulation that supports non-economic activities, such as worker safety and environmental health.

The New Deal of the 1930s was the beginning of the current environment of governmental oversight and regulation in the U.S. The Great Depression caused people to lose faith in a completely free market that was not subject to government oversight. As a result, President Franklin D Roosevelt implemented the New Deal, which gave the government power to intervene in the economy. These laws provided the government with the ability to regulate sales of stock, recognized the rights of workers to form labor unions, established rules for wages and hours, provided unemployment benefits, established Social Security retirement benefits, established farm subsidies, instituted the Federal Deposit Insurance Corporation to insure bank deposits, and created the Tennessee Valley Authority to develop infrastructure in the Tennessee Valley and provide jobs for people in that area.

Since the 1930s, many more laws and regulations have been implemented to provide further protection to consumers and workers. These include employment discrimination based on age, sex, race, religious beliefs, or sexual preference; general prohibitions on child labor; the right of independent labor unions to organize, bargain and strike; workplace safety and health codes; product safety, including food, drugs and transportation; fairness in pricing and truth in advertising.

The social benefits of these regulations are safer products, a cleaner environment, more socially responsible behavior on the part of both consumers and companies, and transparency of the activities of financial institutions. The economic benefits are efficient markets, open competition, relatively low barriers to entry into a market, and a wide variety of goods and services that are available to the consumer.

Concept Reinforcement:

1. Explain the difference between economic and social benefits of government regulation.

2. Describe how the New Deal established the basis for government regulation of the economy.

3. Discuss some of the social and economic benefits of government regulation of the economy.

Section 6.11 – US Anti-Trust Policies

Section Objective:

- Explore the history of United States anti-trust policies

Anti-trust policies were established to ensure that the economy is structured so that competition within an industry or market area exists and to prohibit business practices that stifle competition. The expectation is that if these two goals are met, the market will efficiently allocate goods and services.

The three major antitrust laws in the U.S. are the Sherman Act, the Clayton Act and the Federal Trade Commission Act.

The Sherman Act, was the first antitrust law enacted in the U.S. This law was passed in 1890 in response to a number of mergers that occurred in the tobacco, sugar and oil industries at the time. The goal of the Sherman Act is to prevent monopolies. The primary provisions prohibit restraint of trade resulting from contracts, combinations in the form of trusts or otherwise, or conspiracy; and provide for misdemeanor penalties for those who engage in such behavior. The Supreme Court ruled that the Sherman Act prohibits unreasonable acts to restrain trade when they reviewed the Standard Oil Trust in 1911. The result of this ruling is that both Standard Oil, which controlled 90% of the refinery capacity in the U.S., and American Tobacco, which controlled 75% of the tobacco production market, were split up into smaller companies. The Supreme Court did not restrict monopolies, however, so it refused to break up other large trusts (U.S. Steel, for example) because it could not be proven that they had followed unethical or unfair business practices. The Act does not clearly define unfair or unethical business practice, which resulted in the act being considered ineffective because the courts were unwilling to enforce it. This resulted in the passage of two more antitrust laws in 1914.

The Clayton Act was passed in 1914 to define and prohibit business practices that lessen competition. The business practices must be proven to substantially lessen competition or tend to create a monopoly in order to be prohibited under the Clayton Act. The specific business practices include:

Price discrimination, which occurs when companies charge consumers in different markets different prices that are not related to the costs of transportation of the good to each market. An example is charging people in markets with limited transportation (poor inner city neighborhoods, for example) higher prices than are warranted by the production and transportation costs of getting the goods to market.

Tying contracts, which occur when a buyer requires a seller to purchase an item in order to get the buyer's business. An example is when a heavy equipment producer requires the train company shipping the heavy equipment to purchase train engines from the heavy equipment producer.

Trust busting, a term used to describe the actions of government to break up trusts or monopolies, is most commonly associated with the presidency of Theodore Roosevelt, even though his successor, William Howard Taft, signed twice as many pieces of trust-busting legislation.

Exclusive dealings, which occur when the seller of a good or service is prohibited from selling to a competitor of the purchaser of the good or service. This would occur if the producer of a component of a product (a computer chip, for example) is prohibited by one computer manufacturer from selling that computer chip to competing computer manufacturers.

Interlocking stockholding, which occurs when a company purchases the stock of a competitor. If the company gains 51% or more of the shares of the competing company, competition is reduced because both companies are under the control of the same management team.

Interlocking directorates, which occur when an individual serves on the boards of competing firms. If a person serves on the boards of competing companies, one or both of the companies may gain an unfair advantage because of the information the shared director gains from each company.

The Clayton Act, although more specific than the Sherman Act, was still vague in its definition of when prohibited actions actually become illegal because they substantially lessen competition.

The third major antitrust law is the Federal Trade Commission Act. This declares all unfair methods of competition in commerce illegal. The FTC is composed of five members, who are appointed to seven-year terms by the President. The primary role of the FTC is to enforce consumer protection legislation, prohibit deceptive advertising, and prevent overt collusion. The commission investigates complaints. If a violation has occurred, the FTC will first try to settle the dispute. If that fails, a hearing is conducted before an examiner, the decision of which may be appealed to the full commission. The decision of the full commission may also be appealed to the U.S. Court of Appeals.

These three acts have been supported by further legislation. The Robinson-Patman Act, passed in 1936, prohibits selling at unreasonably low prices when this reduces competition. This act targeted both predatory pricing and more efficient competitors who are able to produce at a lower cost, thus sell at a lower cost. This act has been criticized because it tends to eliminate price competition and protects inefficient producers.

The Wheeler-Lea Act was implemented in 1938 to strengthen sections of the Federal Trade Commission Act, which had been weakened by court decisions. The Wheeler-Lea Act removed the requirement of proof of damage resulting from deceptive or false advertising before action could be taken. This allowed the FTC to prosecute and ban false and deceptive advertising without having to prove any damages to consumers or competitors.

The Celler-Kefauver Act was passed into law in 1950. The purpose of this act is to prohibit a company from acquiring the assets of a competitor if this acquisition substantially lessens competition. This strengthened the Clayton Act by closing the loophole that allowed sale of assets to a competitor to reduce competitive pressures. The intent of this law is to maintain competition within an industry. It prevents both vertical mergers and mergers within the same industry. A vertical merger occurs when a company, for example a car company, acquires a steel company and that transaction results in reduced competition in the market.

Concept Reinforcement:

1. Describe why anti-trust policies have been established in the U.S.

2. List the three key anti-trust laws in the U.S. and what each was designed to achieve.

3. Explain how the Celler-Kefauver Act amended and strengthened the Clayton Act.

Section 6.12 – Price Gouging

Section Objective:

- Define price gouging and describe when it might occur

Price gouging is a term used to describe situations when sellers price goods much higher than is considered fair in a particular circumstance. This can occur in a situation declared a civil emergency, as well as when practices inconsistent with a free market result in high profits. Price gouging occurs when companies increase their monopoly power and customers lose access to substitutes for the goods and services they need. At the same time, demand for specific goods and services becomes more inelastic, meaning that customers are less sensitive to price because they have a greater need and fewer choices for necessary goods and services.

Price gouging often occurs in anticipation of and during a civil emergency. Civil emergencies occur as the result of natural disasters, terrorist attacks, civil unrest, and other unanticipated changes in demand and supply for specific goods. Price gouging as a result of a civil emergency is considered a felony in some states. Some considered the rapidly increasing prices gas prices of the mid-2000s a form of price gouging. Again, gas prices are subject to the forces of supply and demand. As long as customers are willing to pay the price demanded for gasoline, prices will not go down. Once customer demand reduces, prices are likely to follow as suppliers seek to maximize profits and reduce prices to increase demand.

There are conflicting views of price gouging. Some consider that price controls, even in unusual circumstances like civil emergencies, are more detrimental than helpful. Proponents of this viewpoint feel that controlling prices for needed goods and services will reduce the willingness of suppliers to provide enough to meet demand. An opposing view is that emergency situations create increased inequality between demand and supply, which the sellers of goods can exploit to make more profits unless prices are controlled.

Price gouging allegations during civil emergencies are often limited to essential goods and services, which include food, water, medicine, transportation, equipment, shelter, and other items required to sustain and preserve life. Laws and social pressures are used to prevent price gouging during and after natural disasters and other times of civil emergency. Florida, for example, has laws that prohibit price gouging and provide an avenue for citizens to make complaints of price gouging to the police. In areas where no laws prohibiting price gouging are in place, social pressure can be brought to bear on vendors who engage in such behavior. This sometimes discourages vendors for increasing prices to make extraordinary profits.

Price gouging allegations are typically made during natural disasters and during shortages of essential goods and services. Shortages may occur as a result of an overall shortage of a good, such as a particular food or fuel product. They may also occur as a result of resources being diverted to other uses, as can occur during war time. This occurred during World War II when rations were put into place to slow the rise of inflation that would have resulted from the direction of resources to producing the products required by the military to conduct the war.

Concept Reinforcement:

1. Define price gouging.

2. Explain views in support of and against controlling price gouging.

3. List some conditions and events that might result in price gouging.

Section 6.13 – Competition

Section Objective:

• Given a diagram, show why perfect competition is preferred to monopoly, monopolistic competition, and oligopoly

In a free market, under conditions of perfect competition, the market forces work without interference to set the most efficient levels of production and consumption by establishing market equilibrium where demand is equal to supply at a given price.

Equilibrium prices tend to be higher in situations of monopoly, monopolistic competition, and oligopoly, where supply of a good may be restricted to increase price.

Let's look at what might happen to demand and supply of a particular good or service in conditions of perfect competition, monopoly, monopolistic competition, and oligopoly.

In perfect competition, demand is perfectly elastic, meaning that there are many small suppliers who are providing identical goods and services. In perfect competition, marginal costs are equal to average costs. Demand is perfectly elastic, meaning that consumers will purchase the good only at the equilibrium price. Any attempts by a provider to increase the price may result in increased short term profit, but it will not be sustainable.

Perfect Competition

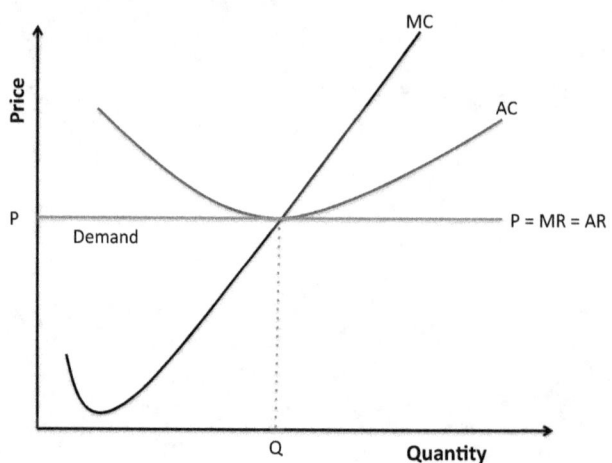

Monopolies exist when one producer controls the market for a good or service. The chart below shows the difference in supply and demand in perfect competition and in a monopoly. A monopolist that seeks to maximize profits will do so at the monopoly output as long as output is less than consumer demand. The supply will be less than demand, driving prices up. In this situation, consumer demand is not completely fulfilled, leading to a loss of economic efficiency.

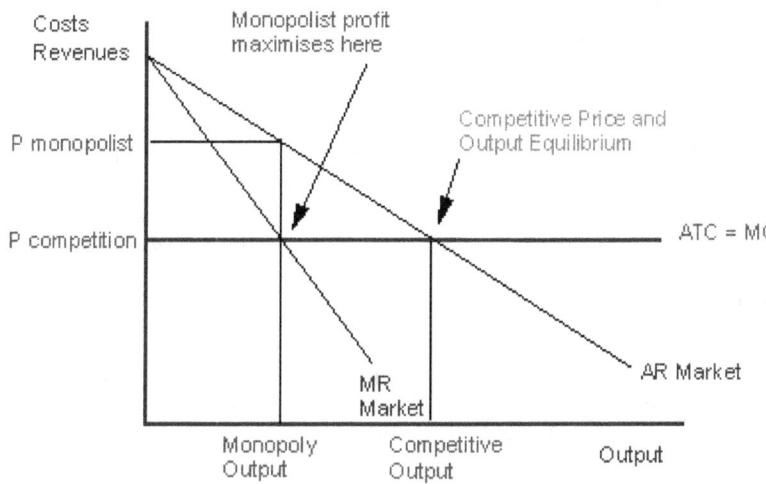

Monopolistic competition occurs when many competitors offer similar, but different products to consumers. The providers differentiate their products using advertising, convenience, quality, supplier reputation, and other characteristics of the product. The chart below shows the long-run equilibrium reached in a monopolistically competitive market. The equilibrium price point is reached where long run average costs for the company equal average revenue. Monopolistically competitive firms are inefficient producers because they produce at a level where marginal cost of production is less than marginal revenue. This allows them to earn more additional revenue than they incur in additional cost for each additional unit of production.

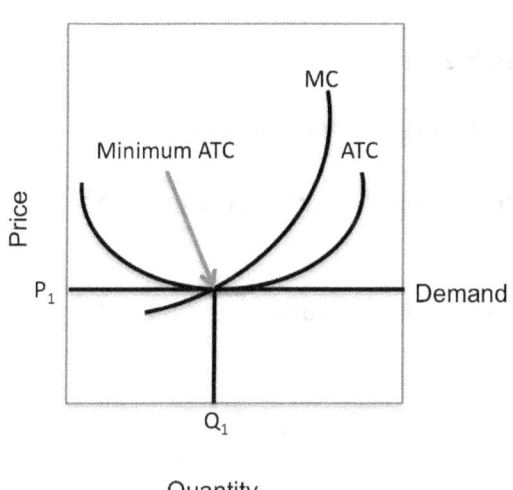

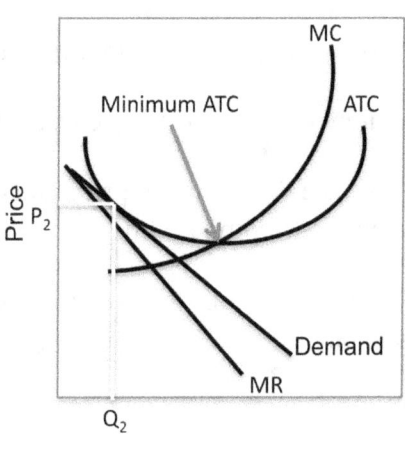

An oligopology is a market that has few sellers, therefore few competitors for their good or service. Firms in an oligopoly are interdependent, meaning that they must consider the reactions of other firms to business decisions. Each member of an oligopoly is affected by the policies of the other firms in the oligopoly. An oligopolistic company must be able to produce goods at a large scale in order to achieve a low per unit cost. Because of this a small number of large scale, cost efficient companies are able to meet the demand for the total market. There are significant barriers to entry to oligopolistic markets and the goods produced may be either the same or differentiated. Because of the interdependence of companies in an oligopoly, price determination is more complex than estimating demand and costs. Oligopolists must also consider how competitors will respond to price and quality adjustments.

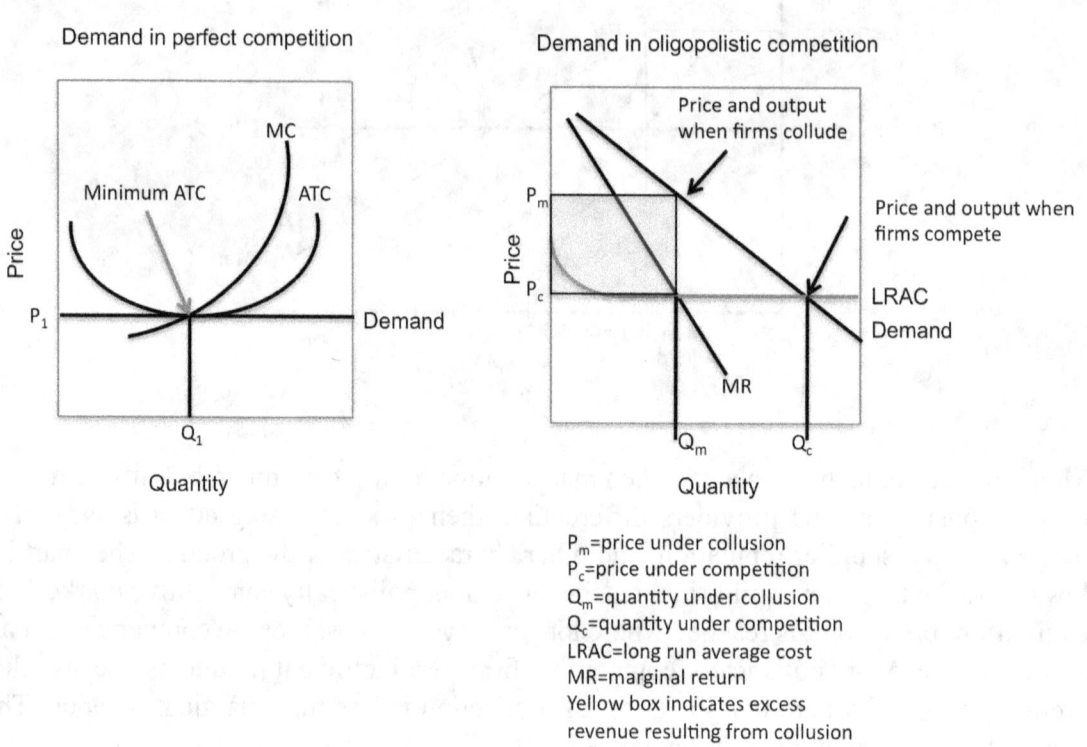

P_m=price under collusion
P_c=price under competition
Q_m=quantity under collusion
Q_c=quantity under competition
LRAC=long run average cost
MR=marginal return
Yellow box indicates excess
revenue resulting from collusion

Concept Reinforcement:

1. Describe why perfect competition is desirable.

2. Explain why monopolies are less efficient than perfect competition.

3. Discuss the difference in price and output between perfect competition and monopolistic competition.

4. Detail the effect on supply and price when oligopolies collude and when they compete.

Section 6.14 – Government Remedies for Market Failure

Section Objective:

- Describe the possible remedies that government may try in each of the cases of market failure in order to achieve an optimal allocation of resources

There are four primary causes of market failure: abuse of market power (monopolies), externalities, public goods, and incomplete or asymmetric information.

Abuse of market power typically occurs when a monopoly exists in a specific market. The U.S. government has enacted several pieces of legislation to deal with monopolies. They are the Sherman Act, the Clayton Act, and the Federal Trade Commission Act. Additional legislation was enacted in the 1900s to refine these three primary antitrust laws. If abuse of power is found to have occurred, the government will break the monopoly into smaller businesses. The goal of action is to increase competition between the small companies, which should result in lower prices, more options and better service to the consumer.

Externalities occur when an economic activity (environmental pollution, noise, or other impacts) have a negative or positive impact on nonconsenting second parties (neighbors, people and businesses downstream from a factory, etc.). Externalities are often managed with regulations imposed by the government. For example, a company that emits pollution into the air via a smokestack will be required to meet maximum pollution standards or pay a fine. In some cases, the cost of meeting the pollution standards is very high, in which case the company will choose to pay the fines as long as that cost is lower than upgrading the equipment to reduce pollution. In other cases, the cost of meeting pollution standards is low, which is an inducement to make the upgrades to the physical plant that will allow the standards to be met or exceeded rather than pay the fines. This approach places the burden of managing the externalities on the companies that create them. These costs, in turn, are included in the production costs of the good or service and passed on to the consumer. Increased price often results in decreased demand unless the demand is inelastic. The shift in the demand of the item results in a new market equilibrium with a higher price and lower supply.

Public goods are those that are provided to everyone in society regardless of their ability to pay. Examples include public schools, police forces, the armed forces, public parks, etc. Everyone benefits from these services whether or not they are able to pay for them. The government imposes taxes to cover the costs of these public goods. The market would typically not pay for public goods at the level provided by the government because the costs are high.

Incomplete or asymmetric information occurs when a producer does not provide full information to the consumer or the consumer does not have the expertise to fully comprehend the information provided. Producers of goods that rely on repeat customers are motivated to provide clear and correct information to consumers because they need the consumers to return. Producers of medications or complex, infrequently purchased items provide information, but the consumer may not be able to make a fully informed decision about the quality of the information and the product. The government addresses these issues by requiring truth in advertising, full disclosure of contents of food, full disclosure of the potential side effects of medications, and the enactment of lemon laws, which apply to vehicles. All of these actions are taken in an effort to ensure that consumers receive full and accurate information to allow them to make informed decisions about the items they purchase and use.

Concept Reinforcement:

1. Describe the expected impact of breaking up a monopoly on competition and price.

2. Explain how externalities can affect demand for a good or service.

3. Discuss why public goods would not be supported by the market at the level the government supports them.

4. Detail how government regulation is used to ensure that consumers receive complete information on goods and services.

Section 6.15 – Government Policy and Monopolies

Section Objective:

- Describe the two major policy positions adopted by the government when a firm exercises monopoly power or is a natural monopoly

Monopolies exist because they have achieved economies of scale that allow them to dominate the market in which they compete. The government has three options when a monopoly exists.

- Allow the monopoly to operate freely. This option is not usually acceptable because it limits consumer choice, and results in higher prices and lower output than would occur under an efficient market situation.

- Governments can regulate the monopolies.

- The government can take over production in the industry that is monopolized.

If the government chooses to regulate a monopoly, it typically establishes a price ceiling on the goods and services provided by the monopoly. This can be done in one of two ways: average cost pricing or marginal cost pricing.

Average cost pricing occurs when the monopolist is required to reduce the price of the good or service to the point where average total cost intersects with demand. This will cause the monopolist to expand output to meet the demand at the average cost. Average cost is still higher than marginal cost, so full efficiency is not achieved even though the cost to the consumer is reduced and supply increased.

Marginal cost pricing occurs when the producer is forced to lower price to the intersection of marginal cost and demand. This results in even higher output on the part of the producer and a lower cost to the consumer.

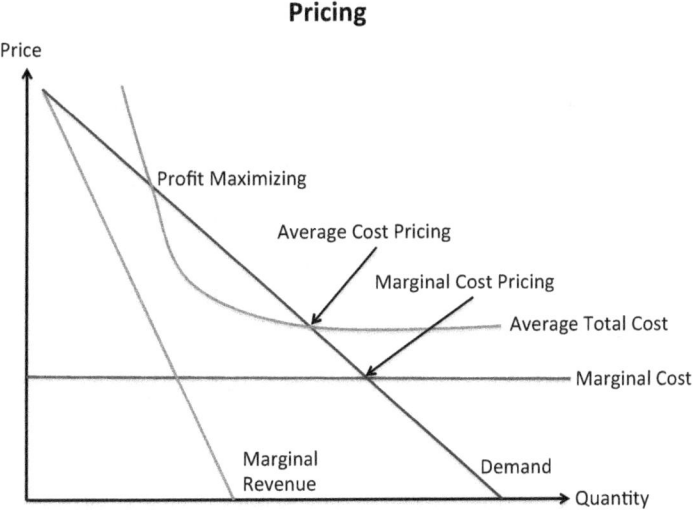

The third option for a government facing a monopoly is to take over the industry. When this occurs, the firm is considered to be a socialized firm, meaning that social, political, and economic factors are considered by the management of the firm. Examples of government-operated firms in the U.S. are the postal service and the Tennessee Valley Authority, as well as many public utilities. The theory of a socialized firm is that it is run efficiently and sets prices equal to marginal cost. Some government-operated firms are able to make a profit and put money back in the public coffers and others require subsidies. It depends upon how efficiently the firms are able to operate.

None of these options are ideal for ensuring economic efficiency. If a monopoly is allowed to operate freely, there will be less supply than can meet demand and prices will be higher than in a perfectly competitive market. Regulation of the monopoly requires allocation of government resources to oversee and enforce the regulations. Regulation often includes imposition of average cost pricing or marginal cost pricing to increase production and lower the price to the consumer. Government operation of a monopoly requires resources to be allocated to the management and oversight of the monopoly.

Concept Reinforcement:

1. List the three choices a government has when faced with a monopoly.

2. Describe how governments use regulation to manage monopolies.

3. Explain a government-operated monopoly.

Appendix

An Easy Introduction to Economics: Microeconomics
Answer Key Unit 1

Section 1.1

1. Define economics

The term economics is derived from the Greek words oikos, which means house, and nomos, meaning custom or law. When combined, they mean "rules of the house."

Economics is a social science, meaning it is a study of human behavior and human systems. It is studied at the micro (small) and macro (large) scales. Ultimately, economics is the study of how individual human behavior and choices affect individual, local, corporate, national and international economies. The human activities that affect the economy are production, distribution, exchange and consumption of goods and services.

2. Define microeconomics and macroeconomics and describe how they differ.

The study of economics on a large scale is called macroeconomics. Macroeconomics is concerned with national and regional economies. Topics of study include income, productivity, diversity of economic sectors, imports,exports, relationships with other countries, and any activities that affect the national economy of a country. Macroeconomists study aggregated (combined) indicators such as gross domestic product, unemployment and employment rates, price indices, national income, output, consumption, inflation, savings, investment, and international trade and finance.

Microeconomics is the study of how individuals, families, households and companies make decisions to allocate limited resources. Decisions made by individuals accumulate to contribute to the patterns of supply and demand for goods and services that micro-economists study. Microeconomists analyze how prices are established in an environment of limited resources and how resources are allocated in these conditions. Other areas of interest to microeconomists are market failure and how it occurs, theoretical conditions for perfect competition, elasticity of products within the market system, and how the market regulates itself.

Section 1.2

1. Describe an economic system.

An economic system is simply the way a society manages the production, distribution and consumption of goods and services for its members. The system consists of both individual people and organizations (governments, companies, etc.) and their relationship to the resources that can be used to produce the goods and services needed by the members of the society. Economics is the way in which scarcity of resources and demand of consumers is managed.

2. Describe the general changes in economic systems from the ancient Greek and Roman systems to the beginning of modern economic thought.

One of the oldest forms of economic systems is the barter system, in which two individuals agree to an exchange of goods and/or services that meet each of their needs. The important thing to understand in a barter system is that each exchange will assign a perceived value to the good or service that is based solely on the perspective of the person making the decision. This eventually led to some standard of value being established for certain resources. For example a cow may have become an accepted standard of exchange for an acre of land.

In addition to the practical aspects of economics – i.e. people getting what they want and need – theories and systems of economics developed beginning back in ancient Mesopotamian, Greek, Roman, Indian, Chinese, Persian and Arab civilizations. Philosophers, such as Aristotle, Thomas Aquinas, Chanakya, Qin Shi Huang and IbnKhaldun were influential through the 14th century, when the late scholastics developed economic theories of money, interest and value in the context of natural law, which is law that is considered to apply everywhere because it is set by nature.

The late scholastics were followed by two groups – mercantilists (16th-18th century) and physiocrats (18th century).

Mercantilists followed the economic model that a nation's wealth is directly dependent upon its accumulation of gold and silver, which could either be mined (if the resource was available to the nation) or traded for using other goods or services the nation was able to produce. This led to the gold standard, which was used to ensure the value of currency until the mid 20th century. This philosophy also encouraged import of cheap raw materials for manufacture of goods and tariffs (an import tax) on imported manufactured goods. This philosophy resulted in complex and burdensome governmental regulation and oversight of trade.

Physiocrats were a group of people who believed that there was a natural order that properly governed society and that land should be the basis of all wealth. They developed the idea of the economy as flowing in a circle in the 18th century. The circle is a relationship between income and output. This group believed that only agricultural production generated a true profit (surplus over cost), therefore that agriculture was the basis of all wealth. Physiocrats disagreed with the mercantilist concept of promoting manufacturing and trade at the expense of agriculture, as well as that tariffs should not be imposed on imported goods. Physiocrats also proposed the idea of a land tax, which is a single tax on land owners, to replace the complex tax system generated by the mercantilist theories, and introduced the concept of laissez faire, which discouraged governmental interference and regulation of trade.

Modern economic systems were first described in a 1776 publication by Adam Smith called "The Wealth of Nations." Adam Smith was a philosopher who was interested in how resources were allocated to meet the needs and wants of the consumers. His work provided the rationale for free trade and capitalism as effective economic models and he is acknowledged as the father of economics. He defined land, labor and capital as the three primary factors of production and the major contributors to the wealth of a nation. Smith promoted a self-regulating free-market system that would automatically meet the needs of the people and businesses. This idea is based on the concept that individuals, while pursuing their own self-interests, will produce the greatest benefit to society as a whole. This idea is also described as the "invisible hand" of the market encouraging individuals to fulfill their own self-interests, resulting in the greatest societal gain. This is a paradox: an individual pursuing selfish interests and advances broader societal interests.

Section 1.3

1. **What are the three basic economics questions?**

   There are three basic questions that must be answered in any economy:

   What will be produced?

   How much will be produced?

   For whom will it be produced?

2. **Discuss how these questions raise more questions before they can be answered appropriately.**

   What will be produced? This question is answered by asking more questions. What does the society already produce? What resources are available to the society? Are those resources appropriate for production of goods and services that will be used by the society or traded to another one? The decision about which goods and services to produce is driven by the availability of resources and the potential benefit to the society of producing specific goods or services.

   How much will be produced? This is a question that requires an assessment of the supply of resources available, the costs incurred to produce a good and the demand for that good. What is the benefit to the group that is producing the good? Is it worth the energy and resource expended to produce the good? Is the demand high enough to produce the good? Is there a benefit to the society of restricting production of a good that is in high demand? In low demand? Is it worth using scarce (valuable) resources to produce this good or service? Is there a reason to be conservative with the use of the resource?

   For whom will the good be produced? Questions to ask before answering this include: Is this an essential good? Is this a luxury good? Are there concerns about justice of distribution, meaning will the good get to the people who will benefit from it? Is the good made from scarce resources or are the resources sufficient to meet demand? Will this benefit the society, the individual or both?

Section 1.4

1. Define the term entrepreneur.

Entrepreneurs are people who organize, operate and assume the risk for a business venture. An entrepreneur can be the chief executive officer (or CEO) of a big company or a high school student who mows lawn for a fee.

The most important characteristics of an entrepreneur are that they are:

- profit-seeking, meaning that they want to earn money by increasing the value of the resources they use

- decision makers, meaning that the entrepreneur decides what projects will be pursued and how they will be conducted

- ultimately responsible for the success or failure of the business they are engaged in

2. What is the most important role of the entrepreneur in a business?

In the case of the CEO of a large company, there are a lot of other people working to carry out the goals and projects set by the CEO. The CEO's job is to look to the future to decide what activities will best serve the success of the business.

Some questions CEOs consider when making decisions about the future of the company are:

- What is the market for the goods or services produced by the company?

- Will the demand for the product stay steady, increase or decrease? Is there a seasonal demand?

- Is technology affecting how the goods and services of the company are able to compete in the marketplace?

- Does the company need to upgrade its products to maintain its competitiveness?

- Does the company need to consider developing new goods and services?

- Does the company need to discontinue existing goods and services?

These questions all boil down to one idea: finding the opportunities the company can use to increase the values of the resources used and generate profits.

Section 1.5

1. Define scarcity in terms of economics.

From the perspective of an economist, scarcity is the problem of the unlimited human wants and needs in an environment of finite resources. Society is unable to fulfill all of the wants and needs because it does not have enough resources to produce the goods and services in demand. If society had enough resources to meet all of the wants and needs of every person, scarcity would not exist.

Scarcity can also refer to the concept that society is unable to pursue all of its goals at the same time. This applies at all levels, from the individual to the national government. In this situation, scarcity of resources results in decisions being made about how to best use existing resources. These decisions are also known as trade-offs.

2. **Define choice in terms of economics.**

Choice comes into play when an individual who has limited resources must decide how to use those resources to maximize their benefit to the individual. Typically, the first choices will ensure his basic needs of food and shelter are met. This reduces the cash resource available for fulfilling other wants and needs. Other needs that are not as critical as food and shelter, but may still be needs, are clothing and transportation. Our individual will make his remaining choices based on the level of satisfaction of wants or needs he receives from using his financial resources to obtain specific goods or services.

3. **How do choice and scarcity affect purchasing decisions?**

Scarcity can lead to rationing. A consumer's choices will be influenced by the price of goods and services, and availability of alternatives that will meet his needs or wants. This is the basis of the economic concept of supply and demand.

Section 1.6

1. **List the three factors of production.**

Land is essential for the physical infrastructure required to produce the product

Labor is essential for the production of goods and services.

Capital is the money available to pay for the production of your goods.

2. **Discuss why each factor is essential to production of a good.**

Land: Production requires buildings for the workers and machines required to make the goods, as well as for storage. In order to have buildings, the business must have the land on which to build the buildings and related infrastructure of parking lots, green space, offices, and any other things necessary for the business to produce goods.

Labor: The infrastructure will not be productive without the people required to operate the machines and do the other tasks required to produce the goods. You may need skilled or unskilled labor for your particular production process. When considering where to locate a production facility, it is important to define the skill level required for your production process and whether an appropriate labor pool is available where you want to locate your business. Another consideration when looking at the labor pool available to you is the cost of the labor. If the cost of labor is too high, you will not be able to produce your goods at a cost that will result in a price that the consumers will pay for the product you produce. You will also need to consider the costs of labor for employees who are in support roles, such as administrative and sales people.

Capital is required to acquire land, build buildings, pay workers, and transport the goods to their final destination. Capital is available from a few sources: self-financing, bank loans, venture capitalists, and others. The type of capital you use will depend upon your unique situation and the business you are establishing.

These three factors of production must all be in place at the appropriate levels for a good or service to be produced. If one is missing or not available at a sufficient level, the production process will not work efficiently if it works at all.

Section 1.7

1. **Define the two types of capital.**

   Financial capital is financing provided by lenders and investors to businesses. Financial capital may be borrowed from a bank or a credit union in the form of a loan. Sometimes it is even possible to get financial capital in the form of grants from state or federal governments to start a small business. Grants are beneficial because they are a gift – not a loan that requires repayment. It is also possible to self-finance a business if you have been able to save enough money or build sufficient assets to support your business venture.

   Real capital takes the form of the tools required to perform the task. Real capital includes the buildings, tools, equipment and other physical things required to produce goods.

2. **Discuss the primary differences between the two types of capital.**

   Financial capital is considered a liability to a company if it is from a loan that requires repayment. It may also be considered shareholders' equity if venture capital is involved. Venture capital is an investment made by a person called a venture investor, who is someone who invests in young businesses with the hope of making a profit when the business becomes established.

   Real capital is considered an asset. Real capital is wealth that can be represented in financial terms. A savings or investment account has a financial value associated with it. Real estate and financial securities (stocks, bonds, CDs, and other financial instruments) may be considered real capital. Real assets are owned by the company and have value, meaning that they can be used as collateral for loans or sold for cash, if necessary. It is important to use caution when considering a sale of real capital because you need to maintain the infrastructure required to produce your good or service.

3. **Define equity.**

Equity is ownership. A person who provides 25% of the funding required to start a business is likely to have 25% ownership equity in the business. Remember that both liabilities and shareholders' equity represent funds that will eventually leave the company, either in the form of loan payments or dividend payments.

Section 1.8

1. **Describe the concept of a trade-off in decision-making.**

Each person and business approaches the decision making process based upon their own sets of values, needs and wants. A mechanic will place a much higher value on a piece of equipment or parts he needs to complete a repair job than will someone who does not know how to use the tool or what the part does to help the vehicle move.

The concept of a trade-off is a result of scarcity of resources. In many cases, people and businesses have limited resources available to acquire what they need or want. Since human beings have unlimited wants, they must learn to make trade-offs to obtain what they need and want within the resources available to them.

The trade-off can be applied to all aspects of economic decision-making. The people making the decisions consider the resources available, the options available, and make a decision about how to use the resources to provide the most benefit/profit to the business and, hopefully, the end user.

2. **Describe how consumers impact the way companies make decisions.**

Trade-offs are not always strictly financial. Many companies are now considering the impact they have on the environment and are changing their business practices because they value the environment enough that they are willing to pay more to reduce their long-term environmental impact. This has been driven in large part by demand on the part of the consumers who are worried about environmental degradation and are making purchases from companies that are actively working to reduce their environmental impact.

Other areas where consumers have had an impact on corporate decision-making are personnel practices, where they obtain their raw materials, how they market their goods, and compensation of workers and executives.

Section 1.9

1. **List the four primary types of profit in economics and describe how they differ.**

Normal profit occurs when total revenues equal total costs. In other words, the company is breaking even. A company that is making normal profits is bringing in enough revenue to ensure that the investors in the company are not losing money.

The rate of return (profit) is at the minimum level required by the investors to maintain their level of investment. Normal profit is considered one of the two components that compose the cost of capital. There is no economic profit to the business owner in the condition of normal profits.

Economic profit occurs when revenues of a company exceed the total opportunity costs of the inputs required to produce the company's goods or services. In this case, the costs include the cost of the equity (loans, venture capital) that are included in normal profit, as well as the costs of raw materials, labor, overhead, and the other costs related to production. Economic profit occurs when the average cost of production is less than the price of the product or service to the consumer.

Accounting profit is a calculation of the company's total earnings, including costs such as depreciation, interest and taxes. Accounting profits tend to be higher because they do not include the opportunity cost of engaging in the business venture.

Social profit is defined as the normal profit plus or minus any effects of the production activity on society. If a company engages in production processes that result in damage to the environment, use unfair employment practices, or do other things that result in a negative social effect, the social profit will be negative. If, on the other hand, the company works to maximize both profits and social good by minimizing environmental impact, engaging in fair employment practices, and doing other things to improve society, the social profit will be maximized.

Section 1.10

1. **Explain why some careers are more susceptible to economic downturns than others.**

   Careers that are more susceptible to changes in economic behavior are those that rely on consumer spending. Economic downturns tend to decrease consumer spending and upswings tend to increase consumer spending.

2. **Describe how a business can weather an economic downturn by understanding the needs and wants of the client base.**

   A business can weather an economic downturn by monitoring trends in population, style, and changes in the customer base, including income level, culture, age groups, and other relevant variables.

3. **Why are publicly funded careers less impacted by an economic downturn than others?**

   Careers that are less affected by economic conditions are those that provide fundamental services to the community. For example, safety services (fire, police, emergency medical services), government positions (administrative, educational, regulatory) and other positions that keep society working at a minimal required level are not as subject to economic downturns as those that rely on consumer spending. Regardless of the economy, people will always need fire, police and emergency medical services. These career fields may be affected somewhat by the economy, but are likely to be less impacted than others.

Section 1.11

1. **Describe an economic cycle.**

   Business cycles are periods of expansion and recession. Business cycles can be predictable – for example, the seasonal nature of certain jobs in climates that have a harsh winter. They can also be the result of other factors, such as changes in the political landscape, addition or departure of large employers from a geographic area, and a shortage or surplus of a key raw material, labor or capital.

2. **Explain how political decisions affect individual and business economics**

   Political change can result in economic disruption. In a time of conflict, essential resources are segregated to support the war effort. Examples of this include manufacturing capacity for war materials (weapons, vehicles, clothing, and other commodities required by the military), food, fuel, and other basic necessities of life. This can result in rationing that affects the entire economy of the nation at war. Another example of economic disruption occurred in the 1970s with the energy crisis. The supply of gasoline to fuel vehicles was extremely limited, resulting in high prices and fuel shortages.

3. **Describe how natural events can affect the economics of the agricultural industry.**

   Seasonality is a key component of many economic situations. All agricultural businesses rely on the rhythms of nature to ensure a successful crop. If all goes well, the crops are planted, grow and are harvested in a predictable cycle. One of the major challenges of agriculture is the unpredictability of Mother Nature. Crops are dependent upon good conditions to grow to a harvestable state. When there is drought, flooding, unusually cold or warm weather, disease outbreaks, or pest infestations, the crop does not follow a predictable pattern, which may result in a smaller crop than expected or no crop at all. Seasonality of jobs, such as those in tourist areas or in agricultural situations, can be predicted and managed. The problems crop up when unexpected situations such as extreme conditions or economic recession occur.

Section 1.12

1. **Describe the factors that affect price**

   Businesses sometimes intentionally set prices too high or too low. Businesses who want their product to be perceived as a luxury product are likely to set their price higher than equilibrium to increase the perceived value of the product. Examples of this are expensive purses and designer clothing.

Businesses may set a price lower than equilibrium when a brand new product is being introduced to the market and the producer wants to make sure that the product is priced at a level that will encourage as many people as possible to purchase it, who then rely on the product. After consumers accept the product, they may be willing to pay a higher price for the product and the producer may increase the price to equilibrium.

Grocery and retail stores use the concept of a loss-leader to attract consumers to the store. A loss-leader is a product that consumers want and that is priced significantly below market value. The store loses money on the loss-leader, but anticipates that the consumer will make other purchases while in the store that will make up for the initial loss.

Other basic factors that affect prices are supply of raw materials, the ease or difficulty of production, the availability of production facilities, and market demand for the good or service. A sudden change in the availability of raw materials, typically a shortage, usually results in a rapid increase in the price of the product to the consumer. Likewise, a surplus of a raw material may drive the price down.

2. **Discuss how a free market defines price based on market variables.**

A free market is a market where prices are established based purely on the supply and demand for a good or service. The price is established where the supply and demand curves meet.

Demand for a product priced above the equilibrium price set by the market is likely to decrease because fewer people will feel that the price of the product is worth the benefit gained by purchasing the product.

When a product price is set below equilibrium, demand may outstrip the available supply, causing a shortage of the product.

Section 1.13

1. **Define microeconomics and discuss the primary concerns of the microeconomist.**

The field of microeconomics is concerned with the behavior of the individual economic entity, including individual people, households, and businesses. Microeconomics also includes the study of individual economic factors, such as employment, unemployment, prices, and labor economics.

2. **Define macroeconomics and discuss the primary concerns of the macroeconomist.**

Macroeconomics is the study of economic systems. Topics of interest to a macroeconomist include national economies, large portions of a national economy, production and distribution systems, indicators of the health of the large system (overall income and productivity of an economy), and the relationships that exist between different parts of the economy.

Economic news is often based in macroeconomic theory. Discussions of markets, recession, inflation, gross domestic product, and national debt are all based in macroeconomics.

3. **Discuss how microeconomics and macroeconomics both affect the individual.**

Microeconomics and macroeconomics both affect the individual consumer, just in different ways. Microeconomics is the economy of the individual household or small business. Each person creates his own unique economy based on income and the choices he makes as far as how he uses this financial resource. It is possible to create a very strong personal economy if he uses his financial resources to acquire the necessities of life (food, shelter, transportation, clothing, etc.), save for the future, and generally lives within his income. It is also possible to create a very weak personal economy if he makes unwise choices about how to use his money. Some people place more importance on having the "right" things than taking care of basic necessities. This leads to debt and other financial problems.

The combined behavior of all the individuals in a country drives the larger economic trends that macroeconomists are interested in. For example, if the majority of individual consumers are not confident about having continued employment, they will scale back their spending, conserving their resources in case they need them later. This, in turn, impacts the businesses that no longer generate sales because people have reduced their spending. The ripple effect of these behaviors eventually leads to changes in the indicators that macroeconomists use to understand the behavior of the national economy.

Section 1.14

1. **Define and describe positive economics.**

Positive economics are also referred to as scientific economics. This field of study attempts to determine what is actually happening in the economy. The scientific method is used to gather and assess data to answer a specific question, or hypothesis, the researcher developed. The hypothesis is developed based on extensive research and a thorough understanding of the topic under study. The essence of positive economics is that we can analyze objective data to determine whether a hypothesis is correct.

2. **Define and describe normative economics.**

Normative economics add ethical, or value, judgment to the methods used in positive economics.

Normative economics are often used to advocate for policy changes based on a specific point of view. The statements used in normative economics are about "what could be" if certain conditions are met. For example, a person might say that if all U.S. citizens are provided comprehensive health care at no charge, the total cost of health care will be reduced. A key aspect of normative economics is that the statements made in support of a particular point of view cannot be proved or disproved using data. This happens because personal values are introduced to the conclusions made. Personal values cannot be proved right or wrong because they are based on opinion and not data.

Section 1.15

1. **Define and describe economic profit.**

   Economic profit includes accounting profit (revenue minus costs for a time frame) AND the opportunity cost of doing business. Economic profit occurs when the revenue generated by a business exceeds the total of expenses plus opportunity cost.

2. **Define and describe accounting profit.**

   Accounting profit is the result of calculating the result of revenue minus costs for the company for a specific time frame, which is typically a year. Accounting profit includes the payments made to investors to ensure a specific rate of return on their investment in the company. This means that what you might logically consider profit is actually listed as a cost because it must be paid out to the investors before the business actually makes a profit. The formal term for this cost is the cost of capital. If the firm's income is greater than the costs, it is making an accounting profit.

3. **Describe opportunity cost.**

   Opportunity cost is the cost of pursuing one option instead of another option, which may be equally interesting or appealing.

An Easy Introduction to Economics: Microeconomics Answer Key Unit 2

Section 2.1

1. **Define production possibility curve and describe what it represents in relationship to efficiency, growth, and cost.**

   The production possibilities curve shows all the possible combinations of total output. Opportunity cost is a key component of the production possibilities curve. Each point on the curve represents a trade-off between the use of one resource and another to produce a good.

The production possibilities curve assumes three things:

1) Utilization of a fixed amount of productive resources.
2) Resources are used fully and efficiently.
3) A specific state of technical expertise.

The production possibilities curve will give an indication of where pricing will increase or decrease. The larger the supply of a good or service relative to demand for that good or service, the lower the price will be. Conversely, the smaller the supply of a good or service, the higher the price will be.

When the economy is growing, the curve will push out to reflect the increased production capacity.

Section 2.2

1. **Describe how the resources available in a country influence its ability to produce goods and services.**

   Natural resources are the resources available from the natural environment. Different areas have different combinations of natural resources available for use in production of goods and services. Each geographic area has a unique grouping of natural resources that can be utilized for producing goods and services to stimulate the economy.

   Technical resources include the infrastructure and expertise required to produce a good or service. Economies that use basic technologies of production are usually not able to take advantage of the increased efficiencies resulting from improvements in production technologies. Developed countries have more technically advanced production and money management systems than developing countries, which typically lead to more efficient systems.

   Human resources, which are also known as human capital, are the people available to do work. The number and skill level of the people available to do work has a strong influence on the production capacity of a country. A highly-educated workforce is able to produce more complex products that have a high value to the consumer. A workforce that does not have a strong education or specialized technical skills will be able to do a lot of work, but not take advantage of the benefits provided by technological advances and higher education.

2. **What societal pressures influence society's decisions to produce specific goods or services?**

   Societal values contribute to the decisions made about production of goods and services. For example, in times of war, a society may choose to sacrifice availability of certain consumer goods to support production of the resources needed to support the war effort.

   Usually however, the three basic economic questions drive the decision about what goods and services a society will produce.

These three questions are:

- What goods and services should be produced?

- How should the goods and services be produced?

- For whom should the goods and services be produced?

Societal values will impact how these decisions are made. A society that values ensuring that all people in that society have their basic needs met will make decisions to support that goal. A society where the decision makers care only about personal gain will produce the goods and services that benefit the few (decision makers) and not the majority of the people, who are the ones actually producing the goods and services.

Of course, all of these production decisions are made based on the natural and technical resources available. A country that is rich in energy will make production decisions based on those natural resources. A country that is rich in highly-skilled labor and technical resources will make its production decisions based on those resources and the availability of the raw materials required to produce their products.

In theory, a society should be able to manage its resources so that all of its members have what they need to survive and be healthy. If the people making the decisions about production are not interested in the well-being of the society as a whole, the decision will probably serve the selfish interests of the decision makers.

Section 2.3

1. **Define the free enterprise system in the U.S.**

   The free enterprise system in the U.S. is a capitalist system. It is a free enterprise system that is subject to government control and regulations. The government control and regulations are designed to protect consumers, workers, the environment, and the society. The free enterprise system in the U.S. is not a true free enterprise system because of the government controls.

2. **Describe how the consumer affects the free enterprise system.**

   The U.S. consumer votes with her dollar. Consumers make choices every day about how to use their resources. Free markets are an extension of personal freedom, which is the result of people making decisions that benefit themselves. A market that is providing what the consumer needs at a reasonable price will thrive. A market that is unable to provide what the consumer needs will not thrive.

   Another way to look at this problem is from the perspective of the individual business. A business may choose to engage in ethical behavior or unethical behavior, which is based on societal norms. A business that chooses to engage in ethical behavior may have a competitive advantage in attracting clients, which will contribute to the behavior of the market.

The consumer also drives the market based on fundamental needs for survival. A consumer will allocate resources to provide for basic needs before providing for unnecessary purchases.

Section 2.4

1. **State the law of demand and discuss how increases and decreases in price are related to demand.**

   The law of demand states that as the price for a good or service increases, demand will decrease. It also states that as the price for a good or service decreases, demand will increase. An alternative way to state this law is that, given a consistent supply, increased demand will increase price and vice versa. In other words, the price of a good or service drives consumer demand for that commodity.

2. **Use the following demand schedule for the product "Flower Power" to draw a demand curve for the product.**

Price	Demand
$50	0
$40	1
$30	5
$20	20
$10	100
$0	175

Flower Power Demand Curve

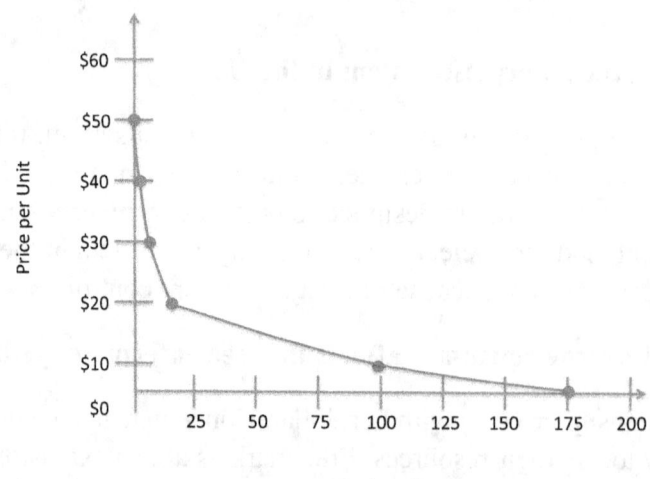

1. **Describe how the change in price of a product can change the demand for complementary products.**

   The demand of a product influences the demand complementary products. If the demand for a product is high, demand for complementary products will probably be high. Likewise, if the demand for the product is low, the demand for the complementary product will probably be low.

2. **Discuss the impact of drastic price changes on related products.**

   Related goods or services are those that substitute easily for on another. Consider what will happen, for example, if pork drops sharply in price compared to related products, such as beef, chicken and fish. In this situation, the demand for the higher priced beef, chicken and fish will fall while the demand for the cheap pork is likely to increase. This occurs because pork is a substitute for other meats.

3. **List and describe the primary factors that cause a shift in the demand curve.**

   Preferences: Societal preferences tend to change over time, which affects demand for products. In the 1970s, for example, people covered their hardwood floors with shag carpeting. Wood floors were considered to have a lower status than carpet, so people added carpet to their homes when they remodeled. Many years later, wood floors are very popular and a sign of quality. As you might imagine, the demand curve for shag increased in the 1970s and decreased as wood floors came back into fashion.

   Population: Populations change over time. These changes can be a result of normal growth. They may also be the result of an influx of people from another place as a result of a natural disaster or economic downturn. Finally, the composition of population changes over time. The U.S. is currently experiencing a rapid growth in the population of people over age 65 as the baby boomers are retiring. Each of these population changes has the potential to shift the demand for products.

   Prices of Other Goods and Services: Related goods or services are those that substitute easily for on another. Consider what will happen, for example, if pork drops sharply in price compared to related products, such as beef, chicken and fish. In this situation, the demand for the higher priced beef, chicken and fish will fall while the demand for the cheap pork is likely to increase. This occurs because pork is a substitute for other meats.

   Income: Increases or decreases in income will affect demand for goods and services. As people have more income (resources), they demand higher quality goods and services and want to enjoy an improved lifestyle. As income decreases, people conserve resources by reducing their demand for goods and services. Normal goods are those for which demand increases as income increases. Inferior goods are those for which demand decreases as income increases. An example of this is a store brand versus a name brand food or household item.

Perception of Future Prices: If people think that the price of a good is going to increase dramatically in the future, demand for that good is likely to increase if it is something people are able to store for future use. For example, if the price of rice is expected to double because of a natural disaster that destroyed a major portion of the world"s rice crop, one would expect the demand for rice to increase as people stock up on it. This factor affects goods more than services because it is not likely that a service can be hoarded.

Section 2.6

1. **Compare and contrast quantity demanded and a shift in a demand curve.**

   Quantity demanded represents any point on a demand curve and is a relationship between price and quantity. As price increases on a demand curve, the quantity demanded falls. Likewise, as price decreases on a demand curve, the demand increases.

   A shift in the demand curve is a result of a fundamental change in the relationship between price and demand. The demand curve may shift down or up. A negative shift in the demand curve means that there is less demand for a good or service. The demand at a specific price point decreases. For example, if demand for car tires decreases because people are driving less, the demand for tires at specific price will decrease. A positive shift in the demand curve means that there is an increased demand for a good or service at that same price point.

2. **Describe a situation in which a demand curve might have negative movement.**

   Many factors can affect demand for a good or service. Politics, raw materials or component availability, labor issues, natural disasters, and a number of other factors can affect demand.

   A demand curve may have negative movement if the price of a good is artificially high, reducing the quantity demanded. It may also have negative movement if a population suddenly has to conserve financial resources because of war, loss of a job, or a natural disaster. In those situations, the demand curve for unnecessary items is likely to have negative movement.

3. **Describe what effects you think political processes might have on a demand curve.**

   Political changes can cause businesses and people to have either increased or decreased confidence in the market. When confidence is up, demand is likely to increase, causing production to increase, which creates increased demand for raw materials. Likewise, if individuals and businesses are not confident in the market, they will conserve resources, reducing demand for the end products, therefore reducing demand for the raw materials required to manufacture the products.

Section 2.7

1. **Define elasticity of demand and describe the three types of elasticity studied in microeconomics.**

   Elasticity of demand is the change in demand for a good or service based on changes in price. Elasticity of demand is the degree to which an increase or decrease in price will change the quantity demanded.

   There are three degrees of elasticity: unitary elasticity, elasticity, and inelasticity.

   Unitary elasticity occurs when the percentage increase in price results in an offsetting decrease in demand. Conversely, a decrease in price will result in an offsetting increase in demand.

   Elasticity is a situation in which a reduction in price increases demand sufficiently to increase revenue.

   Inelastic demand occurs when a price increase does not increase revenue.

2. **Discuss the law of supply and how price affects the supply of goods and services to the market.**

   The law of supply states that there is a direct relationship between the price of a good or service and the amount of it offered for sale. In other words, all other factors being equal, as the price of a good or service increases, the quantity of goods or services offered by suppliers will increase. Conversely, as the price of a good or service decreases, suppliers are less motivated to provide the good or service for sale. If the price drops too low, the company will no longer provide the good or service because there is no opportunity for profit. Higher prices induce producers to offer more of a good or service for sale. The minimum price for a good or service must at least be equal to the opportunity cost of using the resources required for production of the good or service. In other words, the producer is going maximize profit by utilizing the resources available in the most efficient manner. If the producer cannot make a profit, the good or service will not be produced. As the price for the good or service increases, the producer has incentive to increase the supply, which can lead to a surplus if the supply outstrips the demand.

3. **Solve the following problems and state which type of demand elasticity it represents.**

   Calculate the revenue for each of the price and demand combinations and specify which type of elasticity of demand is shown for this set of problems.

   $Demand_1 = 10$; $Price_1 = \$50$
   $Demand_2 = 30$; $Price_2 = \$150$
   $Demand_3 = 20$; $Price_3 = \$100$

251

Solution:

Revenue = Demand × Price

$$R_1 = D_1 \times P_1$$
$$R_1 = 10 \times \$50$$
$$R_1 = \$500$$

$$R_2 = D_2 \times P_2$$
$$R_2 = 30 \times \$150$$
$$R_2 = \$4,500$$

$$R_3 = D_3 \times P_3$$
$$R_3 = 20 \times \$100$$
$$R_3 = \$2,000$$

Type of Elasticity of Demand: Unitary because demand changes at the same rate as increases or decreases in price.

4. **Calculate the revenue for each of the price and demand combinations and specify which type of elasticity of demand is shown for this set of problems**

   $Demand_1 = 50$; $Price_1 = \$35$
   $Demand_2 = 75$; $Price_2 = \$30$

   Solution:

   Revenue = Demand × Price

   $$R_1 = D_1 \times P_1$$
   $$R_1 = 50 \times \$35$$
   $$R_1 = \$1,750$$

   $$R_2 = D_2 \times P_2$$
   $$R_2 = 75 \times \$30$$
   $$R_2 = \$2,250$$

   Type of Elasticity of Demand: Elastic: As demand increased, revenues increased.

5. **Calculate the revenue for each of the price and demand combinations and determine which type of elasticity of demand is shown here.**

   $Demand_1 = 100$; $Price_1 = \$150$
   $Demand_2 = 110$; $Price_2 = \$100$

Solution:

Revenue = Demand × Price

$$R_1 = D_1 \times P_1$$
$$R_1 = 100 \times \$150$$
$$R_1 = \$15,000$$

$$R_2 = D_2 \times P_2$$
$$R_2 = 110 \times \$100$$
$$R_2 = \$11,000$$

Type of Elasticity of Demand: Inelastic. As demand increased, revenues decreased.

Section 2.8

1. **Define elasticity of supply.**

   Supply elasticity is related to the speed with which suppliers are able to respond to changes in price and demand. Production facilities typically have fixed capacity to produce goods and it takes effort, money, and time to increase capacity. This may require bringing in additional equipment, hiring new workers, increasing supply orders or building new buildings to accommodate the increased production capacity.

2. **Discuss how producers of goods and services respond to increases or decreases in price, both in the long and short term.**

   If a supplier is able to plan for an increase in production, the company is better able to respond when the price changes. However, if the change in price is sudden, the supplier will require time to adjust the production capacity of the factory.

   In general, it is less expensive to expand production capacity slowly because careful planning and cost estimation will allow the expansion to be done at the lowest possible cost. If the production capacity expands quickly, it often costs more because of the speed with which the work is done. Once production capacity is established, it is efficient for the company to produce products at different levels, usually lower than the maximum capacity of the plant, while still retaining the ability to ramp up production if necessary to increase supply.

3. **Create a supply curve from the following supply schedule.**

Price per unit	Number of units manufactured
$25.00	3,000
$20.00	2,800
$15.00	2,300
$10.00	1,500
$5.00	750
$1.00	0

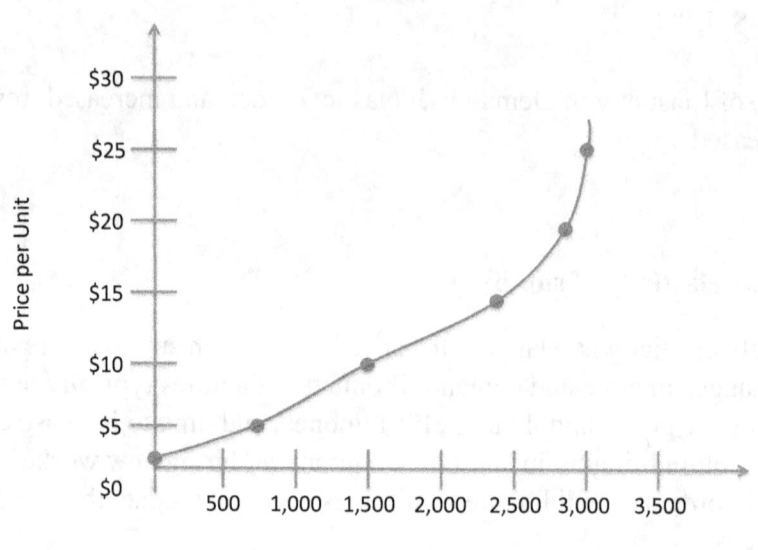

Supply Curve

Section 2.9

1. **Define entrepreneur and describe the role entrepreneurs play in the economy.**

   An entrepreneur is a person who starts a new business venture and assumes all of the risk of the venture's success or failure. Small business owners are considered entrepreneurs, as is anyone who is self-employed.

2. **Describe how fixed and variable inputs are affected by increases or decreases in demand for a good.**

   Production includes two types of inputs: fixed and variable. Fixed inputs are the costs of the building, equipment, and other fixed assets that are required to produce the good. Variable inputs are those that change based on the volume of goods being produced. The primary variable inputs are labor and raw materials.

   The law of diminishing returns is related to production. It states that a production system with fixed and variable inputs will receive proportionally less benefit from additional variable inputs after a certain point. Labor efficiency is maximized at the point where each person is producing as much product as possible while maintaining standards of quality. If demand for a product increases or decreases, the demand for labor to produce that product does the same.

3. **Discuss how the law of diminishing returns and downsizing are related, including how they contribute to production efficiency and profit maximization.**

Downsizing is a response to the law of diminishing returns. A company is motivated by profit and seeks to maximize profit by minimizing production costs through efficient use of resources. Downsizing will also have a negative effect on the entrepreneurs who are supplying the raw materials used in production of a good. If demand for the product decreases, the demand for raw materials decreases, which means that suppliers of the raw materials have reduced demand for their products.

Section 2.10

1. **List the key factors that affect supply.**

There are a number of factors that affect supply. The primary factors are capacity and technology, cost structure, prices of substitutes and complements, and perceptions of future prices. Other factors include politics, and cost and availability of raw materials.

2. **Discuss how changes in technology and capacity affect the supply of a product to the market.**

Capacity is the ability of an industry to produce goods and services. When a product is new to the market, the capacity for production is limited. Production capacity will increase as the product gains acceptance by the market and the price is in line with what consumers are willing to pay for the product. Production capacity also increases as additional producers are able to add to the available supply of product. Sometimes, as with the telecommunications industry in the 1990s, the industry developed too much capacity (overcapacity). This made it possible for the companies to increase the supply of goods and services produced for a specific, lower price point because they had the infrastructure in place to make their production processes highly efficient. Technology is closely related to capacity. In order for a company to remain competitive, it is critical to improve the technology used to produce the good or service provided. Companies that invest in technological improvements improve their efficiency and capacity. Overcapacity can occur within one company or across and entire industry.

The reverse also holds true. If a company or industry has too little capacity, too few producers, or is behind in technological innovation, the supply will decrease.

3. **Describe how politics are able to affect the availability of goods and services, including raw materials.**

The politics of governments can have a direct impact on the supply of goods and services, including raw materials and labor. Governments will sometimes place embargoes (restrictions) on the import of goods from or export of goods to specific countries that have policies that our government does not support. For example, a country that violates human rights, as defined by the U.S. or United Nations may be subject to an embargo. If that country provides a vital raw material for a specific industry, that industry will be unable to supply as much of their final product as they would if the embargo was not in place.

Political pressures may also come from consumers. A highly publicized example is the blood diamonds, also called conflict diamonds, from Africa. The African diamond mining industry has been shown to be very violent. The profits of the African diamond trade have also been used to finance civil wars in Africa. As a result of the poor conditions the African diamond miners work in and the civil wars, consumers have begun boycotting diamonds from these mines, which have become known as blood diamonds to reflect the violence associated with them. The Canadian diamond industry has benefited from this consumer behavior because the working conditions of the mines in Canada are considered more humane than those in Africa.

In some situations, raw materials required for a product become scarce. Scarcity of a raw material will reduce the amount of an end product that can be supplied by the producer. Conservation of raw materials is critical for ensuring the continuation of industries, such as logging. Many logging companies replant forests to ensure a continual supply of wood for future use.

Section 2.11

1. **Describe the global economy and how it is subject to the rules of supply and demand.**

   The global economy follows the same rules of supply and demand as a national economy. International trade involves import and export of goods and services around the world.

   Global trade allows people and companies to purchase goods they need from places that are able to create them less expensively, thereby increasing the efficiency of resource use. In order for this to be the most effective, the importer or exporter must have something that is of value to the other party. Both countries benefit from the exchange by reducing the cost of goods to their producers and consumers.

   Comparative advantage occurs when the opportunity cost for a nation to produce a good is lower than that of another nation. Absolute advantage occurs when a nation can produce a good more cheaply than another nation. Comparative advantage is the measure that should be used to determine whether a good should be exported. Comparative advantage shows that even if a country does not have the absolute advantage in producing any product, it can still benefit by producing goods and services for which it has the lowest opportunity cost.

2. **Discuss the effects of tariffs, quotas, and other factors on the supply of goods in an international economy.**

   In reality, governments put barriers to trade in place in a number of ways. Tariffs and quotas are common barriers to trade put in place by governments. A tariff is a tax levied on an imported good to increase the price of the good to consumers so that it is competitive with similar goods that are produced domestically. This increases the cost to both the producer and the consumer. A quota is a limit on the amount of a good that can be imported or exported. Other barriers to import or export include regulations regarding product content or quality, packing and shipping regulations, harbor and airport permits, and overly difficult customs procedures.

The barriers to trade described above increase the cost of inputs used to produce a good or service. This is likely to result in a reduction in supply of the good or service to the consumer. If the barriers to international trade are reduced, the reduced cost of the inputs should result in an increase in supply.

3. **Draw a supply curve shift from the following data points:**

   $Price_1 = \$4.00$ per unit; $Supply_1 = 500$ units

   $Price_2 = \$5.00$ per unit; $Supply_2 = 700$ units

   $Price_1 = \$4.00$ per unit; $Supply_1 = 500$ units

   $Price_3 = \$3.00$ per unit; $Supply_3 = 275$ units

   Combine the two curves into one summary graphs that shows the increase and decrease in supply.

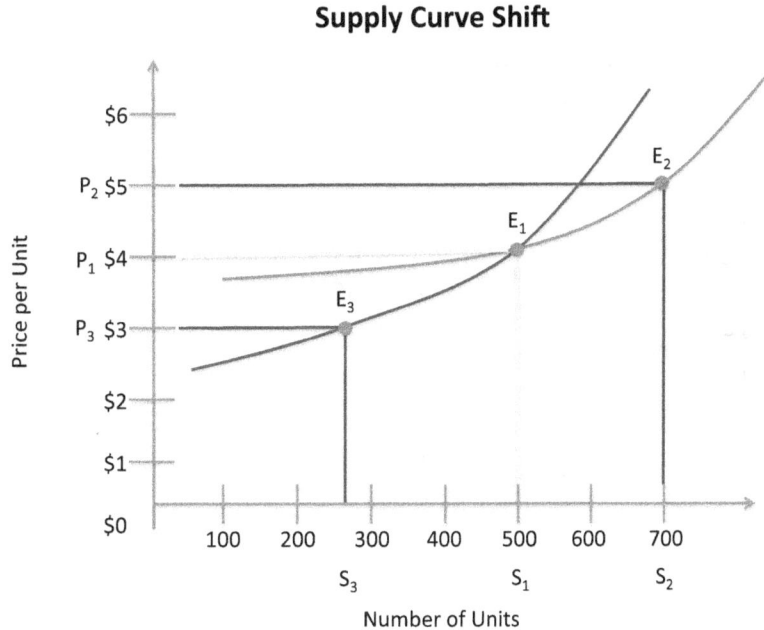

Supply Curve Shift

1. **Describe what market equilibrium is and why it is the preferred state for the market.**

    Markets tend to move toward equilibrium, meaning that supply meets, but does not exceed demand. This can also be stated as demand meeting supply, meaning that demand meets, but does not exceed, supply for a good or service.

2. **Discuss how market disequilibrium occurs and what the results of this disequilibrium are.**

    A market that is not in equilibrium will either have too much supply for the demand (surplus) or too much demand for the available supply (shortage). This is called disequilibrium, meaning that the market forces are out of balance in terms of supply and demand.

3. **Draw a supply and demand curve based on the following variables. Define the point at which the market is in equilibrium. Quantity is shown on the *x*-axis and price on the *y*-axis.**

    $Q_1 = 500$; $P_1 = \$7.00$

    $Q_2 = 750$; $P_2 = \$5.00$

    $Q_3 = 1,000$; $P_3 = \$3.00$

Supply and Demand

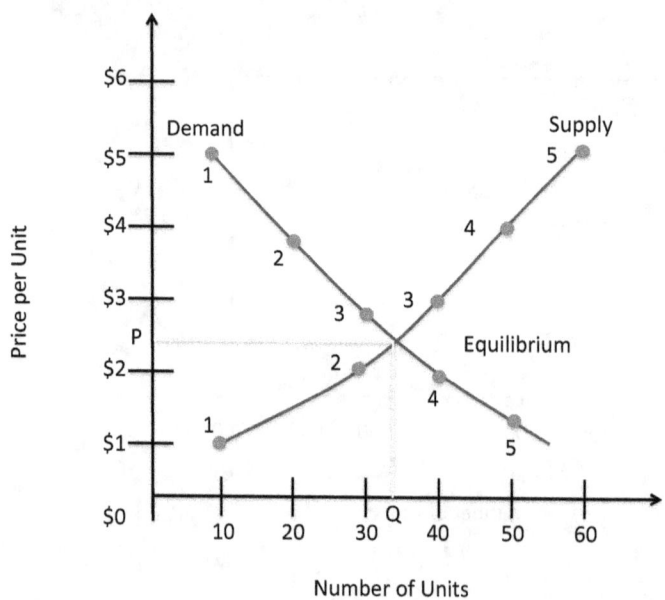

Section 2.13

1. **Describe how the forces of supply and demand interact to move the market into balance, or equilibrium.**

   Supply and demand are pressures that work together to create equilibrium in the marketplace. When the supply and demand for a product are exactly the same, the market is in equilibrium. The market forces of supply and demand push the market to this point for every good and service available.

2. **Discuss what happens when the supply curve shifts left while demand remains constant.**

   The supply line shifts to the left, increasing the price the market will bear for that product when produced at that quantity. The intersection of the new supply line and the demand line moves to the left, as well, resulting in an increased price per unit for the good.

3. **Describe what happens to price when both supply and demand change in the same direction in the same proportion.**

   If supply and demand increase or decrease in relatively the same amount, the equilibrium point will remain at the same price.

Section 2.14

1. **Describe how the equilibrium point and price for a product will change if there is an overall positive shift in demand while the supply remains constant.**

   A shift in demand will have an effect on price if the supply of a good remains constant. If the demand is greater than the supply, the price per unit is likely to increase

   The opposite will occur if the demand curve shifts to the left. Both the supply of the good and the price of the good will decrease, resulting in a new equilibrium point and price.

2. **Discuss what it means for the market to be at equilibrium.**

   The market will react in one of three ways to changes in demand and supply. The equilibrium point will increase, decrease, or simply shift to the left or the right.

   An increase in the price per unit at the equilibrium point is a result of reduced supply for a level of demand, or an increased demand for a given level of supply.

   A decrease in the price per unit at the equilibrium point is a result of an increased supply for a given level of demand, or a decreased demand for a given level of supply.

The price per unit of a good can stay the same if the supply and demand increase or decrease in proportion.

3. **How does the price point for a product remain the same if both supply and demand curves shift?**

The market is self-balancing. Shifts in overall demand or supply for a given product will result in a change in the equilibrium point (the point at which quantity and demand intersect), which also determines the price that the market will bear for the good or service.

Section 2.15

1. **Using the chart below, give the price and quantity for each point on the demand curve.**

   Price: 1. $5.00   2. $3.75   3. $2.90   4. $2.00   5. $1.25
   Quantity: 1. 10   2. 20   3. 30   4. 40   5. 50

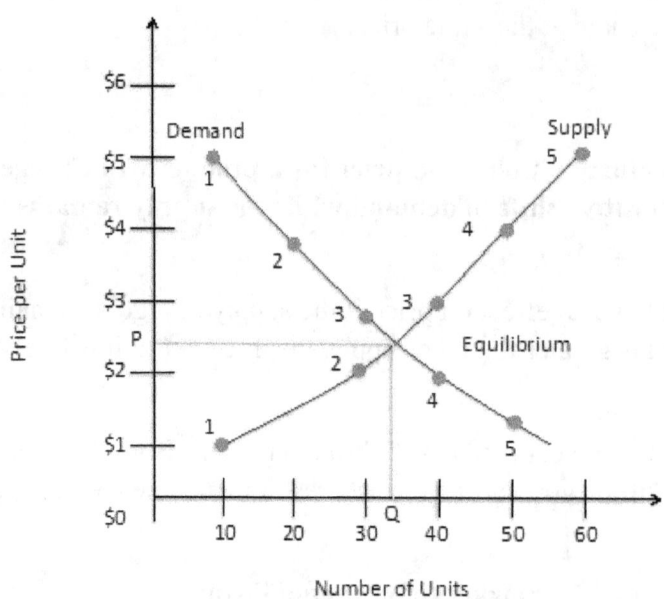

2. **Using the same chart, give the price and quantity of each point on the supply curve.**

   Price: 1. $1.00   2. $2.00   3. $3.00   4. $4.00   5. $5.00
   Quantity: 1. 10   2. 20   3. 30   4. 40   5. 50

3. **Give the equilibrium price and quantity and describe how equilibrium is achieved.**

   Equilibrium point: Price $3.50   Quantity 33

   Equilibrium is achieved where the demand and supply curves cross. This is the price at which the supply available is equal to the demand for the product.

An Easy Introduction to Economics: Microeconomics
Answer Key Unit 3

Section 3.1

1. **Define marginal utility.**

   Consumer use of a product is subject to diminishing marginal utility as more units of the product are used, just as producers face diminishing marginal returns as they increase their output. Consumers continue to gain by purchasing more of a product as long as the marginal utility (benefit) derived exceeds the cost of purchasing additional units.

2. **Describe how people make decisions to increase marginal utility of purchases.**

   Consumers will change their purchasing decisions based on the resources available (money, typically) and the product choices available. The first law of demand states that the amount of a product purchased is inversely related to its price. This means that the number of units of a product purchased increases as the price decreases. This occurs because the opportunity cost to the customer decreases as the price decreases, so the customer is more willing to spend resources on the product than he would at a higher price point. However, as more units of the product are purchased, the marginal utility (added benefit) of each unit to the consumer decreases. A person can only use so many units of a product. Once the marginal utility is lower than the price for a product, consumers are unlikely to purchase the product unless the price is decreased. This effect is dampened by the law of marginal utility, too. The tendency to substitute a relatively cheaper product for a more expensive product is called the substitution effect.

   Another factor is the cost of a product relative to consumer income. The income of consumers tends to be constant. A reduction in the price of a product increases real income, which is the amount of goods and services the consumer is able to purchase. Consumers typically purchase the less expensive products because they can better afford to do so. This is called the income effect. An increase in the price of a good reduces real income, which discourages buying on the part of the consumer.

   When these two effects (substitution and income) are combined, consumers will generally purchase less of a good. When price increases, the opportunity cost of using the product rises when the price rises. Marginal utility per unit increases because the consumer is utilizing fewer units of the product. Remember that marginal utility is the additional benefit the consumer derives from the use of an additional unit of the product.

3. **Discuss how the key economic questions of production are influenced by consumers.**

The key questions of production are influenced by the willingness of consumers to purchase specific products. These factors of production are the following:

- What should be produced?

- How should the goods be produced?

- Who will consume the goods produced?

All three of these concepts are driven by consumer demand. The companies producing goods and services must understand the demand for the goods they are producing. There must be a market for the products or there is no point in producing the goods. Once demand has been established, the next question is how the goods should be produced to maximize profit to the producer and marginal utility to the consumer. A major consideration of the decision to produce a good is who will consume the goods. An expensive product directed at a luxury consumer will have a different level of demand than an economy product directed at a budget-conscious consumer.

Consumers and companies think at the margin to maximize benefit and efficiency in the use of resources. In order to maximize benefit and efficiency, the manufacturers of products must consider what should be produced, how it should be produced, and who the end user for the product will be.

Section 3.2

1. **Describe the circular flow of a free market economy.**

The free market economy is an economic system in which the forces of supply and demand set prices. No government intervention regarding price or production of goods and services exists. Producers decide what they will produce and consumers decide what they will purchase. This is different than a planned economy, in which the central government makes policy and decisions about production levels and prices.

In a free-market economy, money flows between businesses and consumers through product markets and factor markets. A product market is where a business sells goods and services to households. A factor market exists where households engaged in entrepreneurial activities sell labor, land, capital, and entrepreneurial ability, the factors of production, to businesses. Money can flow either through the consumers to the businesses or from the businesses to the consumers.

2. **How does a free market economy regulate itself?**

The free market is a self-regulating environment. Supply and demand are forces that act upon each other to regulate the market. If a consumer good or service is in high demand, the supply will increase to meet demand until it is no longer profitable for the company supplying the good or service to continue increasing production.

3. **Give an example of free market economy self-regulation that was not presented in this section.**

This answer can be anything that shows the effect of supply and demand on regulating the price of a good or service.

Section 3.3

1. **Define public goods and give a couple of examples of public goods. Explain why public goods are difficult to deliver in an efficient manner.**

Public goods are things that everyone wants, but no one wants to pay for. Examples are clean air, a well-educated population, universal health care, and clean water. Markets and governments tend to be very inefficient at delivering public goods, such as education, clean air, and clean water. There are efforts underway in the U.S. to increase the efficiency of the delivery of public goods. These efforts, including tradable emission credits and school voucher programs, have met with limited success so far.

2. **Describe how the substitution effect and income effect interact to influence consumer purchasing decisions.**

The substitution effect is the effect of changes in the relative price of a good on the level of consumption for that good. An increase in the price of one good causes a consumer to purchase more of the other good (substitution) because the first good has become relatively more expensive. The opposite also holds true. A decrease in the price of one good causes a consumer to purchase more of that good because it is relatively less expensive than the second good.

3. **The income effect has different effects of normal goods and inferior goods. Describe the differences.**

The income effect reflects the increase in real income of the consumer, either as a result of a price drop or an increase in wages. A drop in prices allows the consumer to purchase more goods, which is an increase in consumer purchasing power. Higher real income leads to an increase in demand for a normal good (a product for which demand increases as income increases and vice versa). Lower real income, resulting from an increase in prices or loss of wages, leads to a decrease in demand for a normal good.

The income effect has an interesting effect on inferior goods. Inferior goods are those for which demand decreases as real income increases. Examples of inferior goods are generic and non-name brand food products, instant noodles, and discount store clothing.

1. **Define normal goods and give examples of how demand for normal goods changes with real income.**

   Normal goods are goods for which demand increases when real income increases and decreases when real income decreases. Some examples include: a used car versus a new car; fast food versus fine dining; riding a bus versus flying.

2. **Define inferior goods and give examples of how demand for inferior goods changes with real income.**

   Inferior goods are those goods for which demand decreases as real income increases and increases as real income decreases. Some of these goods show such consistent trends that they are used as reliable markers of the health of an economy. Instant noodles are one of these products. They are very inexpensive and are often used as a substitute for higher quality, more expensive foods.

3. **Describe how selfish individual behavior helps the free market reach equilibrium, maximize consumer choice and ensure efficient resource allocation.**

   Adam Smith wrote about the invisible hand in his book "The Wealth of Nations." The fundamental idea behind the invisible hand is that market economies support spontaneous order, meaning that the market will naturally move to its most efficient structure based on each individual pursuing his own self-interests. In other words, people acting to help themselves ultimately contribute to the efficiency of the market. A totally free market is completely neutral. The producers who are most efficient in meeting the needs of the consumer will thrive. The producers who are not efficient will either struggle or fail. The free market is flexible and adapts to changes in technology, resource availability, and society to reach the new point of maximum efficiency. Freedom of choice is key component of the free market. Producers are free to choose what to produce, how much to produce, the price they will charge, and the quality of the goods they produce. Consumers are free to choose whether to purchase goods or not, based on their available resources, needs and wants. Freedom of production and freedom of consumption are directly related to supply and demand of goods and services. Supply and demand meet at the equilibrium point for the product, which is where the producer is willing to supply as much of a good or service as the consumer demands. A free market removes the administrative costs of managing a central government policy on production of a good or service. A free market also diminishes incentives to control the market because everyone receives maximum benefit at equilibrium.

Section 3.5

1. **Discuss two advantages of a price-based system.**

   A price-based system has the advantage of maximizing market efficiency. The system is efficient because the balance of market forces (supply and demand) determines the optimal price for the product. If a resource is limited, the producer is unable to supply as much of the good, so the price increases. Likewise, if resources become more available, supply increases and price drops, which typically generates an increase in demand.

Other advantages include development of a wide variety of goods and services to meet the varying needs of the consumers. A price-based system leads to companies offering discount items, middle-range items, and high end, or luxury, items. The needs and wants of each individual are met.

Companies will sometimes try to set the price of a good higher than it would normally be, based on pure supply and demand, to increase the perceived value of the good. Common examples of this are luxury brands of clothing and accessories. The higher price of the good limits the number of people who are able to purchase it, often making it more desirable to those consumers who brand conscious. Think of what happens when a sports star promotes a particular brand or model of shoe. The fact that the sports star has allowed his/her name to be associated with the shoe increases the perceived value of the shoe to those who find value in celebrity.

2. **List examples of normal and inferior goods and describe why the goods you listed are normal or inferior.**

   Normal Goods: household appliances, automobiles, clothing, computers, are all examples of normal goods because people are able to buy products with real or perceived increases in value as their incomes go up.

   Inferior goods include bus transportation, ramen noodles, and other products that are purchased more frequently as real income declines.

3. **Define substitute and complementary goods and how the demand for each is impacted by a change in the original good.**

   Substitute goods are those that can take the place of one another. The choices consumers make about which goods to purchase are highly influenced by the cost of the goods. This applies to both necessary and luxury goods. The demand for necessities, such as water, food, and energy, is highly influenced by the cost of the good or service. Consumers will begin to change their behavior to conserve resources as the resources become more scarce, thus more expensive to purchase.

   Complementary goods are goods that are consumed with another good. For example, a hamburger and bun are complementary goods, as are pencils and erasers and bread and butter. If the demand for computers increases, for example, the demand for software will increase. Likewise, if the demand for salads decreases, the demand for salad dressings will probably also decrease.

Section 3.6

1. **List four of the major occupational groups and the characteristics of the jobs in those groups.**

   Management: This group of occupations includes management, business and financial operations occupations. A few of the specific jobs included are administrative services managers, computer and information systems managers, education administrators, human resources, accountants, budget analysis, management analysts and top executives. This is a broad category that is present in all industries. Management positions typically require at least a four-year degree and often an advanced degree.

   Professional: Professional occupations include many computer and mathematical jobs, architects, surveyors, cartographers, engineers, drafters, engineering technicians, life scientists, physical scientists, social scientists, science technicians, community and social services professionals, legal professionals, teachers, librarians, museum curators, artists and designers, entertainers, performers, athletes, media, communications, and medical professionals. Professional occupations can require anywhere from a high school (athletes and artists) to doctoral education. Wages in professional occupations range widely, from starving artists to highly-paid physicians and athletes.

   Service: Service occupations range from healthcare to protective services (corrections, police, fire, and security), food service, building and grounds maintenance, and personal care work. The educational requirements for service jobs tend to be lower than for management or professional occupations. High school diplomas may or may not be necessary for some of the occupations, such as grounds keeping or building maintenance. Other occupations require a two- or four-year degree or some other certification of skills.

   Sales: Advertising, cashiers, clerks, product demonstrators, insurance agents, real estate brokers, retail sales people, travel agents, and securities traders are among the occupations included in this category. Many of these occupations require no formal training and pay low wages. Insurance, real estate, and financial sales occupations typically require some formal training and may require certification by an independent certification board. Again, most of the positions demand low wages, but others can result in high incomes, often as a result of sales-based commissions. The more product sold, the more money the salesperson earns.

   Office and Administrative Support: Occupations in this category include financial clerks, information and record clerks, material (recording, scheduling, dispatch and distribution) occupations, and other office and administrative support positions. These jobs tend to demand low to middle-range wages and do not typically require any education beyond a high school education.

   Farming, fishing and forestry: These occupations include agricultural workers, fishers, fishing vessel operators, foresters, conservationists, and loggers. Some of these occupations require degrees (conservationist, forester), but most do not. These are physically-demanding occupations that often demand low to moderate wages.

Construction trades: This group of occupations includes the skilled trades, such as masons, carpenters, plumbers, and electricians, as well as a wide variety of construction-related occupations. Many of the skilled trades require workers to complete apprenticeships that can last up to five years and improve their skills through a variety of training programs.

Installation, maintenance and repair occupations: These include electrical, electronics, vehicle, mobile equipment, and other installation, maintenance, and repair occupations.

Production: The production occupations include factory workers, assemblers, fabricators, food processors, metal and plastic workers, printers, textile, apparel, furnishing and other production-related occupations. Many of these occupations require specialized technical training, often obtained at vocational schools or through apprenticeship programs.

Transportation and material moving: This group of occupations includes air transportation occupations, material moving occupations, motor vehicle operators, rail and water transportation. This group of occupations usually requires a high school diploma, but may also require additional technical training. For example, people who drive semi-trucks are trained at specialized truck-driving schools.

Armed Forces: The armed forces include a wide range of occupations, with different educational and skill level requirements. The enlisted occupations require a high school diploma. The officer positions require a minimum of a bachelor"s degree, and require advanced training as the officer is promoted to higher ranking positions.

2. **Describe how educational levels affect income potential.**

Income potential tends to increase as education levels increase. This is not always the case, but, in general, increased education has a positive effect on income.

3. **Discuss how technological advances have changed the available occupations.**

The occupations available to people have changed dramatically as technology has changed. Mass production opened up a tremendous number of jobs working on the production lines. Computers have had an incredible impact on occupations. Almost every job a person can hold now requires some level of computer skills.

Section 3.7

1. **Describe how labor force statistics are tracked and used.**

The Bureau of Labor Statistics of the U.S. Government collects, analyzes and publishes data about the labor force in the U.S. The data collected include information on job title, responsibilities, salary, occupational category, educational requirements, demographics, geographic area, benefits, unemployment levels, new job creation, job loss, industry, productivity, safety, consumer spending, inflation, imports, exports and a number of other categories.

Each month the Current Employment Statistics (CES) group of the BLS surveys about 150,000 businesses and government agencies, which represent about 390,000 individual work sites. The survey collects detailed industry data on employment, hours and earnings on nonfarm payrolls for all of the state, the District of Columbia, Puerto Rico, the Virgin Islands, and over 300 metropolitan areas. Nonfarm payrolls are the payrolls for jobs that are not related to farming activities.

The CES group analyzes the collected data to understand employment trends based on geographic area, industry, worker demographics, etc. They publish a monthly report that summarizes information.

The U.S. government tracks labor statistics for all components of the U.S. market, as well as internationally. These data are available for analysts to understand the labor market and economy from the local level all the way to the international level. These data are useful indicators of economic health as well as to understand how the economy of this country is changing and developing. Trends in total compensation, including wages and fringe benefits, have been increasing for U.S. workers. The components of fringe benefits are changing because of the rising cost of health care, which is taking a larger and larger portion of the fringe benefits. This increasing cost has led employers to assess the fringe benefits they offer and to sometimes change the mix of benefits to manage costs.

2. **Define the components of total compensation and describe how they are different.**

Employees work to both receive money (wages) and to have fringe benefits (health insurance, retirement, life insurance, dental insurance, vacation, sick leave, and disability insurance). Fringe benefits are provided in addition to the wages the employees are paid. Wages may vary, but the fringe benefits for a particular group of employees are usually the same.

Section 3.8

1. **Summarize the ongoing changes that are affecting the labor supply.**

The U.S. labor force is changing in a fundamental way. The baby boomers (people born between 1946 and 1964 – after World War II) have begun to retire, leaving more job openings than there are experienced people to fill them. In addition, the labor force participation rate, which is the proportion of the working-age population that is either working or actively looking for work, is declining in the population under age 55. The labor force participation rate is directly linked to the health of the economy. When the economy is strong and jobs are plentiful, more people join the labor force because they are able to find work. The opposite occurs, as well, when the economy is weak. The job market shrinks, making it more difficult for people to find work, which reduces the labor force participation rate.

Other changes in the labor force include slowing declining participation by men and a rapid increase in women participating in the labor force after World War II. Fewer high school students are participating in the labor force because they are staying enrolled in school rather than dropping out to work. This is important for the future success of the country because so many careers now require a high level of education and technical skills at the entry level.

2. **Discuss why you think immigration, even though the numbers have remained steady as a percent of the labor force, is such a contentious issue.**

Immigration is a contentious issue because some people immigrate illegally. These people take whatever work they can get and some feel that they take jobs from Americans who would do them. In many cases, the jobs require hard and dirty physical work, which many Americans no longer wish to do. Other people immigrate legally to the United States to attend school. In many cases, they choose to stay in the U.S. and are able to take high paying jobs that require advanced technical skills. In many cases, the government allows this to occur because the demand for these positions is greater than the supply of Americans able to perform the jobs.

3. **Describe how supply and demand apply to labor.**

Labor is a critical component of the U.S. economy. Just as with any other commodity, labor is subject to the forces of supply and demand. Unskilled jobs do not typically have a high wage associated with them. Most unskilled workers are paid at the minimum wage or a little higher for their efforts. As the jobs demand higher levels of skill and education, the wages paid to the workers generally increase. This is not always the case, however. The value the market places on particular jobs will also affect the wages paid to the worker. There are certain professional jobs that are highly valued by society, but for which the pay scales are not consistent.

A rapid increase in demand for a specific skill set increases the cost of labor to the employer because the employees are able to negotiate higher wages and benefits in order to maximize the benefit to the individual. The employer will benefit by hiring the individual, even at a higher rate, because the skill set is scarce. This happened in the information technology (IT) industry in the late 1990s and early 2000s. The demand for skilled programmers and other IT cause a large number of people to get training that would allow them to enter the field. As this large group of people was graduating and actually entering the work force, the changes in computing technology actually reduced the need for additional skilled workers, leading to a reduction in the compensation paid to IT professionals.

The forces affecting the labor supply (baby boomers, participation rate, and increases in the education required to perform jobs) directly affect the wages paid to the workers. Supply and demand apply just as much to labor as to any other raw material. When there is a surplus of labor, the price of the labor goes down. When there is a shortage, the price goes up until equilibrium is reached.

Section 3.9

1. **Discuss how unions have affected labor costs.**

Unions have had a large influence on wages, both positive and negative. Unions originally formed to help workers earn a competitive wage and have safe working conditions. Unions and corporate managers negotiate specific terms of employment for the union members. Unions try to maximize the benefit to the workers and unions while corporate managers try to minimize labor costs while retaining workers. This has sometimes backfired on union members when management and the union were unable to reach an agreement on terms. A lack of agreement can lead to a strike, which means lost wages to the employee.

2. **Describe how government regulations, such as minimum wage and workplace safety laws, affect labor costs.**

The minimum wage is the absolute minimum hourly rate an employee may be paid for work. The minimum wage is set at the federal level, and sometimes raised by local or state governments. The goal of the minimum wage is to provide every worker with a living wage, meaning that all of life's necessities can be purchased with the wages paid. Jobs that pay the minimum wage are typically unskilled jobs that can be done by a wide variety of people. Whenever a proposal is made to increase the minimum wage, there is often pushback from businesses saying that they cannot afford to pay more wages to the workers for various reasons, including whether or not the business will remain open.

Workplace safety laws may affect wages negatively because of the actual costs of implementing safety regulations and the potential cost of a workplace injury. Companies are in business to make a profit. Every additional cost reduces the potential profit. Worker safety is a critical part of every production process. The cost of implementing safety regulations is a basic cost of doing business. It is possible for safety laws to become so stringent that companies, especially small companies, cannot afford to implement them. The balance of reasonable safety regulation and coping with the costs of supporting injured employees will have a downward pressure on wages. Workers may also be willing to reduce the amount of money they demand in wages if they are working in a safe environment.

3. **How does discrimination affect wages?**

Wage discrimination often occurs in the context of race or sex discrimination. When discrimination exists, the people of the race or sex that is being discriminated against typically earn lower wages than the other employment groups. When discrimination results in a lawsuit, this increases the costs to the company and reduces profits. It also damages the reputation of the company accused of the discriminatory behavior. Unions and governmental legislation have also added to the cost of wage discrimination. Unions have formalized procedures in place to address employee complaints. The administrative costs of addressing these complaints can be significant because of the number of hours of employee, union representative and management effort required to address the problems. Additionally, if a company is found to have engaged in wage discrimination, the company is usually forced to review the wages of all the employees of the company for equity (fairness) and increase the wages of those whose wages are low. Governmental legislation mandates a minimum federal, and sometimes state or local, wage be paid to each employee. As the minimum wage increases, wages increase for all employees to ensure that all employees are being paid in an equitable manner.

1. **Describe the general trend showing the relationship between educational level and wages.**

   The U.S. economy is gaining more and more jobs that require highly skilled employees to perform technical jobs. Highly technical jobs require employees with the appropriate technical training and skill sets to perform them. These skills are obtained by continuing education beyond high school in pursuit of Associate, Bachelor, Master and Doctoral degrees. The opportunity cost of attending school rather than working is compensated for by the higher wages typically earned upon graduation. The Bureau of Labor Statistics publishes wage statistics each year. These statistics show a strong relationship between educational level and average weekly earnings. The trend is that as you achieve a higher level of education, you also earn more money. This is not always the case, of course. Many other factors such as work ethic, job availability, and location will also affect your ability to earn money.

2. **Do you think it is possible to have too much education? What effect might highly specialized training have on job availability and wages?**

   Answers that address the relationship between specialized skills, demand for those skills, and job availability are acceptable.

3. **Describe job migration and the various conditions that may lead to job migration within the U.S. and outside the U.S.**

   Job migration is closely connected to wages. Employers are motivated to earn profit. One of the costs they work to carefully control in earning a profit is the cost of labor. If labor costs become too high in one area, companies may decide to move their operations elsewhere, taking the jobs with them (migration). There are many reasons companies move jobs from one place to another, including supply and demand for products and services, business conditions, labor markets, government policies, political reasons, competition, environmental conditions, local business costs, technological obsolescence, outsourcing, and higher productivity.

   It is typically most efficient to manufacture products near the location that has the highest demand for the product or service. Transportation of goods from the factory to the retail store is getting increasingly expensive because of rapidly increasing fuel prices and increases in the costs of labor, and it is often important to be near the client when providing a service because of the time and money cost of travel.

   Business conditions may motivate companies to move jobs elsewhere, especially if the move reduces the cost of production. Labor markets, governmental policy, local business costs, environmental conditions and politics can all affect business conditions and the decision to keep jobs in a location or move them to another location. If a company is in need of a pool of employees with a specific skill set, that company may choose to locate near other companies that require similar skill sets or near an educational institution that trains students in those skills. Another condition could be the availability of raw materials or access to a shipping system (rail, water).

Technological obsolescence (outdated technology) may result in conditions that allow the company to move out of the outdated facilities and relocate where the raw materials and highly skilled talent they need are located. This could even lead to outsourcing of work to other companies that are already set up to do specific processes with state of the art equipment. It is getting to the point where many companies simply outsource portions of their production process to other companies who are able to make the component at a lower cost. In many cases, jobs are outsourced to other countries, such as Mexico and India, which have lower employment costs.

Job migration typically has a negative economic effect on the area losing the jobs, but a positive effect on the community gaining the jobs. Those who lose jobs often face a very difficult transition because they have to learn a new skill set or move to retain their old jobs. This is part of the market balancing itself to produce goods and services at the most efficient quantity and price.

Section 3.11

1. **Discuss some reasons why there is a disparity between the earnings of men and women.**

   Some fundamental factors that may contribute to the disparity between the earnings of men and women are experience and educational attainment.

   Another factor that affects women's earning capacity is the decision of whether to have a family or not. Women traditionally shoulder most of the burden for child care and household chores, although that is changing as more men choose to either be stay-at-home dads or contribute more equally to the child care and household duties. The breaks in careers to allow for child birth and rearing impact the amount of experience a woman has at the same age as a man. If a woman takes two years to have children, then returns to work, she has two years less professional experience on her resume, which may put her at a disadvantage against others who did not take a break from work. Women also tend to take the burden of elder care when aging parents require assistance. This role can also lead to a break in service from a profession. This can put a woman at a disadvantage, especially in rapidly changing, highly technical fields.

2. **Describe how the wage gap is becoming narrower. Do you think the wage gap will ever be totally closed? Why or why not?**

   Women have been gaining traction in the business world by increasing their education achievements. Many women are also choosing to delay having children, which allows them to work and gain experience. However, the time a parent (male or female) takes off to raise children affects the wages they are likely to earn when they want to return to the workplace. They have been working at raising children, but not in their professions, so they technically have less experience and are likely to be paid a lower wage than others who did not take time off for childrearing.

3. **Define how net gains or losses of jobs are used to assess the health of the economy.**

The economy is a dynamic system. As companies are started or fail, jobs are created or lost. Job creation and loss also occur with expansion or contraction of an industry, changes in technology, development of new industries, and the decline of long-time industries. The government constantly monitors the number of jobs created or lost and reports these statistics on a regular basis. If the number of jobs created is greater than the number lost, the economy is likely to be healthy. However, if the number of jobs lost is greater than the number created, it means people are less able to find work and that the economy is weak.

4. **Discuss the relationship between job stress and wages. Be sure to include comments on sources of job stress and how job stress sometimes leads to higher wages.**

Job stress is a part of life for everyone who works. The National Institute of Occupational Safety and Health (NIOSH) studies stress levels in the workplace. NIOSH did a large study in the 1990s to better understand the factors that lead to job stress. An interesting finding is that job stress is more closely linked with health problems than with financial or family problems. In fact, the NIOSH report on the 1990s study indicated that 40% of workers reported that their jobs were very or extremely stressful, and 75% of employees believe that workers have more stress now than they did a generation ago.

Job stress can lead to health problems, stress, behavioral problems, and even violence. Job stress can result from insecurity about continued employment or working too many hours. Job stress results in health problems, such as migraines, back and neck pain, more frequently than financial or family problems. Some high stress jobs demand a higher wage. For example, a person working third shift is paid a night differential for the stress and inconvenience of working at night. There are some jobs that actually pay hazardous duty pay, such as when military members are in a combat zone.

Section 3.12

1. **Discuss Karl Marx's basic economic theory.**

Marx was a student of history and came to believe that capitalism produces internal tensions that eventually lead to its destruction. He developed the concept of communism, which, in its ideal form, is a classless society in which everyone has their needs met and the government is run by the proletariat (the people). Marx authored the "Communist Manifesto," "Das Kapital" and the "Economic and Philosophical Manuscripts of 1844."

Marx was very interested in the relationship between people and the fundamental resource of their own labor power. He felt that giving up one's ability to transform the world (being paid for work) was the same as being alienated from one's own nature, resulting in a spiritual loss. He used the term commodity fetishism to describe this concept, which includes the idea that the things people produce seem to have life and movement of their own, to which humans adapt.

Marx continued to develop this concept and argued that commodity fetishism and the alienation of people from their own labor are the defining features of capitalism. Prior to capitalism rising in Europe, people were self-sufficient, meaning that they used their labor to produce the things they needed to survive. Marx argued that Europe moved to a capitalist society when labor became a commodity. The peasants were able to sell their labor as a commodity, and soon had to sell their labor because they no longer owned land, so they had to obtain work to survive. Marx called those who had to sell their labor the proletariat and those who buy the labor and control the resources required for production, are called capitalists, or the bourgeois.

2. **How does Marx's economic theory relate to capitalism?**

Capitalists, according to Marxist thinking, take advantage of the difference between the labor market and the market for the product being manufactured. He called the difference between the sale price and the production cost per unit surplus value and argued that the surplus value had its origin in surplus labor. Marx defined surplus labor as the difference between what it costs to keep a worker alive and the amount of goods the worker can produce. He believed that the surplus value of labor is the source of profits, and that the rate of profit would fall as the economy grew under a capitalist market.

He considered the capitalists the most revolutionary class in history because they were always reinventing and improving the manufacturing processes and technologies. He was concerned that they would invest more in machines than in labor and would eventually be in crisis as a result of not investing in labor. He believed the cycle of growth, collapse and growth would result in the enrichment of the capitalists and the marginalization of the proletariat (the workers). As a result of this belief, he felt that the proletariat should take control of the means of production (factories, etc.) to protect the production system from the periods of crisis he felt the capitalists would cause to happen. Marx was willing to pursue the revolution required to transition countries from the capitalist society to rule by the proletariat using either peaceful or violent means.

3. **Why has Marxist economic theory not succeeded?**

While communism is a good idea from an academic perspective, it does not work well when applied to society. Centralized socialist economies, as described by Marx, have proven to be far less efficient in producing the goods and services required by the people. In other words, they are less efficient at producing the greatest good for the greatest number than capitalist systems. Additionally, worker's incomes (real income) have risen over time, meaning that workers are sharing in the growth of the economy and the profits of the company. The distribution of profit may not be equal, but it is there.

1. **Describe why the state of the economy in the 1980s and 1990s had a negative effect on union membership.**

   The economic conditions of the 1980s and 1990s led to a reduction in the power of organized labor (unions). Fewer people were members of the work force. In 1945, more than 33% of employees belonged to unions. By 1979, that percent fell to 24.1% and further declined to 13.9 percent by 1989.

   The National Labor Relations Board rulings and court decisions about employees' rights to withhold the portion of their union dues used to influence political candidates reduced union influence. The unions therefore had fewer resources to use in their efforts to influence political campaigns. Another influence that has reduced the power of unions is increased foreign and domestic competition. Management, which has the goal of maintaining the viability and profitability of the company, is less willing to give in to union demands for increased wages and benefits than they were in the past.

   Management has become much more aggressive when opposing establishment of unions (organization of workers). Management became much more willing to employ strike breakers when unions went on strike in the 1980s and 1990s. Management would then retain the strike breakers as employees rather than rehiring the striking union workers. This reduced the effectiveness of the strike as a way of getting additional wages for the union members. It doesn't matter if you win the negotiation if you don't have a job. Part of the reason management changed its approach was President Reagan's 1981 decision to fire illegally striking air traffic controllers employed by the Federal Aviation Administration.

   The shift from manufacturing to service industry employment has been a challenge for labor unions. The service industry unions tend to be weaker and the service industry employees traditionally less willing to join a union. This demographic includes women, young people, temporary, and part-time workers. The service sector also has the largest number of new jobs created over the past several years. This combination has reduced the influence of unions.

   Relocation of industry from the northeast to the south and west parts of the U.S. has reduced union influence, as well, because the southern and western U.S. states have a weaker tradition of union membership and power than the northern or eastern parts of the US.

   Some of the biggest reasons for the unions' loss of influence are the extensive negative publicity about corruption in the Teamsters Union and others. Despite the unions' success in increasing working wages and benefits, and improving working conditions, younger workers do not feel they need a union to represent them. The independent-minded younger workers are not interested in belonging to an organization that they feel limits their independence in their work.

The economy of the late 1990s was so strong that the unemployment rate fell to 4.1%, a record low. This had a negative effect on union membership because the people who wanted jobs had them. Only the chronically unemployed and those between jobs were out of work.

2. **Discuss how automation has affected union workers and what the unions have done to help the workers retain their jobs.**

Automation has been an ongoing challenge for unions and union members. As technology develops more efficient labor-saving devices to perform tasks previously performed by union workers, the need for workers has declined. Examples are robotics on production lines. Unions had some success in protecting jobs and incomes against reductions in staffing due to automation. A few of these successes are free retraining, shorter work weeks to share the available work among employees, and guaranteed annual incomes.

3. **Why do people join unions?**

Unions function by collecting dues from their members and using those resources to negotiate with management for increased wages and benefits. The reason people joined unions was to gain better wages and benefits, as well as job security and improved working conditions. The unions also work hard to maintain political influence, which they accomplish by contributing to political campaigns and working to encourage people to vote. The political power has declined less than union membership because of the relationships the unions have established with political parties and offices. This power is not directly related to membership levels.

Section 3.14

1. **Describe the primary goals of unions.**

The unions worked hard to improve conditions and wages for working Americans, with great success. If negotiations with management did not result in an agreement, the unions would organize strikes, boycotts and protests to bring the situation of the worker to the attention of others and pressure corporate management to accede to the union demands for improved working conditions, wages, and benefits.

2. **Discuss why corporate management resisted union organization.**

Corporate management resisted union organization because a unionized shop was more expensive to run than a non-union shop. This was a threat to profit and to producing goods and services at a competitive price.

3. **Describe how unions gained political influence and were able to help improve worker wages, benefits and conditions.**

Samuel Gompers founded the American Federation of Labor in 1886. The American Federation of Labor (AFL) pushed for more effective union organization to protect workers from changes in the workplace resulting from introduction of automation, subdivision of labor, the use of women and children as labor and the lack of an apprentice system for the skilled trades. The AFL was a federation of unions that represented only skilled workers.

Initially, federal intervention in strikes was harsh. The 1894 Pullman Strike in Chicago resulted in 125,000 railroad workers engaging in a sympathy strike. The government swore in 3,400 special deputies and President Cleveland using federal forces to break the strike. The sympathy strike was ended by a federal court injunction and many of the railroad workers who participated in the strike were blacklisted. The injunction became the key legal weapon used against unions and their efforts to organize and take action in support of the workers.

President Theodore Roosevelt took a different approach to strike resolution in response to the 1902 strike of anthracite coal miners, who were part of the United Mine Workers union. Over 100,000 miners called a strike on May 12 of that year. The mines they worked, which were in Northeastern Pennsylvania, were closed all summer as a result of the strike. Negotiations were unsuccessful and the mine owners refused a request for arbitration, which would have used a third party to help negotiate and finalize the labor agreement. On October 16, President Roosevelt appointed a commission of mediation and arbitration. This commission was charged with developing new terms of employment for the workers. The miners returned to their jobs in 5 days, and 5 months later received a 10% wage increase and shorter work days. They did not, however, obtain the formal union recognition they wanted.

Unions have played a key role in improving safety of workspaces. The 1911 Triangle Shirtwaist Company fire in New York killed about 150 employees, most of which were young women. The workers were unable to escape from the building because the safety exits were locked shot. This was the driving force behind Frances Perkins" efforts to reform industrial safety and fire prevention measures.

Congress created the U.S. Department of Labor (DOL) at the urging of the AFL. The mandate of the DOL is to protect and extend the rights of wage earners. The Clayton Act of 1914 clarified that "the labor of a human being is not a commodity or article of commerce." This is crucial because it means that labor was not subject to the Sherman Act provisions that had been used in the past to prevent union organization. The Clayton Act legalized strikes, boycotts, and peaceful picketing, as well as limiting the use of injunctions in labor disputes.

The Committee for Industrial Organization (CIO) was created in 1935 by John L Lewis. The CIO was composed of about a dozen leaders of AFL unions, with the goal of continuing to develop industrial unions. Industrial unions are different in that they organize an entire industry regardless of skill set or skill level, so they represented unskilled workers. Lewis began to verbally attack his colleagues on the AFL Executive Council, which led to expulsion of the CIO unions from the AFL. The CIO reorganized into the Congress of Industrial Organizations in 1938. The CIO was incredibly successful in organizing large sectors of American industry and continued to gain membership.

During World War II, the AFL and CIO began to work together on some issues, while agreeing to disagree on others. Eventually, this cooperation led to a merger of the two labor groups, which occurred in 1955 when they became the AFL-CIO.

This merger led to further organization of workers in areas and industries where the workers did not have labor representation or had resisted unions.

4. **Why has the membership and influence of unions declined since the 1970s?**

The technology shift that has occurred since the 1970s has made our economy less reliant on factory jobs and resulted in a more highly educated work force that tends to work in professional, white-collar jobs.

Section 3.15

1. **Describe how working conditions in America have improved as a result of union efforts.**

Labor unions can be credited for significant improvements in American working conditions. Unions have been influential in shortening the work day, improving workplace safety, and improving wages and benefits.

Improved working conditions include basic things such as temperature (heating and cooling), scheduled breaks and lunch times, increased wages and improved benefits packages, fire safety, ergonomics and general safety, job training, protection against unfair labor practices, and increased job security.

2. **Define collective bargaining.**

The unions and management negotiated improved working conditions through a process called collective bargaining. The collective bargaining process involves negotiation between union representatives, who represent the collective (the group of workers), and management, which represents the company. Collective bargaining includes the union making demands for certain improvements in wages, benefits, working conditions, etc., of management. Management evaluates the demands and decides whether to accept or reject them. The management decision is then presented to the union representatives, who respond. This process continues until either agreement is reached or they are at a stalemate. If agreement is reached, production continues and business is uninterrupted. If the two sides are unable to come to an agreement on terms, the union may organize a strike, boycott or other action to pressure management into accepting the union demands.

3. **Discuss how collective bargaining is affected by market conditions.**

Collective bargaining is affected by the economy in which it happens. If, for example, the product of the company has a strong and increasing demand, management is going to be more willing to accept significant increases in pay or other benefits. On the other hand, if the market for the product is weak, the company will not be willing to accept increases in labor costs. This is a result of the law of supply and demand. If there is high demand for the product, the equilibrium point for the value of labor will be higher because the company will still make profit even if they are paying more for labor. However, if demand for the product drops, demand for labor drops, and the company will make an economic decision to reject union demands. If the union representatives and management are unable to come to an agreement in this environment, the company is more likely to reduce production, resulting in job losses for the union members.

An Easy Introduction to Economics: Microeconomics Answer Key Unit 4

Section 4.1

1. **Describe the difference between scarcity and poverty.**

   Scarcity drives economics. The more scarce a demanded resource is, the higher its value. If a resource is scarce, but there is no demand, the value does not increase. Scarcity is NOT the same as poverty. Scarcity affects all economic systems regardless of wealth. Poverty is a situation in which people cannot meet their basic needs of food, shelter and clothing. These are two different concepts. As an example, if only one of a certain model of luxury car is produced, it is a scarce good. The only people who will be able to consider purchasing it, however, are those with enough disposable income to allow them to choose to purchase the vehicle. Poverty means that the consumer is often choosing between necessities, such as when people choose between the medications they require to survive and the food they require to survive.

2. **Explain why economists consider all resources to be scarce.**

   Scarce resources include the raw materials, labor, and infrastructure required for production of goods and services. Resources we all need to survive and thrive, such as clean air, clean water, healthy food, green spaces, leisure, and time, are scarce resources. Economists consider all resources scarce because humans want more resources than are freely available from nature. Some of these limited resources are also called economic goods.

3. **Discuss the concept of opportunity cost using an example different than the one presented in the text.**

   Scarcity of resources leads to the concept of choice. Choice means people have to choose one option over another. Opportunity cost is the cost of lost opportunities. The choice to do one thing is also a choice to NOT do another thing. Opportunity cost is the highest valued option that is not selected because another option is chosen.

   Any example, except the value of time, is acceptable as long as it shows an understanding of the concept of opportunity cost.

1. **Discuss the differences between a free market economy and a centrally planned economy.**

   The extremes of the economic models are the centrally planned economy (total government control) and the free market economy (no government control).

   In a centrally planned economy, the government owns the factors of production and determines what is produced and how much is produced. The market does not influence a pure centrally-planned economy.

   A free market economy relies on the forces of supply and demand to determine the availability of goods and the price of those goods. In a pure free market economy, the market experiences no other interference, such as government regulation, so it is extremely efficient.

2. **Why does no country succeed in achieving a fully free economy or a fully centrally planned economy?**

   The free market requires some oversight to ensure consumer safety and fair economic practices on the part of producers and vendors of products. The centrally planned economy is not possible because of the wide variety of economic activity that humans engage in. Imagine trying to control the sale of goods between individuals. It is not possible. People will find a way to make trades for what they need if a centrally planned government does not provide it.

3. **Describe how a country might transition from a centrally planned economy to a free market economy. Be sure to discuss some of the social and governmental influences that influence this process.**

   Many of the eastern European countries have economies that are transforming from centrally planned communist/socialist economies into capitalist economies. As they transition through the state capitalism and state regulated capitalism toward free enterprise, the industries are moved from government ownership to private ownership and often result in a blended economy that reflects some of the former economic system combined with the new economic model. The success of individual countries in making this transition varies. The reasons for the variability are the current government, the ability and willingness of the people to adapt from the centrally planned economy to a free-market economy, and the resources the country has to use in making the transition. A country with abundant natural, technical, and human resources will probably be more successful in transitioning to a free market system than a country with limited resources.

   Alternatively, countries can move from a free-market economy to a more restricted economic system. This occurs when the government imposes new regulations to ensure consumer safety, financial ethics, and other concerns.

1. **Describe how a centrally planned economy is organized. Who makes the decisions? Who owns the resources?**

Centrally planned economies are often described using the political terms of socialism or communism. The primary differences between a centrally planned economy and a free market economy are who owns and controls the means of production and who determines resource allocation. A centrally planned economy includes a government that owns and controls the means of production (factories, natural resources, etc.) and also determines the allocation of resources to suit the goals of the government. An economy of this type represents the idea that society's economic affairs belong in the public, rather than the private, sector of the economy.

The physical resources in a socialist economy are owned by the state. Workers retain the right to sell their labor and gain the benefit of the wage they earn. Because the physical resources belong to the state, all of the profits resulting from the use of those resources go to the state. The state also makes the decisions about resource allocation and use in the economy.

A socialist economy has the following traits:

Property rights	Physical (nonhuman) resources are owned by the state.
Employment	Government or government-controlled cooperatives provide employment opportunities.
Investment	The central planners determine investment strategies that support the objectives they have established for the economy.
Allocation of goods and resources	The central planners allocate all goods and resources.
Income Distribution	The central planners determine income distribution to meet their goals of equality or some other income distribution pattern.

2. **Explain the problems encountered in centrally planned economies. What can happen in the production process? How are consumers affected?**

Often, the output of one state enterprise (steel, for example) was a raw material for another state enterprise (tank factory, for example). If the steel enterprise was unable to meet its production goals, it would directly impact the ability of the tank factory to meet its production goals. In a free market, the steel would increase in price until a new market equilibrium was reached. In a socialist economy, resources are allocated by law and the market does not have an impact on the allocation of resources.

Another problem that could arise was the build-up of bottlenecks in the system. If production of a critical component was halted because of a natural disaster or some other disruptive event, it would cause a bottleneck at the next stage of production because the system did not allow the state enterprise to have alternate sources in place for emergency situations.

The managers of the production facilities were motivated by a combination of reward and punishment. If the production manager was able to meet all of the goals set by the central planning committee, he might receive a bonus and maybe even a promotion. If, however, he failed to meet the quota, he would probably be demoted even if he did his best to meet the goals set by the central planning committee. This led to an emphasis on quantity over quality. In addition to the obvious problem of the production of potential poor quality goods, the managers worked to get the central committee to set low production goals and falsify reports to show higher production than actually occurred to make the factory look good to the central committee.

An interesting result of the wage discrepancies combined with the special privileges of the elite (easy access to cars, special stores that offered products unavailable to the average person, etc.) was that the elite had access to almost anything they wanted, but the common person was unable to get even the basics. The elite were insulated from the shortages of consumer goods because they were treated differently and allowed different access to the goods and services they wanted and needed. The shortages of consumer goods for the average person were a direct result of the production goals and resource allocation established by the central planning committee. Interestingly, the members of the central planning committee were counted among the elite members of society, so they did not often experience the shortages that most of the USSR citizens had to endure. A second interesting result of the central committee's resource allocation and goal setting was that there were surpluses of other products on the shelves of the same stores that had shortages of basic goods. The surplus products may have been poorly made or too expensive, so the consumers did not purchase them.

3. **Discuss the economy of the former USSR and explain how centralized planning and the focus on defense spending impacted all of the sectors of the economy.**

An example of a large centralized economy was that of the former Union of Soviet Socialist Republics (USSR). The USSR was a huge country that was a union of many eastern European countries and had a socialist government. The economy of the USSR is called a command economy, meaning that the central planning committee, called Gosplan, would draft both annual and long-range (5 years) economic plans, which would then be written into law by the Soviet Government. Gosplan economic plans impacted more than 200,000 different state-owned enterprises, setting production targets and allocating resources (raw materials, production capacity, labor, etc.) to each state enterprise. The success of the state enterprise in using the allocated resources to meet the production targets was evaluated and used as the basis for rewarding the enterprise.

The production of goods is one area where the economy of the USSR was inefficient. The wages workers earned were also inefficiently used. First, the wage discrepancies were significant, but not as large as the discrepancies in the U.S. The socialist goal was to provide for each according to his need and get from each according to his skill. In other words, each person would do whatever job he or she was able to do and each person would receive from government everything that he or she needs. In reality, there were wage discrepancies, ranging from twice to many times that of the basic laborer, depending upon the rank of the individual worker.

In most cases, private enterprise was forbidden in the Soviet economy. There were a couple of exceptions, however. The private enterprise allowed was provision of personal services and some agricultural activities. Those who were allowed to moonlight in addition to their day jobs were professionals, such as teachers and physicians, and skilled laborers, such as tailors and painters. These people were allowed to sell their services directly to private individuals. The permitted agricultural activity was the establishment of collectives to grow agricultural products on private plots. Each person was allowed to use about an acre of land, on average, and all the goods grown on that land could be sold in the market at whatever price the market would bear. These were the only parts of the Soviet economy where the forces of the free market were active.

Section 4.4

1. **List the three agencies that collect and analyze economic data for the federal government and the key economic indicators reported.**

   The key data collection and analysis agencies are the Federal Reserve, Bureau of Economic Analysis, and Bureau of Labor Statistics. These three agencies collate, analyze, and publish statistics on the U.S. economy on a regular schedule. The statistics published by these agencies are further analyzed by various industries and used as a basis for planning future activities. Certain trends in the statistics are considered favorable or unfavorable for the economy.

   Key economic indicators include GDP growth, unemployment, interest rates and cycles, inflations, housing starts and sales, auto sales, and retail sales.

2. **Describe how key economic indicators are used to assess the health of the economy.**

   Some of the most important measures are called key economic indicators. These include GDP growth (gross domestic product growth), unemployment, inflation, interest rate movements and cycles, the interest rate cycle, housing starts and sales, retail sales and auto sales.

   GDP growth is the major indicator watched by economists. This statistic is reported monthly, but the quarterly numbers are watched most closely. The Bureau of Economic Analysis (BEA) generates quarterly reports that measure growth in real GDP. It means that the statistics from each quarter are directly comparable due to adjustments for seasonality. The quarterly numbers are also averaged over the three-month period, which provides a longer-term perspective on the short-term fluctuations in the market. Daily ups and downs have less impact over a longer period of time than a shorter one so trends become more apparent. GDP growth is compared to the growth rate from the same quarter of the previous year, as well as to the prior month in the current year. The average annual growth of GDP is three percent, so figures that show higher growth than that represent an economic expansion and figures lower than that may indicate an economic contraction.

Unemployment is strongly linked with economic expansion and contraction. As unemployment increases, economic contraction tends to occur. Conversely, as unemployment decreases, the economy is more likely to expand. Some of the specific measures related to unemployment are jobs lost, jobs created, and net job loss or gain.

Inflation is a major concern of all economists and those who want to maintain a healthy economy. The Fed responds to economic trends by tightening or loosening its economic policy. Increases in inflation that are out of the ordinary may cause the Fed to tighten its policy. The Consumer Price Index (CPI) and the Produce Price Index (PPI) are the two key measures of inflation. The rate of inflation is reflected by the CPI. The PPI is used as an indicator of future trends because it reflects increases in the costs of production, which are eventually passed on to the consumers.

Interest rate movements indicate business outlook because the cost of borrowing money is a big consideration in making an investment decision. Low costs encourage borrowing and high costs discourage borrowing. Key interest rates are the fed funds rate, the prime rate, and the fixed rate for a 30-year home mortgage.

The interest rate cycle is intimately linked with the business cycle. The business cycle includes recovery (low interest rates), expansion (rising rates that peak at the height of the expansion), and then contraction (falling interest rates). When money is cheap, people and businesses are more likely to borrow and when it is expensive, they are less likely to borrow.

Consumer confidence is reflected by the statistics on housing starts and sales and auto sales. Housing is a huge investment for any consumer, one of the biggest purchases most families make. The consumer must be confident of continued employment and ability to make the mortgage payments before committing to a purchase that will take 30 years to pay for. Retail sales, including car sales, are also a good indicator of consumer confidence. People spend more when they feel confident of their economic situation.

3. **Explain how the government attempts to influence business cycles. Discuss a specific change in fiscal policy that the government might implement if the economy is contracting and a specific change that the government might implement during an expansion and describe how the change is expected to impact the economy.**

Governments attempt to influence business cycles using fiscal policy. Fiscal policy is the policy the government established and modifies in an effort to support economic growth. In order to establish fiscal policy, the government collects data on many different sectors of the U.S. and international economies. The data are then analyzed and interpreted by economists and other experts to understand how the economy is actually working.

Keep in mind that government spending in the U.S. is more than 25% of total spending. This means that government fiscal policy can affect the economy. If government spending increases, the money flows through the economy as the workers make purchases with the wages they earn. If government spending decreases, the flow of money through the economy will slow down.

There are four key tools the government uses to affect the economy. The use of these tools is driven by fiscal policy. The tools include implementing taxes, raising or lowering taxes, borrowing money, or printing money.

The government is able to affect its revenue, which is the amount of money it has to spend, by implementing new taxes or changing existing taxes. Increases in taxes will provide the government more revenue, but may not stimulate the economy because increased taxes reduce the money available for the consumer and business to spend on goods and services. Reductions in tax, although they reduce the short-term revenue collected by the government, are often implemented to stimulate the economy because of the trade-off between short-term loss and long-term gains from the taxes paid for goods and services rather than in income tax.

The government may also raise funds by issuing bonds, which are a form of a loan from the consumer to the government. The consumer pays less than face value for the bond in return for being able to receive full face value when the bond matures and is redeemed.

Finally, printing more money obviously puts more money into the economy, but also has the potential of increasing the inflation rate because the dollar is worth relatively less than it was before the money was added to the economy.

Section 4.5

1. **List the three primary forms of elasticity and discuss how they differ.**

There are three basic types of elasticity: unitary elasticity, elasticity, and inelasticity.

Unitary elasticity occurs when changes in demand resulting from a change in price for the good or service always result in the same revenues. The chart below shows unitary elasticity of demand for a good. Point A on the chart shows the starting price and demand for the product. Point A_1 shows the increase in demand resulting from a price reduction and Point A_2 shows the decrease in demand resulting from a price increase.

Price change	Price	Quantity	Revenue
Original (A)	$1.00	150	$150
Price decreases (A₁)	$0.75	200	$150
Price increases (A₂)	$2.00	75	$150

Elasticity occurs when price increases decrease demand or price decreases increase demand for a good or service. This is an inverse relationship, meaning that as one value increase, the other decreases and vice versa. Providers usually reduce prices to increase quantity, therefore increasing revenue. Keep in mind that the producer/seller of the good or service must recover the costs or producing the good or service and make profit, so the price is rarely less than the producer needs to recover costs. Occasionally, products will be designated as loss leaders, meaning that they are price below cost to draw people to a retail location with the expectation that they will be enough other products to recover the loss on the loss-leader product.

Price change	Price	Quantity	Revenue
Original (A)	$50	20	$1,000
Price decreases 50% (A₁)	$25	50	$1,250
Price increases 50% (A₂)	$75	5	$375

Inelasticity occurs when a reduction in price increases demand, but not to the point that would occur in unitary elasticity. Unity is the proportional change in quantity and revenue that occurs in unitary elasticity.

Price change	Price	Quantity	Revenue
Original (A)	$50	20	$1,000
Price decreases 50% (A₁)	$25	50	$1,250
Price increases 50% (A₂)	$75	5	$375

2. **Describe the difference between infinitely elastic demand and perfectly inelastic demand.**

Infinite elasticity occurs when the price for a good or service remains the same regardless of how much of that good or service is used. Examples include monthly internet service charges, gym memberships, and telephone service packages that cost the same each month regardless of how much you use them. Infinite elasticity is shown as a straight horizontal line with price on the y axis and quantity on the x axis.

Perfect inelasticity is similar to infinite elasticity except that it shows that the quantity of a good or service demanded will not change regardless of price. This is shown as a vertical line with price on the y axis and quantity on the x axis.

3. **Explain the four primary considerations of a company in making pricing decisions.**

First, companies have to recover the cost of production of a good or service. This includes recovering all physical plant and infrastructure costs, which are also known as sunk costs, as well as the costs of the raw material, labor, and overhead associated with the product.

Secondly, they will determine whether or not there are good substitutes available for their products.

Third, the short- and long-run demand for the good or service must be taken into consideration.

Fourth, the price of the product as a percentage of income is a key factor in its elasticity. The higher the price of a good or service is, the higher the elasticity of demand for that good or service.

Section 4.6

1. **List the production costs of a firm and describe each.**

Fixed costs are those that the firm will incur regardless of the number of units of a good or service produced.

Variable costs are those that the firm will incur more of less of depending upon the level of production.

Direct costs are those that can be directly attributed to a unit of a good or service.

Indirect costs are those that cannot be directly attributed to a unit of a good.

Sunk costs are those that have been incurred based on past decisions. These are also called historical costs. These costs are real, but should have no direct influence on current decisions. The outcome of the past decision should provide information to help with current decision-making processes, but the costs are no longer relevant.

Total costs are the sum of all of the costs of production of a good or service. Total costs are the sum of the fixed and variable costs. The equation that shows this relationship is: $TC = VC + FC$ where TC = total costs, VC = variable costs, and FC = fixed costs for a specific number of units.

Marginal cost is the increase in total cost divided by the increase in the number of units. In our table above, the marginal cost is calculated by determining the difference in total costs between levels of production and dividing that by the increase in the number of units produced.

2. **Calculate the marginal cost, average fixed cost, average variable cost, and average total cost for the production levels below.**

Quantity	Fixed Costs	Variable Costs	Total Costs	Marginal Cost per Unit	Average Fixed Cost	Average Variable Cost	Average Total Cost
0	$1,000	$0	$1,000	n/a	n/a	n/a	n/a
25	$1,000	$400	$1,400	$16.00/ unit	$40.00/ unit	$16.00/ unit	$56.00/ unit
50	$1,000	$775	$1,775	$15.00/ unit	$20.00/ unit	$15.50/ unit	$35.50/ unit
75	$1,000	$1,100	$2,100	$13.00/ unit	$13.33/ unit	$14.67/ unit	$28.00/ unit
100	$1,000	$1,300	$2,300	$8.00/ unit	$10.00/ unit	$13.00/ unit	$23.00/ unit
150	$1,000	$1,450	$2,450	$3.00/ unit	$6.67/ unit	$9.67/ unit	$16.33/ unit

$MC = (TC_{new} - TC_{previous}) \div \Delta Q$, where MC = Marginal cost of production, TC_{new} is the total cost at the new production level, $TC_{previous}$ is the total cost at the prior production level, and ΔQ is the change in the number of units.

Calculations

Quantity = 0: There is no marginal cost per unit because no units have been produced. No averages can be calculated, either, because no units have been produced.

Quantity = 25:

$MC = (\$1,400 - \$1,000) \div 25$
$MC = \$400 \div 25$
$MC = \$16.00 / unit$

$AFC = \$1,000 \div 25$
$AFC = \$40.00 / unit$

$AVC = \$400 \square 25$
$AVC = \$16.00 / unit$

$ATC = \$1,400 \div 25$
$ATC = \$56.00 / unit$

Quantity = 50

$$MC = (\$1,775 - \$1,400) \div 25$$
$$MC = \$375 \div 25$$
$$MC = \$15.00 / unit$$

$$AFC = \$1,000 \div 50$$
$$AFC = \$20.00 / unit$$

$$AVC = \$775 \div 50$$
$$AVC = \$15.50 / unit$$

$$ATC = \$1,775 \div 50$$
$$ATC = \$35.50 / unit$$

Quantity = 75

$$MC = (\$2,100 - \$1,775) \div 25$$
$$MC = \$325 \div 25$$
$$MC = \$13.00 / unit$$

$$AFC = \$1,000 \div 75$$
$$AFC = \$13.33 / unit$$

$$AVC = \$1,100 \div 75$$
$$AVC = \$14.67 / unit$$

$$ATC = \$2,100 \div 75$$
$$ATC = \$28.00 / unit$$

Quantity = 100

$$MC = (\$2,300 - \$2,100) \div 25$$
$$MC = \$200 \div 25$$
$$MC = \$8.00 / unit$$

$$AFC = \$1,000 \div 100$$
$$AFC = \$10.00 / unit$$

$$AVC = \$1,300 \div 100$$
$$AVC = \$13.00 \,/\, unit$$

$$ATC = \$2,300 \div 100$$
$$ATC = \$23.00 \,/\, unit$$

Quantity = 150

$$MC = (\$2,450 - \$2,300) \div 50$$
$$MC = \$150 \div 50$$
$$MC = \$3.00 \,/\, unit$$

$$AFC = \$1,000 \div 150$$
$$AFC = \$6.67 \,/\, unit$$

$$AVC = \$1,450 \div 150$$
$$AVC = \$9.67 \,/\, unit$$

$$ATC = \$2,450 \div 150$$
$$ATC = \$16.33 \,/\, unit$$

Section 4.7

1. **Describe how a company decides the amount of labor required to produce its product.**

   Production level is an important decision. The number of units of each good produced affects the firm's profitability. The firm wants to maximize profitability, which means setting production at a level that will meet, but not exceed demand at market equilibrium. Market equilibrium is the price and quantity demanded that maximizes both profit and consumer interest in the product. The firm will use the amount of labor required to produce the quantity of goods demanded at equilibrium.

2. **List the three considerations for maximizing profitability and discuss how they interact.**

   The business owner has to consider three things to maximize profitability. The first is the cost structure of the business. The second consideration is finding the right mix of fixed and variable inputs. The third consideration is minimizing total costs by using the most efficient combination of inputs to produce the good provided by the company. This is measured in marginal product per dollar, both for fixed and variable inputs. Marginal product per dollar is the amount of additional output (product) produced by the last dollar spent on input. Costs are minimized where the marginal product per dollar for the variable inputs is equal to the marginal product per dollar for the fixed inputs. If the marginal cost (total of fixed and variable costs) of the last unit produced is greater than the price the good will demand on the market, the company loses money. On the other hand, if the marginal cost is lower than the price the market will bear for the product, the company is not maximizing profits because it is not producing enough units of the product. The company will make a profit as long as the marginal revenue (the money made by selling one more unit of the product) is greater than the marginal cost of producing that unit. Profit is maximized where marginal cost per unit is equal to the price per unit charged to the consumer.

3. **Explain how a company sets output levels. What are some of the key considerations?**

Marginal product is the output resulting from the addition of a unit of labor. If the relationship between total product and units of labor is linear, each additional unit of labor will result in a consistent increase in the total product output.

Average product is the total output divided by the units of labor. The goal is to maximize efficiency of production, which means maximizing the number of products produced per unit of labor (average product). As more people are hired, the fixed physical resources available for production are divided among more workers until the point where the fixed resources are unable to support the capacity of the labor force, so workers are unable to work at their full capacity.

The law of diminishing returns begins to take effect at this point. The law of diminishing returns states that as units of variable input, such as labor, are added to a production process with a fixed resource, the marginal return will increase to a point, and then decrease. The marginal product curve intersects the average product curve at its maximum.

As with other variable inputs, the company will choose to set inputs at the point where marginal utility is maximized.

Section 4.8

1. **List the three keys to maximizing profitability.**

The three key considerations to maximizing profitability are cost structure, mix of inputs, and minimizing total costs.

2. **Describe how marginal product per dollar is used to maximize profitability.**

Marginal product per dollar is the amount of additional output (product) produced by the last dollar spent on either a variable or fixed input. Costs are minimized where the marginal product per dollar for the variable inputs is equal to the marginal product per dollar for the fixed inputs.

Profit is maximized where marginal cost per unit is equal to the price per unit charged to the consumer.

3. **Explain what happens when the price of the inputs required for production increase or decrease.**

The availability and price of the inputs are subject to the same laws of supply and demand as the final product. If the inputs become more scarce, assuming demand stays the same, the price demanded for the inputs will increase. Alternatively, if the inputs become more available, again assuming demand stays the same the price demanded for the inputs will drop.

Section 4.9

1. **Define price floor and state why a price floor might be established.**

Price floors are minimum prices for specific goods or services that are established by law.

Price floors are established to keep the price of a good above its equilibrium point to ensure that there is a surplus of goods on the market.

2. **Define price ceiling and state why a price ceiling might be established.**

Price ceilings are maximum prices for specific goods or services that are established by law. Price ceilings are used to keep prices below the equilibrium point so suppliers produce less than consumers demand.

3. **What are the secondary effects of price ceilings and price floors?**

The secondary effects of price ceilings are shortages and reduction in the quality of goods available.

Secondary effects of price floors are surpluses of goods on the market and buyers who are more selective than they would be if the price were set at market equilibrium. This can result in easier credit, price breaks on other products, and/or better customer service.

Section 4.10

1. **Describe cause and effect relationships.**

Cause and effect relationships are those that require a specific event or condition to occur before the effect is seen. In the economic world, a price increase is a direct result (effect) of an increase in the cost of the inputs or an increase in demand. Likewise, a price decrease is a direct result of either a reduction in the cost of the inputs or a reduction in demand for the good or service provided by the company.

2. **List and discuss the three criteria for establishing cause and effect relationships.**

There are three criteria that must be met: temporal (time) precedence, establishment of a relationship, and a lack of plausible alternative explanations for the effect.

1. *Time Precedence*: In order for a cause and effect relationship to be established, the relationship between the events must be established temporally (in time). In other words, an increase in the cost of inputs to a production process at time point A will result in an increase in price of the final product to the consumer at time point B. Cyclical functions, such as inflation and unemployment, may both cause each other and be affected by each other. In other words, inflation can cause unemployment and unemployment can cause inflation.

2. *Establishment of a Relationship*: Before you can establish a causal relationship, you have to first establish that a relationship of any sort exists. This is done by observation of both the cause and effect. If you observe that whenever X is present, Y is present, and when X is absent, Y is absent, you have established a relationship between X and Y. X (cause) must be present for Y (effect) to be present. A relationship (not necessarily causal) can be described as follows:

    a. if X then Y

    b. if not X then not Y.

3. *No plausible alternative explanations*: There may be other reasons (third variables) that explain the relationship. For example, you may think that you are in a microeconomics class because your teachers are trying to torture you. However, the desire to torture you would not be the cause of your enrollment in this course. The cause of your enrollment in microeconomics is actually that the course is a requirement for your graduation or that you chose to take the course because you are interested in the subject matter.

3. Explain how cause and effect relationships change the price of goods.

Changes in price are caused by a number of factors, including production costs, demand, supply, personal preferences, population, and the price of other goods (complements or substitutes).

1. *Changes in production costs:* Companies are in business to make a profit. The price of the good produced is based on the costs of the inputs required for production, as well as the demand for the good. If the cost of the inputs increases, the price the company charges to the consumer is likely to increase in order for the company to continue to earn a profit.

2. *Demand:* If demand for a product increases and supply remains the same, the price the market will bear for that product will increase. If demand decreases and supply remains constant, the price the market will bear for that product will decrease.

3. *Supply:* If supply of a product increases and demand remains constant, the price of the good will decrease. Likewise, if the supply of a product decreases and demand remains constant, the price of the good will increase.

4. *Personal Preferences:* Personal buying habits can be affected by social trends.

If the demand for a product increases and supply remains constant, the price demanded for that good will probably increase. If the demand for the product goes down and supply remains constant, the price of that good will probably decrease.

5. *Population changes:* Population increases or decreases affect consumption. More people will consume more products. Fewer people will consume less.

6. *The price of other goods:* Substitute products and complementary products affect the price of products. A substitute product is a product that is easily substituted for another. Complementary products are goods or services that are used in conjunction with other products.

Section 4.11

1. **Describe the profit motive.**

The profit incentive, also known as the profit motive, is the reason that companies are in business. Profit is the economic benefit gained by engaging in a specific activity. It is also the financial gain (the difference between price and cost of bringing the product to market) made by the producer.

2. **Explain what a company may do to increase profitability.**

Producers may be tempted to raise the price for a good or service to a point above the market equilibrium in an attempt to increase profits. They may also be tempted to produce goods of lower quality and charge the same price to increase profits. In a free market, these techniques will not work because the market will force the price to move to the equilibrium point where supply equals demand.

3. **How does a market that is not a free market allow prices to be set at levels that are not the most efficient based on supply and demand?**

In a market that is not a completely free market, other forces influence the price of a good or service. In an economy that has governmental restrictions, artificial controls on access to goods and services, finite resources or other forces that restrict free trade, there is an opportunity for prices to be set at a point higher than the free market would bear.

Section 4.12

1. **Describe the difference between total costs and per unit costs.**

Per unit costs are based on both fixed and variable costs of producing one unit of the good. Fixed costs are those that the company incurs regardless of the level of production and variable costs are those that are dependent on the number of units produced. Per unit costs tend to decrease as volume produced increases.

Total costs are based on the total fixed and variable costs of producing a good or service. Fixed costs include all of the costs the producer will incur regardless of the production level (number of units) of the company. These include building, equipment, heat, lights, and other overhead costs that remain the same regardless of production level. Variable costs are the additional costs incurred ffor producing all of the units of the good and vary with the number of units produced.

2. **State the equations used to calculate total costs and per unit costs.**

Total Costs: The equation for this calculation is: $TC = FC + (VC \times Q)$, where TC is total costs, FC is fixed costs, VC is variable costs per unit, and Q is quantity.

Per Unit Costs: In order to calculate the per-unit cost, we need to use the following equation: $UC = TC \div Q$, where UC is unit cost, TC is total cost, and Q is quantity.

3. **Determine the per-unit and total costs given the following variables:**

   a. Fixed Costs = $75,000

   b. Variable Costs = $12.00/unit

   c. Quantity in increments of 50, from 0 to 500.

Solution:

$$TC = FC + (VC \times Q)$$
$$UC = TC \div Q$$

Fixed Costs	Variable Costs	#Units	Total Costs	Per Unit Costs
$75,000	$12	0	$75,000	n/a
$75,000	$12	50	$75,600	$1,512
$75,000	$12	100	$76,200	$762
$75,000	$12	150	$76,800	$512
$75,000	$12	200	$77,400	$387
$75,000	$12	250	$78,000	$312
$75,000	$12	300	$78,600	$262
$75,000	$12	350	$79,200	$226
$75,000	$12	400	$79,800	$200
$75,000	$12	450	$80,400	$179
$75,000	$12	500	$81,000	$162

Section 4.13

1. **Define opportunity cost and give an example of an opportunity cost.**

Opportunity cost is the cost the company incurs by choosing to produce one product rather than another. Opportunity cost is a result of scarcity of resources and the resulting need to make trade-offs when deciding which goods and services to acquire or produce. Any example that shows the cost of choosing one option over another is acceptable.

2. **Define marginal cost and discuss how marginal cost can increase after a certain point in production.**

Marginal Cost is the change in total cost resulting from the production of each additional unit of a good or service. In most cases, the marginal cost per unit of product declines in the short term. In the long term, however, the marginal cost will increase because of the difficulty of using the same production capacity to produce more than the optimal number of units.

3. **Define sunk cost and explain why a sunk cost should not be considered in making current decisions.**

Sunk Costs are the costs associated with past decisions. These are also called historical costs. These costs do not have any influence on current decision-making except to provide knowledge that is relevant to making current decisions. Sunk costs are costs that have been incurred and the decision to incur the costs cannot be changed. This is why any decisions made by the company need to be made based the costs and benefits related to the current market conditions.

Section 4.14

1. **Describe how the profit incentive affects the price of a good or service.**

The total cost-total revenue method of determining maximum profit involves using total cost of production and total revenue to determine the profit-maximizing level of production.

2. **Generate and plot the price demand curve for the following product:**

a. The price at 0 demand is $25.00.

b. $P = 100 - .0003Q$.

c. Use increments of 20,000 from 0 to 80,000 units.

Demand	Price Per Unit
0	$25.00
20,000	$19.00
40,000	$13.00
60,000	$7.00
80,000	$1.00

Price-Demand Curve

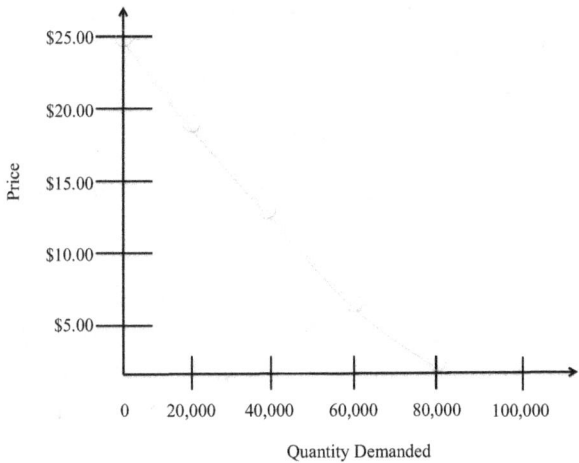

3. **Generate and plot the total revenue, total costs, and total profit curves.**

    a. Fixed costs are $50,000

    b. Variable costs are $1.25/unit

Demand	Price Per Unit	Fixed Costs	Variable Costs	Total Revenue	Total Costs	Total Profit
0	$25.00	$50,000	$1.25	$0	$50,000.00	-$50,000.00
20,000	$19.00	$50,000	$1.25	$380,000	$75,000.00	$305,000.00
40,000	$13.00	$50,000	$1.25	$520,000	$100,000.00	$420,000.00
60,000	$7.00	$50,000	$1.25	$420,000	$125,000.00	$295,000.00
80,000	$1.00	$50,000	$1.25	$80,000	$150,000.00	-$70,000.00

Total Cost, Total Revenue, and Total Profit Curves

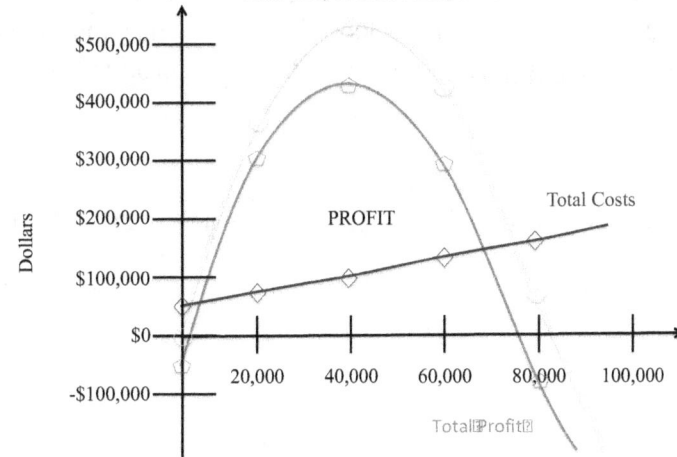

4. **Identify the production level that maximizes profits.**

The production level that maximizes profits is 40,000 units, which results in $520,000 in revenue and $420,000 in profit.

Section 4.15

1. **Define implicit and explicit costs and describe how they differ.**

Implicit costs are resources a company uses, but doesn't directly pay for, such as capital that could be earning a higher rate of return elsewhere. Explicit costs are also known as expenditure costs and include the costs of purchasing additional input that is not already owned by the company. Explicit costs can include both fixed and variable costs. If a company needs to add equipment, buildings, or other costs of production that are not variable once they are acquired, these are additional explicit fixed costs. Explicit variable costs include additional labor and inputs of production. Implicit costs are those costs related to inputs already owned by the firm, as well as the opportunity cost of pursuing a particular production goal. The total cost of a production activity is explicit costs plus implicit costs.

2. **Describe how labor and equipment contribute to marginal revenue product.**

In general, a firm will employ additional units of labor, equipment and other factors of production as long as the marginal revenue product (the additional revenue of a firm resulting from use of one additional unit of a production input) is greater than the marginal cost (the additional cost to the firm of utilizing that additional input of production).

3. **Describe how marginal revenue product is calculated and how it is used to determine the levels of production inputs.**

Marginal revenue product is the increase in revenue generated by an additional unit of labor. When an additional unit of labor brings the marginal revenue product to zero, adding a unit of labor actually increases production costs.

An Easy Introduction to Economics: Microeconomics Answer Key Unit 5

Section 5.1

1. **Describe the characteristics of the three types of economies: traditional, command, and market.**

A traditional economy has some unique characteristics. Resources are typically distributed through inheritance. A traditional economy usually has a strong social network, is based on primitive methods and tools for doing work, such as subsistence farming, raising livestock and hunting. People in an economy like this are very self-sufficient, often making their own clothes and tools. Barter is used to exchange surplus crops or items the people make for other items that they need. Most countries have had traditional economies in the past that have been transformed to command, market or mixed economies. Traditional economies still exist in rural parts of Africa, Asia and South America.

A command economy is also known as a planned economy. In a command economy, the government determines what is produced, how much is produced, and often who will receive the goods. Command economies are associated socialism and communism, which are based on collective ownership of resources and means of production. This power falls with the state (government) making the central government of the country the central authority for planning the economic activities of the country.

A market economy is the result of consumers and producers deciding what they want to produce and purchase in the marketplace. Producers will produce as much of a good or service as they think will meet the demand from consumers. Supply and demand usually set the price that the market will bear in a market economy. Consumers vote with their dollars by purchasing the items they want at the price points they are willing to pay. Producers who are able to provide the goods and services at the price the consumer will pay will succeed. Those who are unable to do so are likely to fail in a market economy. In a market economy, the government has little or no role in regulating economic activity.

2. **Discuss the social values that underlie each type of economy.**

A traditional economy usually has a strong social network and is based on primitive methods and tools for doing work. People in an economy like this are very self-sufficient.

Command economies are associated with socialism and communism, which are based on collective ownership of resources and means of production. This power falls with the state (government) making the central government of the country the central authority for planning the economic activities of the country.

In a market economy, consumers vote with their dollars by purchasing the items they want at the price points they are willing to pay. Producers who are able to provide the goods and services at the price the consumer will pay will succeed. Those who are unable to do so are likely to fail in a market economy.

3. **Explain why markets exist.**

Markets exist to provide a place where goods, services, and the factors of production (raw materials, labor, physical plant, and equipment) are traded (bought and sold).

Section 5.2

1. **Explain the advantages of a free-market economy.**

   A free market economy has three primary advantages over other economies:

   - Freedom to purchase and produce: consumers are free to purchase what they want for the price they are willing to pay. Producers are free to use their factors of production to produce as much or as little of a service as they wish.

   - Pricing based on supply and demand: Producers estimate demand based on consumer behavior and past purchasing trends. Consumers purchase only those items that they feel add enough value to their lives to be work parting with limited resources. When supply and demand are in perfect balance, the market for the product is in equilibrium.

   - Efficient use of the factors of production: If producers are 100% correct in their demand and price estimates, they will be 100% efficient in the use of the factors of production.

2. **Describe why economists use a demand schedule.**

   Demand schedules are used to determine the demand curve of a product, based on the price the consumer is willing to pay and the quantity of good the producer is willing to supply.

3. **Create a demand schedule for a good that you use. Describe how much of that good you are willing to purchase at different price points. Plot your demand schedule on a graph and create a demand curve.**

   Any answer that reflects the students' use of a good or service and includes the demand schedule and graph of the demand curve.

Section 5.3

1. **Explain how market equilibrium is obtained.**

   Market equilibrium for a product is established as a result of the forces of supply and demand. Producers decide how much of a good or service to supply based on the price they can demand and the potential profit. Consumers also decide how much they are willing to pay for a good or service based on the value they place it.

2. **Describe a circular flow economy.**

   The basic concept of the circular flow model is that businesses pay employees, which moves money to the households, which then spend the money they have earned on goods produced by businesses.

3. **Discuss how savings and investment affect the circular flow model of the economy.**

Households save money in banks and other financial institutions. Those banks and financial institutions are then able to loan that money to businesses as financial capital to support the growth of the businesses, including investing financial capital in product markets to make more goods and services available to households. When this market is in equilibrium, the total of the consumption and investment expenditures will equal the flow of income to the resource owners.

Section 5.4

1. **Explain how the U.S. Constitution established the basis for the current mixed economy in the U.S.**

The U.S. Constitution established the entirety of the U.S. as a common (unified) market. This means that all parts of the U.S are able to engage in unrestricted trade between states – that is interstate trade free of taxes and tariffs. The Constitution also granted the federal government the right to regulate commerce within the country and with other nations, establish uniform laws and standards to address bankruptcy, money creation and value, weights and measure, post offices, roads, patents and copyrights. The government went on to establish extensive infrastructure throughout the country in the form of roads, railroads, waterways, a national bank, the postal system, policies related to foreign trade, and oversight of domestic production and trade activities. The oversight developed over time as safety, both for consumers and workers, became more important.

2. **Describe how the federal government's role in the economy has changed.**

Government involvement in the American economy has grown over time. Initially, government was not heavily involved in the private sector, with the exception of transportation, and adopted as laissez-faire approach to the economy. This means that the government is not involved in the economy except to maintain law and order. This began to change in the late 1800s when farmers, small business owners and labor groups began to ask the government for assistance in maintaining free enterprise and competition in the economy. The Progressives, as they were called, favored government regulation of business practices to fight corruption in the public section, and ensure competition and free enterprise.

3. **Discuss the difference between government intervention in the economy for economic and social reasons.**

Governments intervene in economies for many reasons. Economic reasons include regulating industries to ensure fair competition, levying tariffs and other taxes on imported goods, and establishing incentives and tax structures that attract business.

Governments intervene in the market for social reasons to ensure jobs, provide a social safety net for those in need, and

Section 5.5

1. **Describe an entrepreneur.**

   Entrepreneurs are people who organize and manage organizations, particularly businesses, and who are willing to take risks and bring significant initiative to the project. The word entrepreneur is based on the old French word "entreprende," which means "to undertake." Entrepreneurs decide which projects to undertake and how they should be conducted. If an entrepreneur is successful, these entrepreneurial activities will increase the value of the resources used to produce the good or service provided by the entrepreneur, resulting in a profit to the company.

   Entrepreneurs are present in all levels of the American economy, from the biggest companies to single person businesses. Most people think of entrepreneurs as small business owners, but entrepreneurs can be found in all types of businesses. The primary characteristics of entrepreneurs are that they organize and manage businesses, are willing to take risks, and bring initiative to a project. These traits are found in leaders in every organization.

2. **Explain the role of the entrepreneur in the American economy.**

   In a capitalist economy, entrepreneurs organize the factors of production to provide the goods and services demanded by consumers in exchange for making a profit. Entrepreneurs, especially those in small enterprises, are able to be nimble in their response to changing economic conditions and demands.

3. **Identify how prices and output are determined in a perfectly competitive market.**

   In a free market with conditions of perfect competition, supply and demand will determine both output and price. The company will supply only as much of a good or service as the consumer will purchase at a specific price – no more or less. Since the consumer wants to pay the lowest price possible for a good and the producer wants to maximize profit, equilibrium will be reached at the point where demand is satisfied at a given price. The producer must demand a price that will recover the costs of production as well as providing a profit. This means that a minimum price must be demanded. In general, the lower the price of a good or service, the higher the demand will be. However, the price cannot fall below the production cost or the producer will not be willing to supply the product.

Section 5.6

1. **List the four conditions that are in place in a perfectly competitive market.**

   Four conditions must be present for a market to be perfectly competitive.

   1. There are many small suppliers that are each small enough that they are unable to influence the price for the overall market by changing the supply (increasing or decreasing the amount of goods available).

2. The output of each firm must be identical.

3. The market is always in equilibrium. If the market is always in equilibrium, the supply and demand will always maximize benefit for both the consumer and the supplier.

4. Competition is based only on price.

2. Explain why these conditions are not possible to meet in the real world.

There are many small suppliers that are each small enough that they are unable to influence the price for the overall market by changing the supply (increasing or decreasing the amount of goods available). This does not occur in the real world because companies are large and small. Large companies have economies of scale that make it possible for them to produce goods at a lower cost than a small firm.

The output of each firm must be identical. This does not meet the needs of the consumers who want variety in the products they purchase. Each consumer has different needs and priorities for the products they purchase.

The market is always in equilibrium. If the market is always in equilibrium, the supply and demand will always maximize benefit for both the consumer and the supplier. The market, in reality, is always changing due to changes in technology and the availability of alternative products. Consumers have perfect information about the prices being charged by all sellers. This will result in consumers moving away from a producer that demands a higher price for a product than other producers demand.

Competition is based only on price. In reality, consumers are influenced by more than price. Consumers demand quality, reliability, honesty, convenience and good service, and are willing to pay more for a good or service provided by a business that provides these attributes.

Under pure competition, firms face a perfectly elastic demand curve. This means that the firms must accept the price the consumer is willing to pay. Firms will expand production as long as the additional output adds more to revenues than to production costs.

3. Describe two barriers to entry that companies face.

There are three primary barriers to entry: legal barriers, economies of scale, and control over an essential resource. The answer should include two of the following barriers to entry.

Legal barriers to entry include licensing and patents. Licensing is a process of obtaining permission from a government to enter into a specific occupation or business. For example, licenses are often required for barber shops, beauty salons, taxi cabs, drugstores, and funeral homes. Patents are a second legal barrier to entry that allow the owner of the patent to prevent other people from using it for a period of time. In the U.S., patents are limited to 17 years. The patent owner may allow others to use the technology before the patent expires in 17 years, but usually requires payment of a fee to allow the other parties to use the technology.

Economies of scale are important in certain industries. Economies of scale occur when the production capacity of a company grows to a point that the per-unit cost of production is lower than that of a smaller company. Economies of scale often occur in the purchase of raw materials. Companies incur a lower per unit cost when they purchase raw materials in a large quantity because the provider of the raw materials will give them a quantity discount.

Control of an essential resource is a large barrier to entry. For example, if a company controls all of the sapphire mines in the world, no one else will be able to enter the market unless a new mine is discovered.

Section 5.7

1. **Define the term monopoly.**

    Monopolies occur when a single person or company controls the supply of a good or service for which there is no effective substitute and for which there are high barriers to entry.

2. **List some characteristics of a monopoly.**

    Characteristics of monopolies include single person or company control of the supply of a good or service, no effective substitute for the good or service, and high barriers to entry to the market.

    A monopoly usually limits the supply of the goods it provides, which moves the supply curve to the left, raising prices, which does not benefit the consumer. This situation is called forced equilibrium. Forced equilibrium means that consumers are paying a price that is higher than equilibrium for a below-market total quantity of the product.

    Monopolies may be coercive, as in government monopolies of utilities and the US Postal Service. Monopolies may also be natural, which occurs when a supplier controls all or most of a resource or a supplier can meet demand at a lower price than a group of competitors could.

3. **Explain how a government monopoly is formed.**

    Government monopolies are typically coercive monopolies, meaning they are forced upon the market. A government monopoly occurs when the government is the sole provider of a good or service and prohibits competition by law. Examples of government monopolies in different places are the postal service, railroads, public utilities, alcohol sales, and police forces.

Section 5.8

1. **Describe how a monopoly establishes production and price levels.**

   Monopolists, like other capitalist companies, are in business to maximize profits. Monopolists that want to maximize profits will increase production until marginal revenue equals marginal cost. Marginal revenue is the revenue earned for each additional unit produced. Marginal cost is the additional cost for each additional unit produced. A profit-maximizing monopolist will increase production to a point where price is greater than marginal cost.

2. **Define price discrimination and explain why companies engage in price discrimination.**

   Price discrimination occurs when a provider decides to set different price points for different markets or consumers. Providers decide to engage in price discrimination to increase revenues and profits. Three conditions must be met for price discrimination to be beneficial to the producer. First, the demand curve must slope downward, which occurs in monopolistic situations. Second, the provider must have at least two distinct groups of consumers to which the products are sold. The price elasticities of these consumer groups must be different and the groups must be easily separated. Third, the provider must be able to restrict the consumers to whom they sell the goods at a lower cost from reselling them to the consumers they are charging a higher cost.

3. **Explain monopolistic competition.**

   Monopolistic competition occurs when companies offer goods and services that are different than the products produced by other companies, but are also not perfect substitutes for the products produced by the other companies. In this type of imperfect competition, producers may act like monopolists, ignoring the price of competition, in the short term.

Section 5.9

1. **Define the term oligopoly**

   Oligopoly describes a market where a few producers share the market, but no single producer controls the market (price or supply of the product). Oligopolies occur when there are high barriers to entry, high fixed costs, and the need for a large production capacity to reach an efficient level of production. Another characteristic of an oligopoly is that marginal costs continue to decrease as larger quantities are produced. The producers who share the market act in a way that they do NOT undercut the prices of the other producers. Profit is maximized in the long run by maintaining the prices at a certain level.

2. **Describe an oligopoly that has a strong influence on the U.S. economy.**

Cartels are a form of oligopoly, where members agree to limit the supply of a good in order to increase the price they can demand for it. A prime example is the oil cartel (OPEC). Cartel members work together to reduce competition and maximize profits to the cartel members.

3. **Explain how oligopolies compete without reducing prices.**

Oligopolies do not compete on price. They compete more on public perception, advertising, and perceived benefits to consumers. Cereals, shampoos, and other packaged goods are examples of oligopolies. The products are essentially the same, as are the prices. However, the companies invest in significant marketing and advertising activities to differentiate them from one another.

Section 5.10

1. **List the four conditions that must exist for monopolistic competition to develop.**

Monopolistic competition occurs when four specific economic conditions are in place:

1. All firms in the market produce similar products that are NOT perfect substitutes for one another. This differs from perfect competition in that there is variation among the products offered by the suppliers. They are similar, but not the same.

2. All firms are able to enter the market if the profits are attractive enough. Barriers to entry and exit are low, so firms are able to engage in production and supply of a good with relative ease.

3. All firms maximize profits. Profits are maximized based on production factors, demand, and price.

4. All firms have the ability to influence the market (market power), therefore are not price-takers. Firms are able to increase or decrease production to influence price, or increase or decrease price to influence demand, therefore production.

2. **Explain how firms in a monopolistically competitive market set output.**

Monopolistic competition is subject to consumer demand, which is expressed in two ways: love of variety and ideal variety.

The love of variety approach assumes that each consumer will demand different varieties of the same project.

The ideal variety approach that each product consists of a number of characteristics, which can be selected by each consumer based on her individual preferences.

The companies in a monopolistic competition market will set production based on anticipated demand and with a goal of maximizing profits.

3. **Describe how monopolistic competition and oligopoly develop.**

Monopolistic competition and oligopolies occur when the market is not able to support perfect competition. Monopolistic competition allows companies to choose the product they supply to the market and set price based on factors such as consumer demand and differentiation of the product from other suppliers. Some companies may choose to target the high-end market for the product and others will target the consumers who are not willing to pay as much for the good or service being provided.

Oligopolies form when a few firms control the market. They are able to maintain prices above the market equilibrium level by engaging in collusion, sharing markets, and working together to restrict access to the goods and services they offer to the market. Firms may also work together to create stable market conditions for a product, reducing the risks of developing those product markets.

Section 5.11

1. **Describe markets.**

Markets are places where goods and services, as well as the factors of production (raw materials, labor, plant, equipment) are bought and sold. Markets may be better thought of as mechanisms by which these activities occur because markets are not necessarily physical places like grocery stores or farmers markets.

Markets may be described for specific products. For example, if a company is selling musical instruments, the market it is targeting is the group of people and businesses who are likely to purchase instruments. Likewise, the market for luxury automobiles is limited to those who can afford to purchase them. The market for this textbook is high school students enrolled in microeconomics.

2. **Explain how producers of goods target specific markets.**

Companies target specific populations based on their spending patterns, demographics, interests, and needs. Some companies target wealthy populations and others target the poor or middle class consumers. Companies offer products at prices and quality levels that are attractive to their markets.

3. **Discuss how price and market are connected.**

The prices of goods supplied will be influenced by the market being targeted. For example, a company that is targeting a population that is low-income will develop and produce goods that are inexpensive and meet the needs of the low-income consumer. That same company may also target high or middle-income populations. Each of these markets will demand a different product that will sell at a different price point.

The larger a market for a product, the higher the demand is likely to be for that product. Price can be influenced by the producer, which may decide to restrict or expand the amount of a good or service provided. Likewise, consumers influence price by voting with their dollars. Producers will continue to produce goods that the consumers purchase. They will not produce goods if consumers do not purchase them. Market equilibrium is reached when the amount produced is the amount purchased, which occurs at a specific price.

Section 5.12

1. **Define sole proprietorship.**

   A *sole proprietorship* is a form of small business that is owned by a single person and is NOT registered with the state as either a limited liability company (LLC) or a corporation.

2. **Explain situations in which a sole proprietorship may be appropriate.**

   Examples of sole proprietorships are freelance writers, photographers, salespeople working on commission, independent contractors, or artists or craftsmen who take jobs on a contract basis.

3. **Discuss the advantages and disadvantages of a sole proprietorship.**

   Advantages to sole proprietorships are the following:

   1. Easy to establish.

   2. The owner makes all the decisions.

   3. Minimal startup costs

   4. Taxes are reports on the owner's individual income tax forms.

   5. Owner manages and controls all aspects of the company.

   6. No reporting requirements.

   7. Business does not file or pay taxes.

   8. No fees.

   Disadvantages to sole proprietorships include:

   1. The owner faces unlimited personal liability.

   2. Difficult to raise investment capital

   3. Lack of continuity if the owner dies or becomes disabled.

   4. Owner can spend unlimited time responding to business needs.

1. **Describe a partnership.**

   A partnership occurs when two or more people are co-owners of a business. The owners share the risks, responsibilities and rewards of the business. This arrangement is usually established before the partners go into business so the responsibilities of each are clear at the outset of the business venture. Each person involved as a partner contributes money, property, labor or skill. Each partner also expects to share in the profits and losses of the business. Partnerships consist of two or more persons. However, "persons" can include individuals, groups of individuals, companies, and corporations.

   Business partners have the same level of personal liability as sole proprietors. The owners of a partnership are personally liable for all business debts incurred by the firm, meaning that creditors may come after personal assets, including homes, cars and other real property to settle a debt. In a general partnership, all partners are based on their share of ownership. In a limited partnership, the general partner carries personal liability while the limited partners usually are only risking the investment they made in the firm. Common examples of partnerships are law, medical and accounting firms.

2. **Discuss the advantages and disadvantages of partnerships.**

   Partners have both joint authority and joint liability. Any individual partner is typically able to bind the company to a contract for the purchase of goods or some other business deal. There are a few limits on the ability of a partner to bind the company to a contract. A primary limit is that one partner is unable to bind the entire business to a sale of all the assets of the partnership. Joint liability, on the other hand, means that an individual partner can be sued for the full amount of any business debt. If this happens, the individual partner may have to sue the other partners for their shares of the debt.

   From a tax perspective, a partnership has to file an annual information return to the IRS. The annual information return includes information on the income, deductions, gains, and losses of the operation. The partnership does not, however, pay income tax, because it is considered a pass-through entity. Profits or losses of the partnership are passed through to its partners, who then include these profits or losses on their individual tax returns. As with sole proprietorships, partners are not considered employees and are required to make quarterly estimated tax payments to the IRS each year.

   One disadvantage to a partnership is that if one of the partners wants to leave the organization, the partnership is probably going to be dissolved. This means that all partners must fulfill any remaining business obligations, pay off all debts, and split any assets and profits among the partners. This can be avoided by including a buy-sell (buyout) agreement when the partnership is first established. A buyout agreement will allow the business to continue operations as usual if one of the partners becomes incapacitated or decides to leave the business.

3. **Compare and contrast the two types of partnerships.**

Partnerships are not required to file papers with the state to become a corporation or limited liability company (LLC). There are two types of partnerships: general and limited. General partnerships are the most common structure, in which all partners have a role in managing the business. Limited partnerships occur when one of the partners (the general partner) is responsible for running the business and the limited partners are simply passive investors.

Section 5.14

1. **Discuss the advantages and disadvantages of incorporation.**

Corporations and limited liability corporations are slightly different from a tax perspective. Both corporations and LLCs limit the liability of the owners regarding business debts. Corporations pay taxes and the owners pay income tax only on the money they draw from the corporation. This money can be drawn in the form of salaries, bonuses and dividends. The owners of LLCs, however, pay their taxes in a similar manner to partnerships. The owners report their business income on their personal tax returns.

Non-profit corporations are formed to carry out charitable, education, religious, literary or scientific work. Non-profit corporations are able to raise funds by requesting donations from individuals and companies, as well as applying for grant money from public and private sources. Non-profits are usually considered tax-exempt and are not taxed as long as their income is related to their non-profit purpose. This is to encourage them to continue to engage in activities that benefit society. However, non-profit corporations can be taxed on unrelated business income. This is called an unrelated business income tax (UBIT).

2. **Explain the characteristics of corporations.**

A corporation is the most common legal structure for businesses in the U.S. Corporations have several characteristics that distinguish them from sole proprietorships and partnerships.

1. Corporations are separate entities from the owners of the corporations. This provides protection to the individuals who own shares of the company.

2. Corporations issue stocks, or shares of ownership, to the owners. The stocks are easily transferable.

3. The owners of the corporation (stockholders) have limited liability for the company's activities. The owners are not personally liable if the company is sued.

4. The company is considered a going concern, meaning that it will continue to operate indefinitely. This requires the company to be able to generate enough income/assets to continue its operations.

5. Incorporation provides companies flexibility in how they manage their ownership structure.

6. There may be some tax advantages to corporations.

There are three types of corporations: the standard for-profit corporation, the limited liability corporation (LLC), and the non-profit corporation.

3. Describe the role of multinational corporations and how the corporations are changing.

Multinational corporations (MNCs) conduct business in two or more countries. Multinational corporations are also called transnational corporations, or TNCS. These entities are often very large, with budgets that are more than those of some countries. MNCs have significant influence on both local and international economies and play a key role in developing a global economy.

Samel Palmisano, CEO of IBM Corporation, coined the term "globally integrated enterprise" in 2006. He used this term to describe a business enterprise that goes beyond the multinational corporation. This has implications that are both social and economic. The shift to a globally integrated enterprise has taken two forms: production location and producer. In the past, producers have chosen to produce goods near the place they will be sold. This limited who could produce the goods to those who were in the area. The globally integrated enterprise, however, is able to pull together resources (skills, production capacity, infrastructure, etc.) from around the world to produce its goods and services. Think about computer companies. Many technical support aspects of the computer industry are outsourced to India or other places where there is skilled labor that is less expensive than that in the U.S. This can be looked at as a modular approach to business. The individual pieces all work independently and can be reorganized to meet changing business needs. The globally integrated enterprise is based on collaboration and outsources much of its activity to service companies that specialize in sales support, back-office administration, and other services required to run a global company.

An important result of the globally integrated enterprise is the movement of corporate activities to developing countries, which is raising the standard of living for workers in those areas.

There are four primary challenges facing these companies:

1. Access to highly educated and skilled workers who have collaborative management skills.

2. Appropriate management of intellectual property (patented goods and services) to allow collaboration and innovation.

3. Establishment of corporate governance structures that inspire and maintain the trust of all entities involved.

4. Significant changes in organizational culture, primarily movement from a short-term profit perspective to a long-term vision that embraces real earnings (not prospective earnings) and innovation.

Section 5.15

1. **Describe a cooperative business and its unique characteristics.**

Cooperative organizations are businesses that are owned and democratically controlled by their members. The board of directors for a cooperative is elected from within the membership. Examples are agricultural cooperatives, food cooperatives, and credit unions. Co-ops can range from very small operations to multinational companies.

Co-ops follow seven fundamental principles: voluntary and open membership, democratic member control, member economic participation, autonomy and independence, education training and information, cooperation among cooperatives, and concern for the community.

Cooperative organizations have several unique characteristics:

1. Members are the people who use and buy the goods and services provided by the cooperative.

2. The board of directors of the cooperative is elected from within the membership.

3. The cooperative returns surplus revenues to members. The surplus revenue is returned based on the members' use of the cooperative, not the members' ownership share.

4. Cooperatives are motivated by service, not profit. The service cooperatives provide is typically access to affordable and high-quality goods and services.

5. Cooperatives exist only to serve their members.

6. Cooperatives pay taxes on income that is kept within the cooperatives for investment or operational reserves. The surplus revenue received by members is included in individual income taxes.

2. **List and describe the four primary types of cooperative businesses.**

There are four primary types of cooperatives: consumer, producer, worker, and purchasing/shared services cooperatives. Consumer cooperatives are owned by the purchasers of the goods and services of the cooperative. Produce cooperatives are often seen in agricultural situations. Farmers group together to gain bargaining power with buyers and combine resources to market and brand their products. Worker cooperatives are owned and governed by employees of a business. Examples include employee-owned grocery stores and taxicab companies. Purchasing/Shared services cooperatives are groups of small businesses, municipalities and other entities to enhance purchasing power, lower costs, and improve competitiveness.

3. **Explain a franchise and describe the two primary types of franchises.**

A franchise is another form of legal arrangement, called a franchise agreement, between a franchisee and a franchisor. A franchisor owns the trademark or trade name and provides support to the franchisee, who uses the trademark or trade name and expands the business with the support of the franchisor. The franchisee pays fees to the franchisor to use the trademark/trade name and obtain the support of the franchisor in developing the business.

There are two primary types of franchises: those that distribute products and business format franchises.

Product distribution franchises occur when the franchisee simply sells the product of the franchisor. Common examples are car dealers and gas stations.

Business format franchises are the most common franchise you see in the U.S. In addition to using the trademark, product, service, and trade-name of the franchisor, the franchisee also uses the complete method required to run the business. This includes use of marketing and operating plans and manuals. Business format franchises are found in service, restaurants (including fast food), grocery stores, building and construction, retail, automotive, maintenance, and lodging.

A franchisee may be granted the right to operate one franchise (single-unit franchise) or multiple franchises (multi-unit franchise).

An Easy Introduction to Economics: Microeconomics Answer Key Unit 6

Section 6.1

1. **Describe the foundations of free enterprise in the U.S.**

Free enterprise in the U.S. can be traced back to original colonies, before the country was established. Many of the original settlers arrived in the colonies as part of charter companies to engage in profit-seeking trade on behalf of British companies. A group of individuals or businesses would group together to form a charter company to engage in trade in the New World. The charter companies sometimes also furthered the goals of England. The King of England would provide a charter for the project, which would give the company economic rights, as well as political and judicial authority.

The charter companies went into business with a goal of making a quick profit from the New World. It did not prove easy to reach this goal. In many cases, charter companies would turn over their charters to the local settlers, who used them as the basis for developing the infrastructure of a new country.

2. **List the constitutional protections to free trade.**

The U.S. Constitution, which was adopted in 1787, outlined the basic economic structure of this country. The Constitution established the entire country, from east to west and north to south, as a unified, or common, market. Interstate commerce is not subject to taxes or tariffs. The Constitution also establishes the right of the federal government to regulate commerce both within the country and with foreign nations. Other rights provided to the federal government are:

1. Establishment of uniform bankruptcy laws.

2. Creation of money.

3. Regulation of the value of money.

4. Fix standards of weights and measures.

5. Establish post offices.

6. Establish roads.

7. Fix rules governing patents and copyrights.

3. **Explain how the federal government has used these protections to support the U.S. economy.**

The federal government has used its powers to enact laws to regulate and provide services related to transportation, monopolies, banking, agriculture, public welfare, employment, Medicare, food stamps, educational initiatives, and other areas of the economy. The government has also established more than 100 agencies to monitor and regulate the various sectors of the economy. These agencies enforce consumer safety, worker safety, employment, banking, transportation, and other aspects of the economy that benefit from oversight.

Section 6.2

1. **Describe a market failure.**

Market failure occurs when the system fails to meet the ideal allocative efficiency that can by hypothesized with models. In this situation, potential gains exist that have not been realized. In other words, market failure occurs when the costs of goods and services do not reflect the real costs of production and consumption of those goods. Yet another way to look at this is that market failure occurs when a market left to itself does not allocate resources efficiently.

2. **Explain why market failure is not necessarily negative.**

Market failure is not necessarily negative. Sometimes the costs of a perfectly efficient market are higher than the benefit of that perfectly efficient market to the consumer. If it costs $5.00 more per unit to reach ideal efficiency in a market, but the consumer is only willing to pay $2.00 more per unit, the cost of reaching perfect efficiency is more than it is worth to reach that goal

3. **Discuss how monopolies contribute to market failure.**

Monopolies contribute to market failure when they abuse market power by significantly influencing prices or output of a good or service.

Section 6.3

1. **List the four causes of market failure.**

The four sources of market failure are externalities, public goods, incomplete or asymmetric information, and monopoly (abuse of market power).

Externalities are present when production and exchange affect the welfare of non-consenting secondary parties. Externalities may be positive or negative. External costs occur when the welfare of the secondary parties is negatively affected.

Public goods are goods that are available to all if they are available to one. Joint consumption of the goods means that it is impossible to separate the non-payers from the payers for the public goods. There are a few examples of pure public goods. These are national defense, the legal system, the money system, individual rights, and the quality and management of the air, rivers and waterways. Near public goods are those that are jointly consumed even though nonpaying consumers can be excluded.

Asymmetric or incomplete information often results in dissatisfied customers.

Monopolies induce market failure because they are not motivated to be as efficient as possible. Monopolists do not have competition because they control the market. Therefore, inefficiencies will occur due to the lack of competition.

2. **Provide some examples of market failures.**

When external costs and benefits are present, consumers and producers will not receive the proper signals, which results in market failure (inability to meet maximum efficiency). Examples of negative costs include air pollution, noise pollution, junkyards, litterbugs, muggers, and others who adversely affect the secondary parties. External benefits occur when spillover effects benefit the secondary parties. Examples of external benefits include flower gardens, parks, and golf courses.

Cable television is an example of a near public good, as are national parks, interstate highways, and movies. Additional consumption of near public goods, once they are produced, is costless to society. This then begs the question of whether they should be provided at no cost to society. In order for these near public goods to be provided at no cost, taxes will be increased.

Asymmetric or incomplete information: When a consumer receives bad information and is unhappy with a product the consumer is unsatisfied and the company has lost a future customer.

Examples of monopolistic inefficiencies are public utilities and the telephone companies before they were deregulated.

3. **Describe how poor information can lead to a market failure.**

Asymmetric or incomplete information often results in dissatisfied customers. This is a negative effect for producers if the customers are dissatisfied with the good or service provided. In the case of products that are purchased repeatedly, consumers are able to use trial and error to find the products that work best for them, and suppliers are highly motivated to promote customer satisfaction. However, when the goods are difficult to evaluate because they are infrequently purchased or purchased from multiple suppliers, or have potentially serious and lasting harmful effects, trial and error is not a satisfactory means of determining quality.

Section 6.4

1. **List the three ways the government can manage externalities.**

The government is able to respond to externalities in three ways, establishment of property rights, regulation and taxation.

2. **Describe how property rights are used to manage externalities.**

Establishment of property rights is the first tool used by the government to improve the efficiency of resource allocation when externalities are present. There are situations in which property rights can be clearly defined. For example, the granting of property rights to ranchers and homesteaders improve the efficiency of land utilization in the 1800s. This is more difficult to do with air and water rights. The air and water rights of property owners often overlap. For example, people living near a factory may experience negative effects from the air pollution emitted by the factory. Likewise, if the factory is on a river, the landowners downstream from the river may experience negative effects from emissions of the factory into the water. Property owners are able to go to court to enforce their property rights (clean air or water and/or compensation for abuse of the air or water). They must be able to prove three things: 1) the extent of the damage caused by the pollution, 2) that the pollutant actually caused the damage, and 3) the identity of the company or person whose emissions caused the damage. When it is not possible to establish property rights, the government may decide to manage resources by charging user fees, or establish regulations that have significant fines associated with breaking them.

3. **Discuss the difference between regulatory and taxation approaches to managing externalities.**

Taxation is used when the government decides to charge, or tax, companies that engage in activities that may harm the environment. This can be done by assessing the minimal costs of production for the company when no pollution controls are in place, as well as the negative costs to the secondary parties who are affected by the pollution (neighbors, those who share waterways, and those who are affected by emissions). The costs to the secondary parties can be difficult to assess, but the governmental agencies are required to estimate the environmental damage. The per unit damage costs to the neighbors can be assessed against the company generating the pollution, theoretically reducing the motivation for the company to pollute. Again, the theory behind this is that as long as the costs of cleaning up operations to reduce emissions are less than the tax paid, the company will opt for reducing emissions and maximizing profit. Some people consider this approach to be a license to pollute for the companies that would incur a cost higher than the tax to clean up emissions. On the other hand, the companies with lower costs of controlling emissions will opt to implement cleaner production processes rather than pay the taxes.

Regulation is an allocation of government resources to establish regulations that control negative externalities, such as air pollution and water pollution. The government has established agencies to monitor the long and short-term environmental impact of production activities. The Clean Air Act, the Clean Water Act and other regulations have been enacted to address these externalities. The agency primarily responsible for enforcing these regulations is the Environmental Protection Agency. The EPA works with government and industry to develop strategies and incentives for reducing pollution. Other government agencies oversee public safety (police forces, Food and Drug Administration), provide for national defense (the armed forces), and support research and development activities for future economic growth (National Institutes of Health, National Science Foundation, Department of Defense, Department of Energy, etc.).

Continuing to use pollution as an example, regulators typically establish a maximum emission standard that all companies must meet. If the company is unable to meet the standard, they are required to stop production until they are able to meet the standard. This is perceived as an inefficient method of reducing pollution because of the variation in cost for each of the producers to meet the standard and will impose a high cost on society in the form of increased prices.

Section 6.5

1. **Explain why governments redistribute income.**

The government redistributes income from the well-to-do segments of the population to segments of the population that require assistance. In the U.S., this process occurs in several ways: welfare, unemployment insurance, and taxes.

2. Describe the primary ways the U.S. government redistributes income.

Welfare is a primary tool used by the government to redistribute income to those in need. Individuals who are employed are taxed and part of that tax is used to pay for social welfare programs. Social welfare programs include welfare, some social security payments, and Medicaid. Welfare and Medicaid programs are designed to provide basic levels of income and health care to people in need. Some social security payments are made to individuals who are disabled and unable to work and to children of parents who died to help support them until they are 18 years old. Food stamps are another form of social welfare used to ensure that people in need are able to acquire nutritious food.

Unemployment insurance is a social welfare program designed to assist people who are temporarily unemployed for reasons that are out of their control. Unemployment will provide a certain level of benefits for a short time while the individual is seeking other employment. This is also used to help individuals who are in seasonal jobs while they are laid off during the off-season.

Taxes are also an effective way to redistribute income. Marginal tax rates (tax rates that are lower at lower incomes and increase as income increases) are very effective in redistributing income because those who earn less money pay less tax as a percentage of income than those who make more money. The Earned Income Tax Credit is a second tax tool that provides a tax benefit to those with lower incomes, allowing them to retain more of their income.

3. Discuss some of the benefits and drawbacks to income redistribution.

As with everything else, there are differing opinions about the effectiveness of income redistribution. Arthur Okun postulated in the 1970s that government policies that reduce income equality by redistributing income will lead to reductions in economic production. The wealthy will react to having their resources taken away by using their resources in a manner that was less productive. One of the drivers of economic growth and prosperity is risk taking. If those who are willing to take the risk do not see a large reward, they are less likely to take the risk to innovate new products and services. This can lead to economic slow downs. The challenge to the government policy makers is to find the appropriate balance between income redistribution to help those who really need assistance while still encouraging production and economic growth. Okun was willing to see a reduction in efficiency in order to achieve greater equality.

Charles Murray, on the other hand, argues that the social welfare programs of the U.S. have increased poverty. His argument is that if government payments for poverty are attractive enough, it becomes more common. His views are controversial. Long-term studies of government income redistribution programs will show whether or not they are effective

1. **Define the term poverty.**

   Poverty is the state of being poor. People living in poverty are unable to provide for their basic needs of food, shelter and clothing. Poverty is perceived relative to the accepted standard of living in a country.

2. **Explain why poverty is a relative concept.**

   Conditions that may be considered poverty in the U.S. may be considered a high standard of living in other places. For example, almost all Americans have access to clean water, indoor plumbing, decent food and clothing, access to health care, and education. Many Americans who have access to these resources are considered poor by American standards. However, in a 3rd world nation, a family with access to these same resources may be considered well off. Poverty is relative. Often income inequality rather than actual destitution creates poverty in an economy. Poverty is perceived relative to the accepted and average standard of living.

3. **Describe the U.S. debate on poverty.**

   Given the relative nature of poverty, it is logical that there is a political debate in the U.S. about how to fight poverty.

   One of the challenges facing American politicians and the public is how the U.S. defines poverty. The current U.S. poverty standard is based on one measure of income deprivation based on lifestyles of the 1950s. In the 1950s, housing costs required a smaller percentage of the household budget, one worker could support most families, and childcare costs were negligible. The definition of poverty in the U.S. is at the core of the debate.

   Liberal and conservative groups have different, conflicting views on poverty that are based on different definitions of poverty. Liberals tend to believe that more resources are required to alleviate poverty. Conservatives, on the other hand, tend to argue that more resources are unnecessary and that social welfare programs should provide temporary assistance rather than long-term support.

   Different groups use different statistical measures for poverty. Different statistical measures make different assumptions about the populations and collect data in different ways, so they are not usually comparable. Measures can be absolute (they are the same regardless of context) or relative, meaning that they can be perceived differently depending upon what they are being compared to. Based on the different statistics used, some groups feel poverty is overstated and others feel it is understated. This lack of consensus about the level of poverty makes it difficult to develop programs that will be effective in alleviating poverty.

Section 6.7

1. **Explain how sales taxes affect supply and demand.**

   The general effect of a sales tax is to raise the price of a good or service, which will affect the demand for products that are taxed by reducing the amount the producers are willing to supply at the higher price. The increased price caused by a sales tax will reduce demand for a good or service. For example, when gasoline is in short supply, taxes may be raised to reduce demand. Likewise, increasing sin taxes on cigarettes and alcohol makes these products more expensive, which will reduce demand.

2. **Explain how establishment of price ceilings affects supply and demand.**

   Rent controls set a maximum price, also called a price ceiling.

   Rent controls are established in some communities to keep housing affordable for those who work in the community but would not otherwise be able to afford to live there. The general effect of a price control is to keep the price below the market. In the case of rent, rent control will keep the price of rent for the controlled buildings below the market rate. This creates a high demand for the rent-controlled apartments and houses.

3. **Explain how establishment of price floors affects supply and demand.**

   Minimum wage sets a minimum price, which is also called a price floor.

   Minimum wage sets a floor on the price of labor. The primary goal of the minimum wage is to help workers earn a living wage, or enough money to support themselves without being in poverty. The minimum wage keeps a single person just above the minimum poverty threshold, which is a measure established each year by the federal government. The minimum wage, however, will not maintain a family with two or more people above the minimum wage if there is just one breadwinner (or worker).

   The minimum wage affects the supply and demand for labor. If the minimum wage is set above the wage that would be paid at market equilibrium, a minimum wage will generate unemployment, or a surplus of labor

Section 6.8

1. **Describe the costs of government regulation on the cost of goods and services.**

   Government regulation of economic activities has grown over time. Each time the government decides to regulate an economic activity, resources must be allocated for the purposes of regulation and enforcement of the regulations. Government regulation also increases the production costs of the supplier because the supplier must comply with the regulations, in addition to proving to the government that they have complied. This involves changes in production facilities, as well as additional administrative staff to manage the reporting process. The end result of regulation is an increase cost to the consumer for the good or service being provided.

2. **Explain why deregulation of an industry occurs.**

Deregulation of an industry occurs when the government decides that the costs of regulation are higher than the benefit of the regulation. In the 1970s, dissatisfaction with traditional regulations grew, resulting in moves toward deregulation. This led to deregulation in the ground (trucking) and air (airline) transportation systems.

3. **Discuss the results of deregulation on supply, demand and price for a good or service.**

Deregulation affects supply, demand, and price of a good or service in different ways. In many instances, deregulation allows increased competition, which reduces the price and increases the options available to the consumer. However, sometimes goods and services that were subject to price controls or subsidies are no longer subject to those rules and become more expensive for the consumer.

Section 6.9

1. **Explain why the government regulates or prohibits certain market practices.**

Some market practices are detrimental to a competitive market by preventing unfair trade practices and monopolies. These include collusion and price agreements, predatory pricing, exclusive contracts, and reciprocal agreements. Governments generally regulate or prohibit unfair trade practices and monopolies.

2. **Describe the difference between collusion, exclusive contracts and reciprocal agreements.**

Collusion occurs when competitors agree to engage in behavior that will provide them an unfair advantage in the marketplace through deceit, fraud or deception. Examples include wage fixing, price fixing, kickbacks, and misrepresenting the relationship between the colluding parties be presenting the parties as independent of one another. Wage fixing occurs when an industry works together to restrict the wages of employees. Price fixing occurs when an industry colludes to inflate the price of their goods and services. Kickbacks are undocumented payments for engaging in a certain behavior that results in an unfair competitive advantage to the payer. Misrepresentation occurs when companies that colluded to set prices present themselves and unrelated competitors, not disclosing the relationship established to set prices.

Exclusive contracts, also known as dealerships, occur when a distributor (supplier) of a product prohibits retailers from selling competing products from other producers. Under the Clayton Act, exclusive contracts are illegal when they lessen competition. An exclusive contract may occur when an established company, with a variety of product lines, wishes to limit the entry of a potential competitor that offers a related, but more narrow, product line.

Reciprocal agreements occur when sellers of products are required to purchase another product, usually from the buyer, as a condition of sale. For example, if a car company uses a specific trucking company to ship their cars to dealerships, a reciprocal agreement will occur if the car company requires the trucking company to use trucks made by the car maker in order to get the shipping contract.

3. **Discuss predatory pricing and how it is used to stifle competition.**

Predatory pricing occurs when a large firm that is able to take a financial loss temporarily reduces the price of its good or service to a level below the cost of production in certain areas. This is done to damage competitors or eliminate competition altogether. Once the competitors withdraw from the market, the firm that engaged in predatory pricing is essentially a monopoly and uses its monopoly power to raise prices.

Section 6.10

1. **Explain the difference between economic and social benefits of government regulation.**

Economic regulation is generally targeted at controlling prices. Government regulation of the economy is usually enacted to protect consumers, small businesses, and destructive competition between companies of any size.

Social regulations are enacted to protect people and the environment, and encourage socially desirable behaviors. Examples include emissions controls, tax incentives for providing certain benefits, and product safety regulations.

The trends in government regulation swing between the laissez-faire environment of little government regulation to what some consider over-regulation. In general terms, conservatives tend to prefer minimal governmental regulation because it encourages an efficient market and liberals are more likely to encourage regulation that supports non-economic activities, such as worker safety and environmental health.

2. **Describe how the New Deal established the basis for government regulation of the economy.**

The New Deal of the 1930s was the beginning of the current environment of governmental oversight and regulation in the U.S. The Great Depression caused people to lose faith in a completely free market that was not subject to government oversight. As a result, President Franklin D. Roosevelt implemented the New Deal, which gave the government power to intervene in the economy. These laws provided the government with the ability to regulate sales of stock, recognized the rights of workers to form labor unions, established rules for wages and hours, provided unemployment benefits, established Social Security retirement benefits, established farm subsidies, instituted the Federal Deposit Insurance Corporation to insure bank deposits, and created the Tennessee Valley Authority to develop infrastructure in the Tennessee Valley and provide jobs for people in that area.

Since the 1930s, many more laws and regulations have been implemented to provide further protection to consumers and workers. These include employment discrimination based on age, sex, race, religious beliefs, or sexual preference; general prohibitions on child labor; the right of independent labor unions to organize, bargain and strike; workplace safety and health codes; product safety, including food, drugs and transportation; fairness in pricing and truth in advertising.

3. **Discuss some of the social and economic benefits of government regulation of the economy.**

The social benefits of these regulations are safer products, a cleaner environment, more socially responsible behavior on the part of both consumers and companies, and transparency of the activities of financial institutions. The economic benefits are efficient markets, open competition, relatively low barriers to entry into a market, and a wide variety of goods and services that are available to the consumer.

Section 6.11

1. **Describe why anti-trust policies have been established in the U.S.**

Anti-trust policies were established to ensure that the economy is structured so that competition within an industry or market area exists and to prohibit business practices that stifle competition. The expectation is that if these two goals are met, the market will efficiently allocate goods and services.

2. **List the three key anti-trust laws in the U.S. and what each was designed to achieve.**

The three major antitrust laws in the U.S. are the Sherman Act, the Clayton Act and the Federal Trade Commission Act.

The Sherman Act, was the first antitrust law enacted in the U.S. This law was passed in 1890 in response to a number of mergers that occurred in the tobacco, sugar and oil industries at the time. The goal of the Sherman Act is to prevent monopolies. The primary provisions prohibit restraint of trade resulting from contracts, combinations in the form of trusts or otherwise, or conspiracy; and provide for misdemeanor penalties for those who engage in such behavior. The Act does not clearly define unfair or unethical business practice, which resulted in the act being considered ineffective because the courts were unwilling to enforce it. This resulted in the passage of two more antitrust laws in 1914.

The Clayton Act was passed in 1914 to define and prohibit business practices that lessen competition. The business practices must be proven to substantially lessen competition or tend to create a monopoly in order to be prohibited under the Clayton Act. The specific business practices include:

1. Price discrimination, which occurs when companies charge consumers in different markets different prices that are not related to the costs of

transportation of the good to each market. An example is charging people in markets with limited transportation (poor inner city neighborhoods, for example) higher prices than are warranted by the production and transportation costs of getting the goods to market.

2. Tying contracts, which occur when a buyer requires a seller to purchase an item in order to get the buyer's business. An example is when a heavy equipment producer requires the train company shipping the heavy equipment to purchase train engines from the heavy equipment producer.

3. Exclusive dealings, which occur when the seller of a good or service is prohibited from selling to a competitor of the purchaser of the good or service. This would occur if the producer of a component of a product (a computer chip, for example) is prohibited by one computer manufacturer from selling that computer chip to competing computer manufacturers.

4. Interlocking stockholding, which occurs when a company purchases the stock of a competitor. If the company gains 51% or more of the shares of the competing company, competition is reduced because both companies are under the control of the same management team.

5. Interlocking directorates, which occur when an individual serves on the boards of competing firms. If a person serves on the boards of competing companies, one or both of the companies may gain an unfair advantage because of the information the shared director gains from each company.

The Clayton Act, although more specific than the Sherman Act, was still vague in its definition of when prohibited actions actually become illegal because they substantially lessen competition.

The third major antitrust law is the Federal Trade Commission Act. This declares all unfair methods of competition in commerce illegal. The FTC is composed of five members, who are appointed to seven-year terms by the President. The primary role of the FTC is to enforce consumer protection legislation, prohibit deceptive advertising, and prevent overt collusion. The commission investigates complaints.

If a violation has occurred, the FTC will first try to settle the dispute. If that fails, a hearing is conducted before an examiner, the decision of which may be appealed to the full commission. The decision of the full commission may also be appealed to the U.S. Court of Appeals.

3. **Explain how the Celler-Kefauver Act amended and strengthened the Clayton Act.**

The Celler-Kefauver Act was passed into law in 1950. The purpose of this act is to prohibit a company from acquiring the assets of a competitor if this acquisition substantially lessens competition. This strengthened the Clayton Act by closing the loophole that allowed sale of assets to a competitor to reduce competitive pressures. The intent of this law is to maintain competition within an industry. It prevents both vertical mergers and mergers within the same industry. A vertical merger occurs when a company, for example a car company, acquires a steel company and that transaction results in reduced competition in the market.

Section 6.12

1. Define price gouging.

Price gouging is a term used to describe situations in which sellers price goods much higher than is considered fair in a particular circumstance. This can occur in a situation declared a civil emergency, as well as when practices inconsistent with a free market result in high profits. Price gouging occurs when companies increase their monopoly power and customers lose access to substitutes for the goods and services they need. At the same time, demand for specific goods and services becomes more inelastic, meaning that customers are less sensitive to price because they have a greater need and fewer choices for necessary goods and services.

2. Explain views in support of and against controlling price gouging.

There are conflicting views of price gouging. Some consider that price controls, even in unusual circumstances like civil emergencies, are more detrimental than helpful. Proponents of this viewpoint feel that controlling prices for needed goods and services will reduce the willingness of suppliers to provide enough to meet demand. An opposing view is that emergency situations create increased inequality between demand and supply, which the sellers of goods can exploit to make more profits unless prices are controlled.

3. List some conditions and events that might result in price gouging.

Price gouging allegations during civil emergencies are often limited to essential goods and services, which include food, water, medicine, transportation, equipment, shelter, and other items required to sustain and preserve life. Laws and social pressures are used to prevent price gouging during and after natural disasters and other times of civil emergency. Florida, for example, has laws that prohibit price gouging and provide an avenue for citizens to make complaints of price gouging to the police. In areas where no laws prohibiting price gouging are in place, social pressure can be brought to bear on vendors who engage in such behavior. This sometimes discourages vendors for increasing prices to make extraordinary profits.

Price gouging allegations are typically made during natural disasters and during shortages of essential goods and services. Shortages may occur as a result of an overall shortage of a good, such as a particular food or fuel product. They may also occur as a result of resources being diverted to other uses, as can occur during war time. This occurred during World War II when rations were put into place to slow the rise of inflation that would have resulted from the direction of resources to producing the products required by the military to conduct the war.

1. **Describe why perfect competition is desirable.**

   In a free market, under conditions of perfect competition, the market forces work without interference to set the most efficient levels of production and consumption by establishing market equilibrium where demand is equal to supply at a given price.

   Equilibrium prices tend to be higher in situations of monopoly, monopolistic competition, and oligopoly, where supply of a good may be restricted to increase price.

2. **Explain why monopolies are less efficient than perfect competition.**

   In perfect competition, demand is perfectly elastic, meaning that there are many small suppliers who are providing identical goods and services. In perfect competition, marginal costs are equal to average costs. Demand is perfectly elastic, meaning that consumers will purchase the good only at the equilibrium price. Any attempts by a provider to increase the price may result in increased short term profit, but it will not be sustainable.

   Monopolies exist when one producer controls the market for a good or service. A monopolist that seeks to maximize profits will do so at the monopoly output as long as output is less than consumer demand. The supply will be less than demand, driving prices up. In this situation, consumer demand is not completely fulfilled, leading to a loss of economic efficiency.

3. **Discuss the difference in price and output between perfect competition and monopolistic competition.**

   Monopolistic competition occurs when many competitors offer similar, but different products to consumers. The providers differentiate their products using advertising, convenience, quality, supplier reputation, and other characteristics of the product. The equilibrium price point is reached where long run average costs for the company equal average revenue. Monopolistically competitive firms are inefficient producers because they produce at a level where marginal cost of production is less than marginal revenue. This allows them to earn more additional revenue than they incur in additional cost for each additional unit of production.

   Perfect competition results in an efficient market, in which supply exactly matches demand at the equilibrium price.

4. **Detail the effect on supply and price when oligopolies collude and when they compete.**

   An oligopology is a market that has few sellers, therefore few competitors for their good or service. Firms in an oligopoly are interdependent, meaning that they must consider the reactions of other firms to business decisions. Each member of an oligopoly is affected by the policies of the other firms in the oligopoly. An oligopolistic company must be able to produce goods at a large scale in order to achieve a low per unit cost. Because of this a small number of large scale, cost efficient companies are able to meet the demand for the total market. There are significant barriers to entry to oligopolistic markets and the goods produced may be either the same or differentiated. Because of the interdependence of companies in an oligopoly, price determination is more complex than estimating demand and costs. Oligopolists must also consider how competitors will respond to price and quality adjustments.

Section 6.14

1. **Describe the expected impact of breaking up a monopoly on competition and price.**

   Abuse of market power typically occurs when a monopoly exists in a specific market. The U.S. government has enacted several pieces of legislation to deal with monopolies. They are the Sherman Act, the Clayton Act, and the Federal Trade Commission Act. Additional legislation was enacted in the 1900s to refine these three primary antitrust laws. If abuse of power is found to have occurred, the government will break the monopoly into smaller businesses. The goal of action is to increase competition between the small companies, which should result in lower prices, more options and better service to the consumer.

2. **Explain how externalities can affect demand for a good or service.**

   Externalities occur when an economic activity (environmental pollution, noise, or other impacts) has a negative or positive impact on nonconsenting second parties (neighbors, people and businesses downstream from a factory, etc.). Externalities are often managed with regulations imposed by the government. For example, a company that emits pollution into the air via a smokestack will be required to meet maximum pollution standards or pay a fine. In some cases, the cost of meeting the pollution standards is very high, in which case the company will choose to pay the fines as long as that cost is lower than upgrading the equipment to reduce pollution. In other cases, the cost of meeting pollution standards is low, which is an inducement to make the upgrades to the physical plant that will allow the standards to be met or exceeded rather than pay the fines. This approach places the burden of managing the externalities on the companies that create them. These costs, in turn, are included in the production costs of the good or service and passed on to the consumer. Increased price often results in decreased demand unless the demand is inelastic. The shift in the demand of the item results in a new market equilibrium with a higher price and lower supply.

3. **Discuss why public goods would not be supported by the market at the level the government supports them.**

   Public goods are those that are provided to everyone in society regardless of their ability to pay. Examples include public schools, police forces, the armed forces, public parks, etc. Everyone benefits from these services whether or not they are able to pay for them. The government imposes taxes to cover the costs of these public goods. The market would typically not pay for public goods at the level provided by the government because the costs are high.

4. **Detail how government regulation is used to ensure that consumers receive complete information on goods and services.**

Incomplete or asymmetric information occurs when a producer does not provide full information to the consumer or the consumer does not have the expertise to fully comprehend the information provided. Producers of goods that rely on repeat customers are motivated to provide clear and correct information to consumers because they need the consumers to return. Producers of medications or complex, infrequently purchased items provide information, but the consumer may not be able to make a fully informed decision about the quality of the information and the product. The government addresses these issues by requiring truth in advertising, full disclosure of contents of food, full disclosure of the potential side effects of medications, and the enactment of lemon laws, which apply to vehicles. All of these actions are taken in an effort to ensure that consumers receive full and accurate information to allow them to make informed decisions about the items they purchase and use.

Section 6.15

1. **List the three choices a government has when faced with a monopoly.**

Monopolies exist because they have achieved economies of scale that allow them to dominate the market in which they compete. The government has three options when a monopoly exists.

1. Allow the monopoly to operate freely. This option is not usually acceptable because it limits consumer choice, and results in higher prices and lower output than would occur under an efficient market situation.

2. Governments can regulate the monopolies.

3. The government can take over production in the industry that is monopolized.

2. **Describe how governments use regulation to manage monopolies.**

If the government chooses to regulate a monopoly, it typically establishes a price ceiling on the goods and services provided by the monopoly. This can be done in one of two ways: average cost pricing or marginal cost pricing.

Average cost pricing occurs when the monopolist is required to reduce the price of the good or service to the point where average total cost intersects with demand. This will cause the monopolist to expand output to meet the demand at the average cost. Average cost is still higher than marginal cost, so full efficiency is not achieved even though the cost to the consumer is reduced and supply increased.

Marginal cost pricing occurs when the producer is forced to lower price to the intersection of marginal cost and demand. This results in even higher output on the part of the producer and a lower cost to the consumer.

3. **Explain a government-operated monopoly.**

The third option for a government facing a monopoly is to take over the industry. When this occurs, the firm is considered to be a socialized firm, meaning that social, political, and economic factors are considered by the management of the firm. Examples of government-operated firms in the U.S. are the postal service and the Tennessee Valley Authority, as well as many public utilities. The theory of a socialized firm is that it is run efficiently and sets prices equal to marginal cost. Some government-operated firms are able to make a profit and put money back in the public coffers and others require subsidies. It depends upon how efficiently the firms are able to operate.

www.ingramcontent.com/pod-product-compliance
Lightning Source LLC
Chambersburg PA
CBHW081105170526
45165CB00008B/2336

* 9 7 8 1 4 8 1 8 7 4 0 2 1 *